Christmas

RDA ENTHUSIAST BRANDS, LLC
MILWAUKEE, WI

Taste of Home

EDITORIAL

Vice President, Content Operations **KERRI BALLIET**
Creative Director **HOWARD GREENBERG**

Managing Editor, Print & Digital Books **MARK HAGEN**
Associate Creative Director **EDWIN ROBLES JR.**

Editor **HAZEL WHEATON**
Associate Editor **MOLLY JASINSKI**
Art Director **JESSIE SHARON**
Layout Designer **NANCY NOVAK**
Editorial Production Coordinator **JILL BANKS**
Copy Chief **DEB WARLAUMONT MULVEY**
Copy Editors **DULCIE SHOENER (SENIOR), RONALD KOVACH, CHRIS MCLAUGHLIN, ELLIE PIPER**
Editorial Intern **STEPHANIE HARTE**

Content Director **JULIE BLUME BENEDICT**
Food Editors **JAMES SCHEND; PEGGY WOODWARD, RDN**
Recipe Editors **SUE RYON (LEAD), IRENE YEH**

Culinary Director **SARAH THOMPSON**
Test Cooks **NICHOLAS IVERSON (LEAD), MATTHEW HASS**
Food Stylists **KATHRYN CONRAD (LEAD), LAUREN KNOELKE, SHANNON ROUM**
Prep Cooks **BETHANY VAN JACOBSON (LEAD), ARIA C. THORNTON**
Culinary Team Assistant **MARIA PETRELLA**

Photography Director **STEPHANIE MARCHESE**
Photographers **DAN ROBERTS, JIM WIELAND**
Photographer/Set Stylist **GRACE NATOLI SHELDON**
Set Stylists **MELISSA FRANCO (LEAD), STACEY GENAW, DEE DEE SCHAEFER**
Contributors **MARK DERSE (PHOTOGRAPHER); DIANE ARMSTRONG (FOOD STYLIST); KAREN PONTERI (SET STYLIST); PAM STASNEY (SET STYLIST, CRAFTER); STEPHANIE CHOJNACKI, SUZANNE KERN HARPER, STEPHANIE SLIWINSKI, SARAH VANDERKOOY (CRAFTERS)**

Business Architect, Publishing Technologies
AMANDA HARMATYS
Business Analysts, Publishing Technologies
DENA AHLERS, KATE UNGER
Junior Business Analyst, Publishing Technologies
SHANNON STROUD

Editorial Business Manager **KRISTY MARTIN**
Editorial Business Associate **ANDREA MEIERS**
Rights & Permissions Assistant **JILL GODSEY**

Editor, *Taste of Home* **EMILY BETZ TYRA**
Art Director, *Taste of Home* **KRISTIN BOWKER**

BUSINESS

Publisher, *Taste of Home* **DONNA LINDSKOG**
Strategic Partnerships Manager, Taste of Home Live
JAMIE PIETTE ANDRZEJEWSKI

TRUSTED MEDIA BRANDS, INC.

President & Chief Executive Officer **BONNIE KINTZER**
Chief Financial Officer **DEAN DURBIN**
Chief Marketing Officer **C. ALEC CASEY**
Chief Revenue Officer **RICHARD SUTTON**
Chief Digital Officer **VINCE ERRICO**
Senior Vice President, Global HR & Communications
PHYLLIS E. GEBHARDT, SPHR; SHRM-SCP
General Counsel **MARK SIROTA**
Vice President, Product Marketing **BRIAN KENNEDY**
Vice President, Consumer Acquisition **HEATHER PLANT**
Vice President, Operations **MICHAEL GARZONE**
Vice President, Consumer Marketing Planning **JIM WOODS**
Vice President, Digital Product & Technology **NICK CONTARDO**
Vice President, Digital Content & Audience Development
KARI HODES
Vice President, Financial Planning & Analysis **WILLIAM HOUSTON**

COVER PHOTOGRAPHY

Photographer **JIM WIELAND**
Food Stylist **LAUREN KNOELKE**
Set Stylist **STACEY GENAW**

© 2017 RDA Enthusiast Brands, LLC.
1610 N. 2nd St., Suite 102, Milwaukee WI 53212-3906

International Standard Book Number: 978-1-61765-700-9
International Standard Serial Number: 1948-8386
Component Number: 119600039H

PICTURED ON THE FRONT COVER: White Candy Bark (p. 184), Pineapple & Macadamia Nut Cake (p. 181) and Creamy Coconut Snowballs (p. 183).
PICTURED ON THE BACK COVER: Roasted Sage Turkey with Vegetable Gravy (p. 59), Classic Candy Cane Butter Cookies (p. 161).
ADDITIONAL ART: Romanova Ekaterina/Shutterstock

WHITE CANDY BARK, P. 184

PINEAPPLE & MACADAMIA NUT CAKE, P. 181

CREAMY COCONUT SNOWBALLS, P. 183

Contents

Small Plates, Big Celebrations 6

Slow Cooker Side Dishes 22

Holiday Feasts.............................38

Merry Cranberries 66

Christmas Comfort Food....................84

Seasonal Get-Togethers....................102

Make-Ahead Entertaining.................122

Red Hot Christmas..........................138

Cookie Exchange 152

White Christmas Desserts................168

Holiday Gift Mixes 186

Homemade Gifts & Decor 200

Index...230

1

2

Make your holidays merry and bright with Taste of Home Christmas

1. SMALL PLATES, BIG CELEBRATIONS.
Why not build a perfect party around elegant, bite-sized delicacies? From dips to drinks to savory treats, try 20 great dishes for your holiday buffet.

2. SLOW COOKER SIDE DISHES.
Save your oven space for the roast; use your slow cooker for the sides! Choose from 24 traditional dishes and new favorites.

3. HOLIDAY FEASTS.
Produce one of three full seven-course feasts—poultry, pork or seafood—or design your own menu with tasty a la carte options.

4. MERRY CRANBERRIES.
Bright color and lively flavor make cranberries an ideal holiday item. Explore drinks, sauces, desserts and entrees—all with a touch of berry.

5. CHRISTMAS COMFORT FOOD.
When your loved ones gather for the holidays, welcome them home with these heartwarming recipes.

6. SEASONAL GET-TOGETHERS.
For Christmas morning breakfasts, merry kids parties and casual holiday open houses, these brilliant menus promise to make your home the place to be all season long.

12

11

10

3

4

5

7. MAKE-AHEAD ENTERTAINING.
To be sure you don't spend all your time in the kitchen during your holiday event, simply plan—and make—ahead. Check out 20 delicious dishes that will be ready long before the guests arrive.

8. RED HOT CHRISTMAS.
Winter get-togethers don't have to be subzero! From appetizers to desserts, this collection of 17 recipes raises the heat by grilling, broiling, or upping the spice factor.

9. COOKIE EXCHANGE.
When the plates of cookies are passed around, will your treats stand out? Here are 20 impressive choices, from traditional favorites to new flavor combinations, that will make your cookie creations the stars of the show.

10. WHITE CHRISTMAS DESSERTS.
Cakes, candies and pies—those are just some of the 22 stunning sweets you'll find here. The elegant edibles, all dressed in frosty shades, are sure to keep you dreaming of a white Christmas this year.

11. HOLIDAY GIFT MIXES.
Soups, spices, cookies and cakes! These mixes make the perfect gifts for teachers, co-workers and friends and will warm them twice: once when given, and once when prepared.

12. HOMEMADE GIFTS & DECOR.
Whether it's cards, gifts, ornaments, table settings or an inventive way to deck your halls, homemade adds a personal touch to the holidays. These 30 fun and easy craft projects help you make the holiday your own.

6

9

8

7

SMALL PLATES, BIG CELEBRATIONS

Sophisticated and meant for sharing, small-plate dishes are the key ingredient for a perfect holiday party. Choose your favorites, and create your own amazing spread!

STRAWBERRY-CHAMPAGNE PUNCH

START TO FINISH: 5 MIN.
MAKES: 8 SERVINGS

Sweet strawberries blend with the tang of cranberries to flavor this crowd-pleasing pink punch. Add the sparkling champagne, and you have the perfect holiday party cocktail.
—Linda Foreman, Locust Grove, OK

- 1 package (10 ounces) frozen unsweetened strawberries, thawed
- 2 cups cranberry juice, chilled
- 1 bottle (750 milliliters) champagne, chilled

Place strawberries in a blender; cover and process until smooth. Press through a fine-mesh strainer into a pitcher; discard seeds. Pour into a 2-qt. pitcher. Stir in cranberry juice and champagne. Serve immediately.

HOLIDAY STUFFED BABY PORTOBELLOS

PREP: 30 MIN.
BAKE: 15 MIN.
MAKES: 2 DOZEN

I call these "holiday" mushrooms because I always make them over Christmas, but the tasty bites are popular any time!
—Rd Stendel-Freels, Albuquerque, NM

- 24 baby portobello mushrooms (about 1 pound)
- 2 tablespoons olive oil, divided
- 1 celery rib, finely chopped
- 2 tablespoons finely chopped onion
- 2 garlic cloves, minced
- 4 bacon strips, cooked and crumbled, divided
- ½ cup shredded cheddar–Monterey Jack cheese
- ¼ cup seasoned bread crumbs
- 1 slice provolone cheese, diced

1. Preheat oven to 350°. Carefully remove stems from mushrooms; place caps in a foil-lined 15x10-in. pan coated with cooking spray. Finely chop stems.

2. In a large skillet, heat 1 tablespoon oil over medium heat. Add the chopped mushrooms, celery and onion; cook and stir until tender, 3-4 minutes. Add garlic; cook and stir 1 minute more. Remove from heat. Stir in 3 tablespoons of the bacon, the shredded cheese and the bread crumbs.

3. Spoon mixture into mushroom caps. Top with provolone cheese and the remaining bacon. Drizzle with remaining oil. Bake until mushrooms are tender and cheese is melted, 15-20 minutes.

SPINACH SOUFFLE DIP

PREP: 25 MIN.
BAKE: 30 MIN.
MAKES: 3 CUPS

My mother received a copy of this recipe from a 90-year-old friend who got the recipe from a sharecropper who worked in the kitchen at harvesttime. This dip has been part of my Christmas for about 30 years, and I always keep the recipe handy—everyone asks for it!
—Nancy Needy, Spartanburg, SC

- ½ cup water
- 1 teaspoon sugar
- 1 package (10 ounces) frozen chopped spinach
- 1 can (10¾ ounces) condensed cream of chicken soup, undiluted
- 1 cup shredded cheddar cheese
- 1 large egg, beaten
- 2 slices white bread, cubed
- 1 teaspoon butter, melted
  Dash garlic salt
  Dash cayenne pepper
  Assorted crackers

1. Preheat oven to 350°. In a small saucepan, bring water and sugar to a boil. Add spinach; cover and boil for 10 minutes. Drain the spinach; squeeze dry.

2. Combine spinach, soup, cheese and egg. Transfer to a greased 1½-qt. baking dish. In a bowl, mix bread cubes, butter, garlic salt and cayenne. Sprinkle over the spinach. Bake, uncovered, until the bread cubes are golden brown and the spinach mixture is heated through, about 30 minutes. Serve with crackers.

"This dip has been part of my Christmas for about 30 years."
—NANCY NEEDY

ONE-BITE TAMALES

PREP: 40 MIN.
COOK: 3 HOURS 20 MIN.
MAKES: ABOUT 5½ DOZEN

Clever little meatballs deliver the flavor and rich sauce of a traditional tamale in a bite-size portion. They're a delightfully different addition to a holiday spread.
—Dolores Jaycox, Gretna, LA

> 1¼ **cups cornmeal**
> ½ **cup all-purpose flour**
> 5¾ **cups V8 juice, divided**
> 4 **teaspoons chili powder, divided**
> 4 **teaspoons ground cumin, divided**
> 2 **teaspoons salt, divided**
> 1 **teaspoon garlic powder**
> ½ **to 1 teaspoon cayenne pepper**
> 1 **pound bulk spicy pork sausage**
> **Tortilla chip scoops**

1. Preheat oven to 350°. Mix cornmeal, flour, ¾ cup V8 juice, 2 teaspoons chili powder, 2 teaspoons cumin, 1 teaspoon salt, garlic powder and cayenne. Add the sausage; mix lightly but thoroughly. Shape into 1-in. balls.
2. Place the meatballs on a greased rack in a 15x10-in. pan. Bake until cooked through, 20-25 minutes.
3. In a 4-qt. slow cooker, mix the remaining V8 juice, chili powder, cumin and salt. Gently stir in the meatballs. Cook, covered, on low until heated through, 3-4 hours. Serve with tortilla chip scoops.

RICOTTA PUFFS

PREP: 20 MIN.
BAKE: 15 MIN.
MAKES: 1½ DOZEN

Ricotta cheese gives these pastry puffs a creamy, rich texture, while roasted red peppers add sweetness, Romano cheese adds tang and herbs lend their own spark.
—Maria Regakis, Saugus, MA

> 1 **package (17¼ ounces) frozen puff pastry, thawed**
> ½ **cup ricotta cheese**
> ½ **cup roasted sweet red peppers, drained and chopped**
> 3 **tablespoons grated Romano or Parmesan cheese, divided**
> 1 **tablespoon minced fresh parsley**
> 1 **teaspoon dried oregano, crushed**
> ½ **teaspoon pepper**
> 1 **teaspoon 2% milk**

1. Preheat oven to 400°. On a lightly floured surface, unfold puff pastry. Cut each sheet into nine squares. Mix ricotta cheese, red peppers, 2 tablespoons Romano cheese, parsley, oregano and the pepper.
2. Brush pastry edges with milk; place 2 rounded teaspoonfuls of the cheese mixture in the center of each square. Fold the edges of the pastry over the filling, forming a rectangle; seal the edges with a fork. Cut slits in the pastry; brush with milk. Sprinkle with the remaining Romano cheese.
3. Place pastries 2 in. apart on lightly greased baking sheets. Bake until golden brown, 15-20 minutes. Remove to wire racks. Serve warm. Refrigerate leftovers.

CRANBERRY-PECAN HOLIDAY CHEESE BALL

PREP: 15 MIN. + CHILLING
MAKES: 3 CUPS

Cheese balls can be made in advance and people love the variety. This one makes a wonderful holiday gift or hostess gift. To use as a spread, omit the 1 cup of pecans and ½ cup cranberries used to coat the ball.
—Donna-Marie Ryan, Topsfield, MA

- 1½ cups white shredded cheddar cheese
- ¾ cup whipped cream cheese
- ½ cup butter, softened
- ¼ cup Dijon mustard
- 1⅓ cups chopped pecans, toasted, divided
- 1 cup dried cranberries, divided
  Assorted crackers

1. Beat the cheddar cheese, cream cheese, butter and mustard until blended. Fold in ⅓ cup of the pecans and ½ cup of the dried cranberries. Spread the remaining pecans and dried cranberries in an even layer on a 12x12-in. piece of plastic; place the cheese mixture on top of the cranberry mixture. Bring the corners of the plastic up over the cheese mixture and shape it into a ball. Refrigerate for at least 1 hour.
2. Remove from refrigerator 10 minutes before serving. Serve with crackers.

Holiday Helper

To toast chopped nuts, spread them in a baking pan and bake at 350° until golden brown, stirring often. Generally, nuts toast in 6-10 minutes; the timing depends on how finely the nuts are chopped and the thickness of the baking pan.

BACON-WRAPPED BLUE CHEESE SHRIMP

PREP: 30 MIN.
COOK: 10 MIN.
MAKES: 16 APPETIZERS

Blue cheese, bacon and basil pack big flavor into a couple of bites. To save time, you can assemble the skewers the night before and then serve them hot from the broiler on the day.
—Vivi Taylor, Middleburg, FL

- ¼ cup butter, melted
- 1 garlic clove, minced
- 1 teaspoon hot pepper sauce
- 16 uncooked shrimp (16-20 per pound), peeled and deveined
- ¼ teaspoon salt
- ⅛ teaspoon pepper
- 16 cubes blue cheese (½ inch)
- 16 fresh basil leaves
- 8 bacon strips, halved
- ¼ cup finely chopped celery
- ¼ cup crumbled blue cheese
- 1 tablespoon minced fresh basil

1. Preheat broiler. Combine butter, garlic and pepper sauce. Cut a slit in each shrimp along the inside curve; flatten slightly. Sprinkle shrimp with salt and pepper. Press a cheese cube into slit. Wrap a basil leaf and bacon piece around each shrimp; secure with a toothpick.
2. Place shrimp on a greased rack of a broiler pan. Broil 6-8 in. from heat until shrimp turn pink and bacon is crisp, about 5-6 minutes on each side; baste occasionally with the butter mixture.
3. Arrange the shrimp on a serving platter; sprinkle with celery, crumbled blue cheese and basil.

"People couldn't believe this delicious bread had pretzels in the mix!"
—ANDREA JOHNSON

PRETZEL BREAD BOWL WITH CHEESE DIP

PREP: 30 MIN. + RISING
BAKE: 30 MIN. + COOLING
MAKES: 16 SERVINGS

Our town is known as Pretzel City—even our local sports teams are known as The Pretzels. I came up with this recipe for an annual local recipe contest. People couldn't believe that this delicious bread had pretzels in the mix! For variety, try different flavors of pretzels.
—Andrea Johnson, Freeport, IL

- 1 **cup finely crushed cheddar miniature pretzels**
- 1 **envelope ranch salad dressing mix**
- 1 **package (¼ ounce) quick-rise yeast**
- 2 **teaspoons sugar**
- ⅛ **teaspoon baking soda**
- 2 **to 2½ cups all-purpose flour**
- 1 **cup water**
- ¼ **cup 2% milk**
- 2 **tablespoons butter**
- 1 **cup shredded pepper jack cheese**
- 1 **teaspoon yellow cornmeal**

EGG WASH
- 1 **large egg white**
- 1 **tablespoon water**
  Kosher salt, optional

DIP
- 2 **cups sour cream**
- 1 **cup shredded pepper jack cheese**
- 1 **envelope ranch salad dressing mix**
  Chopped seeded jalapeno peppers and additional shredded pepper jack cheese, optional
  Assorted fresh vegetables

1. Mix the crushed pretzels, dressing mix, yeast, sugar, baking soda and 1 cup of the flour. In a small saucepan, heat water, milk and butter to 120°-130°. Add to the dry ingredients; beat on low speed until moistened. Add cheese; beat on medium for 3 minutes. Stir in enough of the remaining flour to form a stiff dough.
2. Turn dough onto a floured surface; knead until smooth and elastic, about 6-8 minutes. Cover with plastic and let rest 10 minutes.
3. Grease a baking sheet; sprinkle with cornmeal. Shape the dough into a round loaf; place on the prepared pan. Cover and let rise in a warm place until doubled, about 1 hour.
4. Preheat oven to 375°. Whisk egg white with water; brush over the top of the loaf. If desired, sprinkle with salt. Bake until golden brown and bread sounds hollow when tapped, 30-35 minutes. Cool on pan for 5 minutes. Remove to a wire rack to cool completely.
5. For dip, mix sour cream, pepper jack cheese and dressing mix. Refrigerate until serving.
6. To serve, cut one fourth off the top of the bread loaf. Hollow out the bottom of the loaf, leaving a ½-in.-thick shell. Cut the removed bread into cubes. Fill bowl with dip. If desired, top with peppers and additional cheese. Serve dip with bread cubes and vegetables.

Holiday Helper
To hollow out a bread loaf: Cut off the top, then cut around the inside perimeter of the bread, about ½ inch from the crust. Slide your fingers into the cut and work your way around the loaf to loosen the bread from the bottom.

CRANBERRY COCKTAIL

START TO FINISH: 10 MIN.
MAKES: 4 SERVINGS

I adore the combination of flavors in this recipe. The secret is to thaw the lemonade so that it's still slightly icy—this way the cocktail will be cool and refreshing. For a no-alcohol option, use peach juice and lemon-lime soda instead of schnapps and vodka.
—Julie Danler, Bel Aire, KS

- **Ice cubes**
- 4 **ounces vodka**
- 4 **ounces peach schnapps liqueur**
- 4 **ounces frozen lemonade concentrate, thawed**
- 4 **ounces cranberry-raspberry juice**
- 16 **maraschino cherries**

1. Fill a shaker three-fourths full with ice cubes.
2. Add the vodka, peach schnapps, lemonade concentrate and juice to the shaker; cover and shake for 10-15 seconds or until condensation forms on the outside of the shaker. Strain into four cocktail glasses. Place a skewer with four cherries in each glass.

PIMIENTO CHEESE DEVILED EGGS

START TO FINISH: 15 MIN.
MAKES: 1 DOZEN

For my mother's 92nd birthday, we had deviled eggs topped with pimientos as part of the spread. They're timeless and always in good taste.
—Linda Foreman, Locust Grove, OK

- 6 **hard-cooked large eggs**
- ¼ **cup finely shredded sharp cheddar cheese**
- 2 **tablespoons mayonnaise**
- 4 **teaspoons diced pimientos, drained**
- 2 **teaspoons finely chopped sweet onion**
- 1 **teaspoon Dijon mustard**
- 1 **small garlic clove, minced**
- ¼ **teaspoon salt**
- ⅛ **teaspoon pepper**
  Additional diced pimientos and finely shredded sharp cheddar cheese

Cut eggs lengthwise in half. Remove yolks, reserving whites. In a bowl, mash yolks. Stir in cheese, mayonnaise, pimientos, onion, mustard, garlic, salt and pepper. Spoon or pipe into egg whites. Sprinkle with additional pimientos and cheese. Refrigerate, covered, until serving.

CAMEMBERT & CRANBERRY PIZZAS

START TO FINISH: 30 MIN.
MAKES: 2 DOZEN

Appetizer pizza takes several steps up in elegance with creamy Camembert cheese. The bright red color and tangy flavor of the cranberries make this a welcome addition to any holiday party.
—Sue Sans, Buckeye, AZ

- 1 **tube (13.8 ounces) refrigerated pizza crust**
- 1 **can (14 ounces) whole-berry cranberry sauce**
- 1 **round (8 ounces) Camembert cheese, cut into ½-inch cubes**
- ½ **cup chopped pecans**
  Chopped fresh parsley, optional

1. Preheat oven to 425°. Unroll dough and press it onto the bottom and ½ in. up the sides of a greased 15x10-in. pan. Bake until golden brown, 6-8 minutes.
2. Place the cranberry sauce in a bowl; stir to break into pieces. Spoon sauce over crust. Sprinkle with cheese and pecans. Bake until the cheese is melted, 6-8 minutes. If desired, sprinkle with parsley. Cool on a wire rack 5 minutes. Cut into squares.

Holiday Helper
Here's a handy way to serve deviled eggs. Put them in paper cupcake liners and set them in muffin tins to serve. They stay upright and neat, and the eggs in the paper cups won't slide around on people's plates.
—Sally T., Las Cruces, New Mexico

BAKED BRIE WITH MUSHROOMS

PREP: 30 MIN.
BAKE: 15 MIN.
MAKES: 8 SERVINGS

My sister craves this appetizer so much that I made a batch and carried it on the plane when I flew to New Mexico to visit her. The combination of creamy brie with earthy sauteed mushrooms is scrumptious.
—Melody Ansell, Portland, OR

- 1 **tablespoon butter**
- 1 **tablespoon olive oil**
- 1 **pound sliced fresh assorted mushrooms**
- 2 **small red onions, chopped**
- ¼ **teaspoon salt**
- ¼ **teaspoon pepper**
- 5 **garlic cloves, minced**
- ⅔ **cup port wine**
- 1 **round (8 ounces) Brie cheese**
  Toasted French bread baguette slices

1. Preheat oven to 400°. In a large skillet, heat butter and oil over medium-high heat. Add mushrooms, onions, salt and pepper; cook until golden brown, 12-14 minutes, stirring occasionally. Add garlic; cook 1 minute longer. Stir in wine. Bring to a boil; cook until liquid is almost evaporated.
2. Remove rind from top of cheese. Transfer to a 1½-qt. round baking dish. Top with mushroom mixture. Bake, uncovered, until cheese is melted, 15-20 minutes. Serve with baguette slices.
NOTE For assorted mushrooms, we recommend a mixture of white button, baby portobello, shiitake and oyster mushrooms.

HOLIDAY HOT BUTTERED RUM MIX

START TO FINISH: 10 MIN.
MAKES: 52 SERVINGS (13 CUPS HOT BUTTERED RUM MIX)

My family loves serving this rich and delicious beverage around the holidays. It can be made with or without alcohol, so everyone enjoys it!
—Alisa Pirtle, Browns Valley, CA

- 2 **cups butter, softened**
- 3¾ **cups confectioners' sugar**
- 2¼ **cups packed brown sugar**
- 1 **teaspoon vanilla extract**
- 2 **quarts vanilla ice cream, softened**

EACH SERVING
- ¾ **cup boiling water**
- 1 **to 2 tablespoons rum or brandy**
  Ground cinnamon and nutmeg to taste

Cream butter and sugars until smooth. Beat in vanilla and ice cream. Store in freezer containers in freezer. To prepare buttered rum: Place ¼ cup butter mixture in a 10- or 12-ounce mug. Stir in boiling water and rum. Sprinkle with cinnamon and nutmeg to taste.

Divide dough in half; flatten each into a disk. Wrap in plastic; refrigerate 1 hour or until dough is easy to handle.

2. Preheat oven to 400°. In a large skillet, heat butter and oil over medium-high heat. Add onions; saute until tender. Add the mushrooms; saute until most of the liquid has evaporated, about 3 minutes. Reduce heat.

3. Combine flour, curry, salt and pepper; stir into the skillet. Gradually add cream. Bring to a boil; cook and stir 1-2 minutes or until slightly thickened. Remove from the heat.

4. On a lightly floured surface, roll one disk of dough to ⅛-in. thickness. Cut out circles with a floured 3-in. round biscuit cutter. Place circles 2 in. apart on parchment paper-lined baking sheets. Place 1 tablespoon filling on one side of each circle. Brush edges of pastry with water; fold circles in half. With a fork, press edges to seal; prick tops with a fork. Bake until golden brown, 12-15 minutes. Serve warm, with chutney if desired.

HAM & CHEESE PUFFS

START TO FINISH: 30 MIN.
MAKES: 2 DOZEN

These marvelous little bites go over well with kids of all ages. They're also good with soups and many of the items you'd expect to find on a buffet table.
—Mrs. Marvin Buffington, Burlington, IA

  1 **package (2½ ounces) thinly sliced deli ham, chopped**
  1 **small onion, chopped**
  ½ **cup shredded Swiss cheese**
  1 **large egg**
1½ **teaspoons Dijon mustard**
  ⅛ **teaspoon pepper**
  1 **tube (8 ounces) refrigerated crescent rolls**

1. Preheat oven to 375°. Combine the first six ingredients. Divide crescent dough into 24 portions. Press into greased mini-muffin cups.

2. Spoon 1 tablespoon ham mixture into each cup. Bake until golden brown, 13-15 minutes.

CURRIED MUSHROOM EMPANADAS

PREP: 20 MIN. + CHILLING
BAKE: 15 MIN./BATCH
MAKES: 3 DOZEN

A rich mushroom filling is spiced with mild curry and wrapped in flaky pastry. These two-bite treats cross Indian flavor with classic Mexican empanadas for an appetizer that will disappear like magic!
—Pat Cronin, Cotuit, MA

  1 **cup butter, softened**
  1 **package (8 ounces) cream cheese, softened**
  3 **cups all-purpose flour**

FILLING
  3 **tablespoons butter**
  3 **tablespoons olive oil**
  2 **medium onions, finely chopped**
  ½ **pound sliced fresh mushrooms, diced**
  ½ **pound sliced baby portobello mushrooms, diced**
  2 **tablespoons all-purpose flour**
  2 **teaspoons curry powder**
  ½ **teaspoon salt**
  ⅛ **teaspoon pepper**
  ½ **cup half-and-half cream**
      Mango chutney, optional

1. Cream butter and cream cheese until light and fluffy. Gradually beat in flour.

HONEY-MINT LAMB SKEWERS

PREP: 15 MIN. + MARINATING
BROIL: 10 MIN./BATCH
MAKES: 3 DOZEN (2 CUPS DIP)

My hearty lamb bites are delicious and convenient. Assemble them the day before, then pop them under the broiler when the party starts.
—Trisha Kruse, Eagle, ID

- ½ **cup olive oil**
- 5 **tablespoons lemon juice**
- ¼ **cup minced fresh mint**
- 2 **tablespoons honey**
- 5 **garlic cloves, minced**
  Dash salt
  Dash pepper
- 3 **pounds lamb stew meat**

LEMON FETA DIP
- 1 **cup sour cream**
- 2 **tablespoons lemon juice**
- 2 **cups crumbled feta cheese**
- 2 **pepperoncini, minced**

1. Mix the first seven ingredients in a shallow dish. Add lamb; turn to coat.

Refrigerate for 4-6 hours.

2. For dip, place sour cream, lemon juice, feta cheese and pepperoncini in a blender; cover and process until smooth. Cover and refrigerate until serving.

3. Preheat broiler. Drain lamb and discard the marinade. Thread two pieces of lamb on each of 36 soaked wooden skewers; place in two 15x10-in. pans. Broil 6-8 in. from the heat until the lamb reaches desired doneness, 10-12 minutes, turning occasionally. Serve with dip.

SHRIMP IN PHYLLO CUPS

PREP: 20 MIN. + CHILLING
BAKE: 5 MIN.
MAKES: ABOUT 3½ DOZEN

I almost didn't make these appetizers for last year's Christmas party because I was running out of time, but I knew they'd be a tasty hit. Simple to make, the cups have few ingredients and look beautiful on the plate—very gourmet! This turned out to be one of the night's favorites, and they just flew off the plate.
—Terri Edmunds, Naperville, IL

- 1 **pound peeled and deveined cooked shrimp (61-70 per pound), finely chopped**
- 1 **medium celery rib, finely chopped**
- ½ **cup Thousand Island salad dressing**
- 2 **tablespoons mayonnaise**
- 1 **tablespoon lemon juice**
- 3 **packages (1.9 ounces each) frozen miniature phyllo tart shells**
- 2 **tablespoons chopped fresh parsley**

1. Mix shrimp and celery. In a bowl, mix salad dressing, mayonnaise and lemon juice; pour over the shrimp mixture. Stir to combine. Refrigerate, covered, 1 hour.
2. Meanwhile, bake and cool tart shells according to package directions. Just before serving, fill the shells with the shrimp mixture. Sprinkle with parsley.

TROPICAL CANDY CANE FREEZE

START TO FINISH: 10 MIN.
MAKES: 10 SERVINGS

When the midwestern winter drags on and on, this frosty cold drink takes me away to a warm tropical beach! The recipe can easily be made family-friendly by substituting water for the alcohol.
—Jennifer Stowell, Montezuma, IA

- 1 **can (10 ounces) frozen nonalcoholic pina colada mix**
- 10 **cups ice cubes, divided**
- 1⅓ **cups rum or 2 cups water, divided**
- 1 **can (10 ounces) frozen nonalcoholic strawberry daiquiri mix**

In a covered blender, process pina colada mix, 5 cups of ice and ⅔ cup rum or 1 cup water until blended. Repeat with strawberry daiquiri mix and the remaining ingredients. Slowly pour the prepared pina colada and prepared strawberry daiquiri by ¼ cupfuls into the center of 10 highball glasses, alternating layers. Serve immediately.

GOAT CHEESE & ONION PASTRIES

PREP: 30 MIN.
BAKE: 20 MIN.
MAKES: 1 DOZEN

A flaky puff pastry crust holds sweet caramelized onions and creamy goat cheese for an easy yet upscale appetizer. The recipe is a must on all our entertaining menus.
—Heidi Ellis, Monument, CO

- 6 **bacon strips, chopped**
- 2 **large onions, finely chopped**
- 3 **shallots, thinly sliced**
- ½ **teaspoon sugar**
- ½ **cup white wine**
- 2 **teaspoons minced fresh thyme or ½ teaspoon dried thyme**
- 2 **garlic cloves, minced**
- ¼ **teaspoon pepper**
- 1 **sheet frozen puff pastry, thawed**
- 1 **large egg white, beaten**
- 1 **log (4 ounces) fresh goat cheese, cut into 12 slices**

1. Preheat oven to 400°. In a large skillet, cook bacon over medium heat until crisp, stirring occasionally. Remove with a slotted spoon; drain on paper towels. Discard drippings, reserving 2 teaspoons in pan. Add onions, shallots and sugar to the drippings; cook and stir over medium heat until vegetables are golden brown, 15-20 minutes.
2. Add wine, stirring to loosen browned bits from pan. Stir in thyme, garlic and pepper. Cook, uncovered, until liquid is evaporated, 2-3 minutes. Stir in bacon.
3. On a lightly floured surface, unfold the puff pastry dough. Cut into three 9x3-in. rectangles.
4. Transfer dough to a parchment paper-lined baking sheet. Brush with egg white; top with onion mixture and goat cheese. Bake until golden brown, 16-20 minutes. Cut each rectangle into four individual appetizers.

MINI CRAB CAKES

PREP: 20 MIN. + CHILLING
COOK: 10 MIN./BATCH
MAKES: 16 APPETIZERS

Fresh crab is one of my all-time favorite foods. Whenever I get the chance to cook with it, I'll make this dish. These minis are amazing for appetizers; larger ones make a fantastic dinner paired with a simple salad.
—Ellen Riley, Murfreesboro, TN

- ½ **cup mayonnaise**
- 1 **tablespoon dill pickle relish**
- 1 **teaspoon prepared horseradish**
- 1 **teaspoon Dijon mustard**
- ½ **teaspoon hot pepper sauce**
- ½ **teaspoon Worcestershire sauce**

CRAB CAKES
- 1 **large egg**
- ¼ **cup seasoned bread crumbs**
- ¼ **cup mayonnaise**
- 1 **green onion, chopped**
- 1 **tablespoon minced fresh parsley**
- 1 **tablespoon Dijon mustard**
- ½ **teaspoon seafood seasoning**
- ¼ **teaspoon hot pepper sauce**
- 3 **cups lump crabmeat, drained**
- ¼ **cup canola oil**
- 16 **dill pickle slices**
  Minced chives

1. Mix the first six ingredients. Refrigerate, covered, until serving. Combine the egg, bread crumbs, mayonnaise, onion, parsley, mustard, seafood seasoning and pepper sauce. Fold in crab. Refrigerate for at least 30 minutes.
2. With floured hands, shape the crab mixture into ½-in.-thick patties, each containing 2 tablespoonfuls of the crab mixture. In a large skillet, heat oil over medium heat. Add crab cakes in batches; cook until golden brown, 3-4 minutes on each side. Top each with a dill pickle slice and sauce. Sprinkle with chives.

SLOW COOKER SIDE DISHES

With all the bustle involved in preparing a holiday dinner, take advantage of the busy cook's best friend. All these side dishes can be made in the slow cooker while you devote your oven to the main course, and your time to your family.

CHEESE-STUFFED SWEET ONIONS

PREP: 25 MIN.
COOK: 4 HOURS
MAKES: 8 SERVINGS

These onions are stuffed with a delicious blend of cheeses and cooked in vegetable broth. Experiment to find the blend you like. Instead of goat cheese, try cream cheese or mascarpone cheese. For the blue cheese, you can use Gorgonzola, and in place of Romano, you can use Parmesan. It's all delicious!
—Sonya Labbe, West Hollywood, CA

- 4 **large Vidalia or other sweet onions**
- ¾ **cup crumbled goat cheese**
- ¾ **cup crumbled blue cheese**
- 1 **teaspoon minced fresh thyme**
- 2 **cups vegetable stock**
- 1 **tablespoon olive oil**
- ¼ **teaspoon salt**
- ⅛ **teaspoon pepper**
- ¼ **cup grated Romano or Parmesan cheese Fresh thyme leaves**

1. Peel onions. Cut a ½-in. slice off top of each onion; remove the centers with a melon baller, leaving ½-in.-thick shells. Chop the removed onion. Mix together goat and blue cheeses, minced thyme and 3 cups of the chopped onion (save the remaining onion for another use). Spoon the onion and cheese mixture into the onion shells.
2. Place filled onions and stock in a 6-qt. slow cooker; drizzle with oil. Sprinkle with salt, pepper and Romano cheese. Cook, covered, on low until the onions are tender, 4-5 hours. Sprinkle with thyme leaves.

Holiday Helper
To save leftover chopped onions for future use, place them in an airtight container and freeze for up to 3 months. Before sauteing, thaw the onions and pat them dry. Frozen chopped onions can be added directly to soups or casseroles.

HOLIDAY TURKEY GRAVY

PREP: 30 MIN.
COOK: 5 HOURS
MAKES: 6 CUPS

I make this recipe a day ahead so I can get the food on the table faster on the big day. The aroma while this cooks permeates the whole house and gets everyone ready for the feast. I save the turkey meat and use it in recipes that call for cooked turkey or chicken.
—Isabelle Rooney, Summerville, SC

- 2 **turkey wings, halved (about 3 pounds)**
- 2 **medium onions, halved**
- 1 **cup water**
- 8 **cups reduced-sodium chicken broth, divided**
- ¾ **cup chopped carrots**
- ½ **teaspoon dried thyme**
- 2 **tablespoons butter**
- ¾ **cup all-purpose flour**
- ½ **teaspoon coarsely ground pepper**

1. Preheat oven to 425°. Place turkey wings and onions in a roasting pan. Roast, uncovered, until well browned, about 1 hour. Transfer wings and onions to a 5-qt. slow cooker. Add water to pan; stir to loosen browned bits. Add to slow cooker. Stir in 6 cups broth, carrots and thyme. Cook, covered, on low 4 hours.
2. Remove wings; discard or save for another use. Strain and discard the vegetables from turkey stock; skim fat. In a 6-qt. stockpot, melt butter over medium-low heat; whisk in the flour, pepper and remaining broth until smooth. Slowly whisk in stock; bring to a boil, stirring constantly. Reduce heat; simmer and stir until gravy reaches the desired consistency.

TRULY TASTY
TURNIP GREENS

PREP: 20 MIN.
COOK: 5 HOURS
MAKES: 14 SERVINGS

These savory greens are a hit at every church dinner. Adjust the seasonings as you please to make this recipe your own.
—Amy Inman, Hiddenite, NC

- 2¾ pounds turnips, peeled and cut into ½-inch cubes
- 1 bunch fresh turnip greens (about 12 ounces), chopped
- 8 ounces cubed fully cooked country ham or 2 smoked ham hocks (about 1½ pounds)
- 1 medium onion, chopped
- 3 tablespoons sugar
- 1½ teaspoons coarsely ground pepper
- 1¼ teaspoons salt
- 2 cartons (32 ounces each) chicken broth

In a greased 6- or 7-qt. slow cooker, combine all the ingredients. Cook, covered, on low until the vegetables are tender, 5-6 hours, stirring once. If using ham hocks, remove the meat from the bones when they are cool enough to handle; cut the ham into small pieces and return to the slow cooker. Serve with a slotted spoon.

TANGY
CRANBERRY BEANS

PREP: 20 MIN. + SOAKING
COOK: 6 HOURS
MAKES: 10 SERVINGS

Whenever I take these beans to barbeques, they're always eaten up right away.
—Wendie Osipowicz, New Britain, CT

- 3 cups dried navy beans
- 4 cups unsweetened cranberry juice
- ½ pound bacon strips, cooked and crumbled
- 1 medium onion, chopped
- ½ cup ketchup
- ⅓ cup packed brown sugar
- ¼ cup molasses
- 1½ teaspoons salt
- 1½ teaspoons ground mustard
- ⅛ teaspoon ground ginger

1. Rinse beans. Place in a saucepan; add water to cover by 2 in. Bring to a boil; boil for 2 minutes. Remove from heat; let soak, covered, 1-4 hours. Drain and rinse the beans, discarding liquid.
2. Transfer the beans to a 4-qt. slow cooker. Stir in the remaining ingredients. Cook, covered, on low until the beans are tender, 6-8 hours.

NICOLE'S SLOW COOKER BROCCOLI

PREP: 10 MIN.
COOK: 3 HOURS
MAKES: 6 SERVINGS

My sister is a huge inspiration to me and a powerful force in shaping my life. This is one of her favorite dishes. It's an amazing side, and usually little to none of it is left over!
—Toni Ann Moschello, Manahawkin, NJ

- 2 packages (12 ounces each) frozen broccoli with cheese sauce, thawed
- 1 can (10½ ounces) condensed cream of celery soup, undiluted
- 2 cups shredded cheddar cheese
- ½ cup chopped onion
- 2 teaspoons coarsely ground pepper
- 1 teaspoon Worcestershire sauce
- 16 Ritz crackers, crushed
- 2 tablespoons butter, cubed

Mix the first six ingredients. Transfer to a greased 3-qt. slow cooker. Sprinkle with crackers; dot with butter. Cook, covered, on low until the broccoli is tender, 3-4 hours.

CREAMY RANCHIFIED POTATOES

PREP: 15 MIN.
COOK: 6 HOURS
MAKES: 8 SERVINGS

My daughter-in-law gave me this recipe and, over the years, I've tweaked it to our tastes. It's so nice to come home from work to a hot tasty potato dish that's ready to serve! You can use any cheese you like and also any leftover meats that you have—chicken, for one.
—Jane Whittaker, Pensacola, FL

- 2 pounds small red potatoes, quartered
- 1 cup cubed fully cooked ham
- 1 can (10¾ ounces) condensed cream of potato soup, undiluted
- 1 carton (8 ounces) spreadable chive and onion cream cheese
- 3 tablespoons minced chives
- 1 envelope ranch salad dressing mix
- 1 teaspoon pepper
- 6 ounces pepper jack cheese, grated

In a 4-qt. slow cooker, combine the first seven ingredients. Cook, covered, on low until the potatoes are tender, 6-8 hours. Top with cheese; stir to combine.

SLOW COOKER ITALIAN MUSHROOMS

PREP: 10 MIN.
COOK: 5 HOURS
MAKES: 8 SERVINGS

I love to make these mushrooms for big family gatherings—everyone wants to know what the secret ingredients are! They're a star as a side dish, and leftovers go well with steaks or a roast.
—*Becky Schmitz, Fond du Lac, WI*

- 3 **pounds medium fresh mushrooms**
- ¾ **cup butter, melted**
- ¼ **cup Italian salad dressing**
- 3 **tablespoons chicken bouillon granules**
- 1 **envelope zesty Italian salad dressing mix**
- ½ **teaspoon onion powder**
- ½ **teaspoon dried oregano**
- ½ **teaspoon Worcestershire sauce**

Place mushrooms in a 6-qt. slow cooker. Mix the remaining ingredients; pour over the mushrooms. Cook, covered, on low until the mushrooms are tender, 5-6 hours. Serve with a slotted spoon.

CORN & ONION STUFFING

PREP: 10 MIN.
COOK: 3 HOURS
MAKES: 8 SERVINGS

I like something different for a side dish and this is it. This stuffing is perfect with pork, beef or chicken. You can leave it in the slow cooker until it's time to eat—or make it early, refrigerate it until almost serving time and then reheat it.
—*Patricia Swart, Galloway, NJ*

- 1 **can (14¾ ounces) cream-style corn**
- 1 **package (6 ounces) stuffing mix**
- 1 **small onion, chopped**
- 1 **celery rib, chopped**
- ¼ **cup water**
- 2 **large eggs**
- 1 **teaspoon poultry seasoning**
- ⅛ **teaspoon pepper**
- ¼ **cup butter, melted**

Combine the first eight ingredients. Transfer to a greased 3-qt. slow cooker. Drizzle with butter. Cook, covered, on low until set, 3-4 hours.

SLOW-COOKED CHEESY CAULIFLOWER

PREP: 10 MIN.
COOK: 5 HOURS
MAKES: 16 SERVINGS

Since the turkey took up the entire oven, I needed a vegetable that I could make in the slow cooker. After searching for a recipe, I ended up writing my own and trying it out on feast day. My dish turned out even better than I could have hoped!
—*Heather Corson, Casper, WY*

- 2 **medium heads cauliflower, cut into florets (about 18 cups)**
- 1 **can (10¾ ounces) condensed cream of chicken soup, undiluted**
- 2 **cups shredded cheddar cheese**
- 1 **cup sour cream**
- ½ **teaspoon salt**
- ½ **teaspoon pepper**
- ¼ **cup butter, cubed**
- 1 **cup dry bread crumbs**

1. In a 6-qt. slow cooker, combine cauliflower, soup and cheese. Cook, covered, on low until cauliflower is tender, 5-6 hours. Stir in sour cream, salt and pepper.
2. In a small skillet, melt butter over medium heat. Add bread crumbs; cook and stir until golden brown, 2-3 minutes. Sprinkle over the cauliflower.

Holiday Helper

This cauliflower recipe also can be made in the oven in a 13x9-in. dish. Mix the bread crumbs with the melted butter and sprinkle them on top of the cauliflower. Bake at 350° for 30-45 minutes or until bread crumbs are browned and the cheese is bubbly.

"My dish turned out even better than I could have hoped!"
—HEATHER CORSON

2. With a slotted spoon, remove the potatoes and apples to a bowl, reserving the cooking liquid. Mash the potato mixture, gradually adding enough reserved cooking liquid, if necessary, to reach desired consistency.

SLOW COOKER CORN PUDDING

PREP: 10 MIN.
COOK: 4 HOURS
MAKES: 8 SERVINGS

Sweet and creamy, my corn pudding couldn't be simpler to prepare. So satisfying with so little effort—this dish never disappoints!
—Kay Chon, Sherwood, AR

> 2 cans (11 ounces each) whole kernel corn, undrained
> 2 packages (8½ ounces each) corn bread mix
> 1 can (14¾ ounces) cream-style corn
> 1 cup sour cream
> ½ cup butter, melted
> 3 bacon strips, cooked and crumbled

In a greased 3- or 4-qt. slow cooker, combine all the ingredients. Cook, covered, on low until set, 4-5 hours.

BROWN SUGAR SWEET POTATOES WITH APPLES

PREP: 25 MIN.
COOK: 5 HOURS
MAKES: 12 SERVINGS

This foolproof winner is easy to prepare and makes a beautiful alternative to traditional sweet potatoes. To save time, make it ahead, allow it to cool, and refrigerate up to two days. On feast day, put it in the slow cooker set to low about two hours before serving, and reheat while the turkey roasts. Add a bit of apple cider or water if needed.
—Judy Batson, Tampa, FL

> 5 pounds sweet potatoes (about 10 medium)
> 3 medium Granny Smith apples, peeled and cut into 1-inch slices
> ¾ cup butter, cubed
> 1 cup packed brown sugar
> 2 teaspoons pumpkin pie spice

1. Peel and cut sweet potatoes lengthwise in half; cut crosswise into ½-in. slices. Place sweet potatoes and apples in a 6-qt. slow cooker. In a small saucepan, mix butter, brown sugar and pie spice. Bring to a boil over medium heat; cook until blended, 1-2 minutes. Pour over the potato mixture. Cook, covered, on low until potatoes are tender, 5-6 hours.

SLOW-COOKED WILD RICE

PREP: 15 MIN.
COOK: 4 HOURS
MAKES: 8 CUPS

This recipe has become such a family heirloom that I asked permission from my mother before passing it along. It has traveled to weddings, baptisms, landmark birthdays and wedding anniversaries—and it always makes people happy.
—Janet Mahowald, Rice Lake, WI

- 1   **pound bulk pork sausage**
- 4   **celery ribs, chopped**
- 1   **small onion, chopped**
- 1   **can (10¾ ounces) condensed cream of mushroom soup, undiluted**
- 1   **can (10¾ ounces) condensed cream of chicken soup, undiluted**
- 1   **cup uncooked wild rice**
- 1   **can (4 ounces) mushroom stems and pieces, drained**
- 3   **cups chicken broth**

1. In a large skillet, cook and crumble sausage with celery and onion over medium heat until the sausage is no longer pink and the vegetables are tender, 6-8 minutes; drain. Transfer to a 3-qt. slow cooker. Add soups, rice and mushrooms. Stir in broth.
2. Cook, covered, on low until the rice is tender, 4-5 hours.

Holiday Helper
Wild rice actually isn't a grain—it's a seed. You can store uncooked wild rice in an airtight container indefinitely. Always rinse wild rice before cooking to get rid of any dust or debris. Just put it in a strainer and rinse it under cold water.

CRANBERRY-APPLE RED CABBAGE

PREP: 15 MIN.
COOK: 3 HOURS
MAKES: 8 SERVINGS

When I was looking for something new, I started playing with flavors and came up with this very tasty dish. My German grandmother would be impressed, I think! The colorful side dish is just right with pork.
—Ann Sheehy, Lawrence, MA

- 1   **medium head red cabbage, coarsely chopped (8 cups)**
- 1   **can (14 ounces) whole-berry cranberry sauce**
- 2   **medium Granny Smith apples, peeled and coarsely chopped**
- 1   **large white onion, chopped**
- ½   **cup cider vinegar**
- ¼   **cup sweet vermouth or white wine, optional**
- 1   **teaspoon kosher salt**
- ¾   **teaspoon caraway seeds**
- ½   **teaspoon coarsely ground pepper**

Combine all ingredients; transfer to a 5-qt. slow cooker. Cook, covered, on low until cabbage is tender, 3-4 hours. Serve with a slotted spoon.

GOOEY OLD-FASHIONED STEAMED MOLASSES BREAD

PREP: 20 MIN.
COOK: 3 HOURS + COOLING
MAKES: 16 SERVINGS

When I was growing up, the smell of this bread greeted me as I walked in the door from school. I thought everyone baked bread in a slow cooker. My grandmother, mother and I—and now my daughters—all bake this. It's comfort food at its best!
—Bonnie Geavaras-Bootz, Scottsdale, AZ

- 2 cups All-Bran
- 1 cup all-purpose flour
- 1 cup whole wheat flour
- 1 cup dried cranberries
- 1½ teaspoons baking powder
- 1 teaspoon baking soda
- 1 teaspoon salt
- ½ teaspoon ground cinnamon
- 1 large egg
- 1¾ cups buttermilk
- ½ cup molasses
- 2 tablespoons honey

1. Layer two 24-in. pieces of foil. Starting with a long side, roll up foil to make a 1-in.-wide strip; shape into a coil. Place coil on the bottom of a 5-qt. slow cooker to make a rack.

2. In a large bowl, combine cereal, all-purpose and whole wheat flours, cranberries, baking powder, baking soda, salt and cinnamon. In a second bowl, beat egg, buttermilk, molasses and honey. Stir into the flour mixture just until blended (do not overbeat). Pour into a greased and floured 2-qt. baking dish. Tightly cover with lightly greased foil. Place in prepared slow cooker. Cook, covered, on high until a thermometer reads 190-200°, about 3 hours.

3. Remove baking dish to a wire rack; cool 10 minutes before inverting loaf onto the rack. Serve warm or cold.

SLOW COOKER MUSHROOM STUFFING

PREP: 30 MIN.
COOK: 3 HOURS
MAKES: 16 SERVINGS

My grandmother created this recipe after my grandfather left the well-drilling business and invested all their money in a mushroom farm. The farm was a success and saw the family through the Great Depression.
—Eric Cooper, Durham, NC

- ¼ cup butter, cubed
- 1 pound baby portobello mushrooms, coarsely chopped
- 4 celery ribs, chopped
- 1 large onion, chopped
- 12 cups unseasoned stuffing cubes
- ¼ cup chopped fresh parsley
- 1½ teaspoons rubbed sage
- 1 teaspoon salt
- 1 teaspoon dried thyme
- 1 teaspoon poultry seasoning
- ½ teaspoon dried marjoram
- ½ teaspoon pepper
- 2 large eggs, lightly beaten
- 3 cups vegetable broth

1. In a 6-qt. stockpot, heat butter over medium-high heat. Add mushrooms, celery and onion; cook and stir until crisp-tender, 5-7 minutes. Transfer to a bowl. Add stuffing cubes, parsley and seasonings; toss. Whisk together eggs and broth. Pour over the stuffing mixture; stir to combine.

2. Transfer to a greased 6-qt. slow cooker. Cook, covered, on low until heated through, 3-4 hours.

BACON LIMA BEANS

PREP: 15 MIN. + SOAKING
COOK: 6 HOURS
MAKES: 8 SERVINGS

An unusual twist on traditional baked beans, this sweet and spicy version is easy to make and is a surefire crowd pleaser—winter or summer!
—Bette Banjack, Norristown, PA

- 1 pound dried lima beans
- ½ pound bacon strips, cooked and crumbled
- 1 can (10¾ ounces) condensed tomato soup, undiluted
- 1⅓ cups water
- 1 cup packed brown sugar
- 1 garlic clove, minced
- 1 teaspoon salt
- 1 teaspoon paprika
- ½ teaspoon ground mustard

Rinse and sort beans; soak according to package directions. Drain and rinse the beans, discarding liquid. In a 3-qt. slow cooker, combine beans and the remaining ingredients. Cook, covered, on low until beans are tender, 6-8 hours.

¼ cup cider vinegar
2 tablespoons butter
1½ teaspoons whole cloves

1. Place beets in a 3-qt. slow cooker. Mix sugar, brown sugar, cornstarch and salt. Stir in orange juice and vinegar. Pour over the beets; dot with butter.
2. Place cloves on a double thickness of cheesecloth. Gather corners of cloth to enclose spice; tie securely with string. Place bag in slow cooker. Cook, covered, on low until tender, 7-8 hours. Discard the spice bag.

GINGER APPLESAUCE

PREP: 25 MIN.
COOK: 4 HOURS
MAKES: ABOUT 5 CUPS

When it's apple-picking time, it's also time for all the delightful treats you can make with them, including my favorite— applesauce! This is my favorite way to prepare it.
—Renee Pajestka, Brunswick, OH

4 pounds apples (about 12 medium), peeled and cubed
¼ cup water
2 tablespoons brown sugar
2 teaspoons ground cinnamon
2 teaspoons minced fresh gingerroot
2 teaspoons vanilla extract

In a 4-qt. slow cooker, combine all the ingredients. Cook, covered, on low until apples are tender, 4-5 hours. Mash if desired. Refrigerate leftovers.

SMOKY HASH BROWN CASSEROLE

PREP: 10 MIN.
COOK: 3½ HOURS
MAKES: 6 SERVINGS

Making this delicious, savory casserole in the slow cooker saves oven space, but you can bake it in the oven if you prefer.
—Susan Hein, Burlington, WI

1 teaspoon butter
1 package (28 ounces) frozen O'Brien potatoes, thawed
1 can (10¾ ounces) condensed cream of chicken soup, undiluted
1 cup smoked cheddar cheese, shredded
½ teaspoon pepper
¼ teaspoon salt

Grease a 3-qt. slow cooker with butter. Combine potatoes, soup, cheese, pepper and salt. Transfer to prepared slow cooker. Cook, covered, on low until potatoes are tender, 3½-4½ hours.

BAKE OPTION Preheat oven to 350°. Place potato mixture in a greased 13x9-in. baking dish. Add more cheese on top if desired. Bake, uncovered, until potatoes are tender, 45-55 minutes.

SWEET AND TANGY BEETS

PREP: 15 MIN.
COOK: 7 HOURS
MAKES: 6 SERVINGS

Fresh beets are delicious when combined with aromatic spices and a hint of orange. These have the ideal balance of sweet and sour flavors.
—Taste of Home Test Kitchen

2 pounds small fresh beets, peeled and halved
½ cup sugar
¼ cup packed brown sugar
2 tablespoons cornstarch
½ teaspoon salt
¼ cup orange juice

Holiday Helper
A friend taught me a smart trick to stop wasting ginger: Peel the whole root and freeze it. Grate just the amount needed for the recipe and return the unused portion to the freezer for the next time.
—Jennifer C., London, OH

SLOW-COOKED GREEN BEANS

PREP: 10 MIN.
COOK: 2 HOURS
MAKES: 12 SERVINGS

I spent hours in search of side dishes for a cooking demo to present to women from my church. These easy green beans became my star attraction. They add a lovely splash of green veggies to a traditional holiday meal.
—Alice White, Willow Spring, NC

- 16 **cups frozen french-style green beans (about 48 ounces), thawed**
- ½ **cup butter, melted**
- ½ **cup packed brown sugar**
- 1½ **teaspoons garlic salt**
- ¾ **teaspoon reduced-sodium soy sauce**

Place beans in a 5-qt. slow cooker. Mix the remaining ingredients; pour over the beans and toss to coat. Cook, covered, on low until heated through, 2-3 hours. Serve with a slotted spoon.

WINTER FRUIT COMPOTE

PREP: 10 MIN.
COOK: 1¼ HOURS + COOLING
MAKES: 2½ CUPS

You can make this versatile fruit relish up to a week ahead. It's an outstanding accompaniment to poultry or pork f/or the holiday season, and it's sweet enough to top waffles anytime!
—Esther Chesney, Carthage, MO

- 1 **package (12 ounces) fresh or frozen cranberries, thawed**
- ⅔ **cup packed brown sugar**
- ¼ **cup orange juice concentrate**
- 2 **tablespoons raspberry vinegar**
- ½ **cup chopped dried apricots**
- ½ **cup golden raisins**
- ½ **cup chopped walnuts, toasted**

1. In a 1½-qt. slow cooker, combine cranberries, brown sugar, orange juice concentrate and vinegar. Cook, covered, on low until cranberries pop and mixture is thickened, 1¼-1¾ hours.
2. Turn off heat; stir in apricots, raisins and walnuts. Cool to room temperature. Refrigerate any leftovers.

HOT FRUIT SALAD

PREP: 10 MIN.
COOK: 3 HOURS
MAKES: 16 SERVINGS

If you're looking for something easy to round out a brunch, try this spiced fruit salad. With its pretty color, it's perfect around the holidays or for any special occasion.
—*Barb Vande Voort, New Sharon, IA*

- 1 jar (25 ounces) unsweetened applesauce
- 1 can (21 ounces) cherry pie filling
- 1 can (20 ounces) unsweetened pineapple chunks, undrained
- 1 can (15 ounces) sliced peaches in juice, undrained
- 1 can (15 ounces) reduced-sugar apricot halves, undrained
- 1 can (15 ounces) mandarin oranges, undrained
- ¼ cup packed brown sugar
- 1 teaspoon ground cinnamon

Combine the first six ingredients in a 5-qt. slow cooker. Mix brown sugar and cinnamon; sprinkle over the fruit mixture. Cook, covered, on low until heated through, 3-4 hours.

POTLUCK MACARONI & CHEESE

PREP: 25 MIN.
COOK: 2 HOURS
MAKES: 16 SERVINGS

Here's a no-fuss way to make America's most popular comfort food. The dish turns out cheesy, rich and extra creamy.
—*Jennifer Babcock, Chicopee, MA*

- 3 cups uncooked elbow macaroni
- 1 package (16 ounces) process cheese (Velveeta), cubed
- 2 cups shredded Mexican cheese blend
- 2 cups shredded white cheddar cheese
- 1¾ cups whole milk
- 1 can (12 ounces) evaporated milk
- ¾ cup butter, melted
- 3 large eggs, lightly beaten

1. Cook macaroni according to package directions for al dente; drain. Transfer to a greased 5-qt. slow cooker. Stir in the remaining ingredients.
2. Cook, covered, on low until a thermometer reads at least 160°, 2-2½ hours, stirring once.

APPLE & BROWN SUGAR GLAZED CARROTS

PREP: 10 MIN.
COOK: 3¼ HOURS
MAKES: 4 SERVINGS

Carrots seem so simple, but this recipe is something special. Sweet and buttery, this was a favorite my mother always used to serve at holiday time.
—*Darlis Wilfer, West Bend, WI*

- 2 pounds medium carrots, cut into 1-inch pieces
- ½ cup unsweetened apple juice
- ½ cup packed brown sugar
- ¼ cup butter, cubed
- ¼ teaspoon salt
- ¼ cup chopped pecans or walnuts, toasted, optional

1. In a 3-qt. slow cooker, combine carrots and apple juice. Cook, covered, on high until the carrots are tender, 3-4 hours.
2. Remove the carrots from slow cooker; discard juices. Return carrots to slow cooker. Stir in brown sugar, butter and salt. Cook, covered, on high until carrots are glazed, 15-20 minutes longer. Sprinkle with pecans before serving, if desired.

"This was a favorite my mother always used to serve."
—DARLIS WILFER

HOLIDAY
FEASTS

When family and friends gather around the table, give
them a feast to remember. These three menus—with
some extra options—are sure make the season bright.

Poultry Dinner

Lemon Herb Game Hens, p. 41

Crunchy Spinach Casserole, p. 41

Nutty Pumpkin Bisque, p. 42

Spiced Orange-Cranberry
Chutney, p. 43

Bourbon-Infused
Fingerling Potatoes, p. 43

Company Mashed Carrots, p. 44

Caramel Apple Pie with
Streusel Topping, p. 44

LEMON HERB GAME HENS

PREP: 20 MIN.
COOK: 1¼ HOURS
MAKES: 6 SERVINGS

My mom made game hens for my dad once a week. When my sister and I were little, we would try to sneak some of the chicken from his plate. For this dish, use whatever herbs you have on hand. If you have some in the garden, even better!
—*Meagan Meyer, Irving, TX*

- 6 Cornish game hens (20 to 24 ounces each)
- 3 medium lemons
- 1 whole garlic bulb, separated into 18 cloves
- ¾ cup olive oil
- 1 teaspoon onion powder
- 1 teaspoon garlic powder
- 1 teaspoon salt
- 1 teaspoon pepper
- 1 cup coarsely chopped fresh basil
- 1 tablespoon minced fresh rosemary
- 1 tablespoon minced fresh thyme

1. Preheat oven to 375°. Place hens in a roasting pan. Cut 1½ lemons into six wedges. Rub a lemon wedge over each hen; place wedges in roasting pan. Peel and cut garlic cloves in half. Rub cut side of a garlic half over each hen; place in cavity with five additional garlic halves. Rub 2 tablespoons oil over each hen; sprinkle with the onion powder, garlic powder, salt and pepper.
2. In a small bowl, mix basil, rosemary and thyme. Sprinkle half over hens; place remaining herbs in cavities. Cut remaining lemons into 12 slices; place over the hens. Roast 1¼-1½ hours or until a thermometer inserted in thickest part of the thigh reads 170°.

CRUNCHY SPINACH CASSEROLE

PREP: 15 MIN.
BAKE: 35 MIN.
MAKES: 4 SERVINGS

Our holidays would not be the same without this family tradition. My mother made it every Thanksgiving when I was growing up; now I make it every Christmas and Thanksgiving, and my children and grandchildren absolutely love it! We triple the recipe because the kids can't get enough.
—*Sharon Scaletta, Johnstown, PA*

- ½ cup butter, divided
- 2 celery ribs, finely chopped
- 1 small onion, finely chopped
- 2 packages (10 ounces each) frozen chopped spinach, thawed and squeezed dry
- 1 can (10¾ ounces) condensed cream of mushroom soup, undiluted
- 2 cups cubed bread (½ inch)

1. Preheat oven to 350°. In a large skillet, heat ¼ cup butter over medium heat. Add celery and onion; cook and stir 4-5 minutes or until tender. Stir in spinach and soup.
2. Transfer to a 1½-qt. round baking dish. In a small saucepan, melt the remaining butter over medium heat. Stir in bread cubes. Sprinkle over top. Bake for 35-40 minutes or until bubbly and the bread cubes are golden brown.

NUTTY PUMPKIN BISQUE

PREP: 15 MIN.
COOK: 20 MIN.
MAKES: 4 SERVINGS

Hearty and comforting pumpkin soup is the perfect starter to a holiday meal or the star performer of an autumn luncheon. The addition of the toasted pecans and pumpkin seeds creates a wonderful depth of flavor. This soup can be served immediately or made a day in advance and then reheated.
—Lauri Knox, Pine, CO

  2 **tablespoons butter**
  1 **medium onion, chopped**
  2 **garlic cloves, minced**
  3 **cups chicken stock**
  1 **can (15 ounces) solid-pack pumpkin**
  ½ **cup sherry or chicken stock**
  2 **teaspoons brown sugar**
  ½ **teaspoon dried thyme**
  ½ **teaspoon ground cumin**
  ½ **teaspoon dried rosemary, crushed**
  ¼ **teaspoon salt**
  1 **cup heavy whipping cream**
  ¾ **cup chopped pecans, toasted**
  ½ **cup salted pumpkin seeds or pepitas, toasted**
    Optional toppings: sour cream, fresh rosemary sprigs, and additional toasted chopped pecans and pumpkin seeds

1. In a 6-qt. stockpot, heat butter over medium-high heat. Add onion; cook and stir 2-3 minutes or until tender. Add garlic; cook 1 minute longer. Stir in stock, pumpkin, sherry, brown sugar and seasonings; bring to a boil. Reduce heat; simmer, uncovered, 10 minutes or until slightly thickened.

2. Stir in cream, pecans and seeds. Remove from heat; cool slightly. Process in batches in a blender until smooth. Return all to pan; heat through. If desired, serve with optional toppings.

BLING RINGS

Create eye-catching napkin rings with ribbon and costume jewelry. See page 222 for detailed instructions.

SPICED ORANGE-CRANBERRY CHUTNEY

PREP: 15 MIN.
COOK: 55 MIN. + CHILLING
MAKES: 8 CUPS

The aroma of simmering chutney signals the start of the holidays and sets the mood for my seasonal baking. Try it as an appetizer along with cream cheese and graham crackers.
—Pat Stevens, Granbury, TX

 2¼ **cups packed brown sugar**
 1½ **cups cranberry juice**
 ½ **cup cider vinegar**
 ½ **teaspoon ground ginger**
 ¼ **teaspoon ground allspice**
 3 **packages (12 ounces each) fresh cranberries**
 2 **tablespoons grated orange peel**
 2 **medium oranges, peeled and sectioned**
 1 **medium tart apple, peeled and coarsely chopped**
 ½ **cup dried currants**
 ½ **cup coarsely chopped dried apricots**

In a 6-qt. stockpot, combine the first five ingredients. Cook, uncovered, over medium heat until brown sugar dissolves. Stir in cranberries, orange peel, oranges, apple, currants and apricots. Bring to a boil. Reduce heat; simmer, uncovered, 50-60 minutes or until thickened, stirring occasionally. Serve chilled.

BOURBON-INFUSED FINGERLING POTATOES

PREP: 15 MIN.
COOK: 30 MIN.
MAKES: 10 SERVINGS

These saucy potatoes turn out so full of flavor from the combination of bourbon, Worcestershire sauce and garlic. What an easy way to do something different with potatoes!
—JoAnn Mathias, Hoschton, GA

 2 **pounds assorted fingerling or other small potatoes**
 5 **tablespoons butter, divided**
 2 **medium red onions, finely chopped**
 2 **medium green peppers, finely chopped**
 ½ **cup bourbon**
 ¼ **cup reduced-sodium soy sauce**
 2 **tablespoons brown sugar**
 2 **tablespoons canola oil**
 2 **tablespoons Worcestershire sauce**
 2 **garlic cloves, minced**
 ½ **teaspoon salt**
 ½ **teaspoon pepper**

1. Place potatoes in a large saucepan; add water to cover. Bring to a boil. Reduce heat; cook, uncovered, 10-15 minutes or until tender. Drain.
2. In a 12-in. skillet, heat 2 tablespoons butter over medium-high heat; add onions and green peppers. Cook and stir until tender; remove from pan.
3. In the same pan, heat the remaining butter over medium-high heat; add the potatoes. Using a fork or potato masher, flatten the potatoes slightly. Cook 3-4 minutes on each side or until lightly browned. Return the onion mixture to the pan.
4. In a small bowl, whisk the remaining ingredients until blended; add to pan. Bring to a boil; cook 1-2 minutes or until liquid is absorbed.

COMPANY MASHED CARROTS

START TO FINISH: 30 MIN.
MAKES: 6 SERVINGS

Although I call these "company carrots," I'll often serve them on a weeknight to my family. No matter who's eating it, the fast, easy dish is always a favorite.
—Cynthia Hanus-Beard, Tamarac, FL

- 2 **pounds carrots, sliced**
- ½ **cup butter, cubed**
- 2 **tablespoons sugar**
- 1 **tablespoon orange liqueur**
- ½ **teaspoon salt**
- ½ **teaspoon pepper**
- ¼ **teaspoon ground nutmeg**

1. Place carrots in a Dutch oven; add water to cover. Bring to a boil. Cook, covered, 15-20 minutes or until very tender. Drain carrots; return to pan.
2. Mash carrots with the remaining ingredients by hand or puree in a food processor until blended.

CARAMEL APPLE PIE WITH STREUSEL TOPPING

PREP: 50 MIN. + CHILLING
BAKE: 35 MIN.
MAKES: 12 SERVINGS

I developed this recipe through the years to get it exactly where we want it. I've entered several pie contests with it and placed first each time—one bite and you'll know why this pie's a winner!
—Laurel Dalzell, Manteca, CA

- 1⅔ **cups all-purpose flour**
- 2 **teaspoons sugar**
- ¾ **teaspoon salt**
- ¾ **cup cold butter, cubed**
- 4 **to 5 tablespoons ice water**

FILLING

- 9 **medium Golden Delicious or Braeburn apples (about 3 pounds), peeled and cut into ¾-inch chunks**
- ½ **cup butter, cubed**
- ½ **cup packed brown sugar**
- 2 **tablespoons all-purpose flour**
- 1 **tablespoon pumpkin pie spice**

TOPPING

- 1 **cup all-purpose flour**
- ½ **cup packed brown sugar**
- ¼ **teaspoon salt**
- ½ **cup cold butter, cubed**
- ½ **cup finely chopped walnuts**
- 1 **large egg, optional**
- 2 **tablespoons water, optional**

1. In a large bowl, mix flour, sugar and salt; cut in butter until crumbly. Gradually add water, tossing with a fork until dough holds together when pressed. If desired, separate one-fourth of the dough for decorative cutouts; shape both portions into disks and wrap in plastic wrap. Refrigerate 1 hour or overnight.
2. Preheat oven to 450°. In a Dutch oven, combine the filling ingredients. Cook over medium heat 10-15 minutes or until the apples are almost tender, stirring occasionally; remove from heat.
3. On a lightly floured surface, roll the larger portion of dough to a ⅛-in.-thick circle; transfer to a 9-in. deep-dish pie plate. Trim pastry to ½ in. beyond rim of plate; flute the edge. Line unpricked pastry with a double thickness of foil. Fill with pie weights, dried beans or uncooked rice.
4. Bake for 8 minutes. Remove foil and weights; bake 5 minutes longer. Cool on a wire rack. Reduce oven setting to 375°. For topping, in a small bowl, combine flour, brown sugar and salt; cut in butter until crumbly. Stir in walnuts. If desired, make decorative cutouts with the remaining pastry dough.
5. Spoon filling into crust; sprinkle topping over the filling. If desired, arrange cutouts over the topping. In a small bowl, whisk egg and water; brush over the cutouts. Bake pie for 35-45 minutes or until golden brown and the filling is bubbly. Cool on a wire rack.
NOTE Let pie weights cool before storing. Beans and rice may be reused for pie weights, but not for cooking.

"One bite and you'll know why this pie's a winner!"
—LAUREL DALZELL

Pork Dinner

Italian Herb-Crusted Pork Loin, p. 47

Spinach Salad with Raspberries & Candied Walnuts, p. 47

Quick & Easy au Gratin Potatoes, p. 48

Cranberry Pesto, p. 48

Dove Dinner Rolls, p. 49

Blackberry Brandy Slush, p. 50

Pina Colada Bundt Cake, p. 50

ITALIAN HERB-CRUSTED PORK LOIN

PREP: 15 MIN. + CHILLING
BAKE: 50 MIN. + STANDING
MAKES: 8 SERVINGS

I like to change things up during the holidays by roasting pork loin with my favorite herbs and veggies. This showpiece dish really dazzles my family.
—Kim Palmer, Kingston, GA

- 3 tablespoons olive oil
- 5 garlic cloves, minced
- 1 teaspoon salt
- 1 teaspoon each dried basil, thyme and rosemary, crushed
- ½ teaspoon Italian seasoning
- ½ teaspoon pepper
- 1 boneless pork loin roast (3 to 4 pounds)
- 8 medium carrots, halved lengthwise
- 2 medium onions, quartered

1. In a small bowl, mix oil, garlic and seasonings; rub over roast. Arrange carrots and onions on the bottom of a 13x9-in. baking pan. Place roast over the vegetables, fat side up. Refrigerate, covered, 1 hour.
2. Preheat oven to 475°. Roast the pork for 20 minutes.
3. Reduce oven setting to 425°. Roast 30-40 minutes longer or until a thermometer reads 145° and the vegetables are tender. Remove roast from oven; tent with foil. Let stand 20 minutes before slicing.

Holiday Helper
Don't overcook the pork! Conventional wisdom told us pork was done at 160°, leading to a lot of pale, dry roasts. The USDA's new guideline is 145° for doneness; it's all right if you see a little bit of pink in the meat.

SPINACH SALAD WITH RASPBERRIES & CANDIED WALNUTS

PREP: 15 MIN.
BAKE: 25 MIN. + COOLING
MAKES: 8 SERVINGS

I created a bright spinach salad with raspberries for a big family dinner, and the festive colors fit right in on a holiday table. Even those who don't like spinach change their mind at the very first bite.
—Robert Aucelluzzo, Simi Valley, CA

- 1 large egg white
- ¾ teaspoon vanilla extract
- 2 cups walnut halves
- ½ cup sugar

DRESSING
- ¼ cup canola oil
- 2 tablespoons cider vinegar
- 1 tablespoon sugar
- 1½ teaspoons light corn syrup
- 1 teaspoon poppy seeds
- ¼ teaspoon salt
- ¼ teaspoon ground mustard

SALAD
- 8 ounces fresh baby spinach (about 10 cups)
- 1½ cups fresh raspberries

1. Preheat oven to 300°. In a small bowl, whisk egg white and vanilla until frothy. Stir in walnuts. Sprinkle with sugar; toss to coat evenly. Spread in a single layer in a greased 15x10x1-in. baking pan.
2. Bake for 25-30 minutes or until walnuts are lightly browned, stirring every 10 minutes. Spread on waxed paper to cool completely.
3. In a small bowl, whisk the dressing ingredients until blended. Place spinach in a large bowl. Drizzle with dressing; toss to coat. Sprinkle with raspberries and 1 cup of the candied walnuts (save remaining walnuts for another use).

1. Preheat oven to 350°. In a large bowl, mix sour cream, condensed soup, salt and pepper; stir in potatoes, cheese and onion. Transfer to a greased 13x9-in. baking dish.

2. In a small bowl, mix crushed cornflakes and melted butter; sprinkle over the potato mixture. Bake, uncovered, for 50-60 minutes or until golden brown.

CRANBERRY PESTO

START TO FINISH: 10 MIN.
MAKES: 1¼ CUPS

I updated a classic Italian pesto to include cranberries and walnuts. It's so good slathered on pork loin, pasta or turkey sandwiches!
—Aysha Schurman, Ammon, ID

- ⅔ cup loosely packed basil leaves
- ½ cup dried cranberries
- ¼ cup chopped walnuts
- 1 green onion, chopped
- 3 garlic cloves, coarsely chopped
- ½ teaspoon pepper
- ¼ teaspoon salt
- ⅔ cup olive oil

Place the first seven ingredients in a food processor; pulse until coarsely chopped. Continue processing while gradually adding oil in a steady stream. Store in an airtight container in the refrigerator for up to 1 week.

QUICK & EASY AU GRATIN POTATOES

PREP: 10 MIN.
BAKE: 50 MIN.
MAKES: 12 SERVINGS

At the holidays, a good friend serves these creamy, cheesy potatoes when we gather together to celebrate with lifelong friends and grown children.
—Carol Blue, Barnesville, PA

- 2 cups sour cream
- 1 can (10¾ ounces) condensed cream of chicken soup, undiluted
- ½ teaspoon salt
- ¼ teaspoon pepper
- 1 package (30 ounces) frozen shredded hash brown potatoes, thawed
- 2 cups shredded cheddar cheese
- 1 small onion, chopped
- 2 cups crushed cornflakes
- ¼ cup butter, melted

DOVE DINNER ROLLS

PREP: 50 MIN. + RISING
BAKE: 10 MIN.
MAKES: 2 DOZEN

Fluffy dinner rolls shaped like doves are a sweet nod to the holidays. They dash away faster than Santa himself!
—Frances Wirtz, West Allis, WI

- 2 **cups whole wheat pastry flour**
- ½ **cup sugar**
- 3 **packages (¼ ounce each) active dry yeast**
- 2 **teaspoons salt**
- 1 **cup water**
- 1 **cup 2% milk**
- ½ **cup butter, cubed**
- 1 **large egg**
- 4 **to 4½ cups bread flour**

ASSEMBLY

- 48 **dried currants**
- 24 **slivered almonds**
- 1 **large egg**
- 2 **tablespoons 2% milk**

1. In a large bowl, mix pastry flour, sugar, yeast and salt. In a small saucepan, heat water, milk and butter to 120°-130°. Add to the dry ingredients; beat on medium speed 1 minute. Add egg; beat on high 2 minutes. Stir in enough bread flour to form a soft dough (dough will be sticky).

2. Turn onto a floured surface; knead until smooth and elastic, 6-8 minutes. Place in a greased bowl, turning once to grease the top. Cover with plastic wrap and let rise in a warm place until doubled, about 45 minutes.

3. Punch down dough. Let stand, covered, 15 minutes. Turn onto a lightly floured surface; divide and shape into 24 balls. Roll each into a 10-in. rope; tie into a loose knot. Tuck one end into center of roll to form head. Flatten the opposite end; cut four slits to form five tail feathers. Press in two currants for eyes and one almond for the beak. Place 2 in. apart on greased baking sheets.

4. Cover with kitchen towels; let rise in a warm place until doubled, about 30 minutes. Preheat oven to 400°.

5. Whisk egg and milk; brush over rolls. Bake for 10-12 minutes or until golden brown. Remove from pans to wire racks; serve warm.

HEAD START After tying dough in a loose knot, use the shorter end to form each dove's head.

SPRAY AND GO Coat a sharp knife with nonstick cooking spray to keep it cutting tail feathers freely.

PINA COLADA BUNDT CAKE

PREP: 15 MIN.
BAKE: 45 MIN. + COOLING
MAKES: 12 SERVINGS

We named this cake "pina colada" because it has coconut, pineapple and rum. It's a soothing finish at the end of a big spread.
—Debra Keil, Owasso, OK

- 1 **package white cake mix (regular size)**
- 1 **package (3.4 ounces) instant coconut cream pudding mix**
- 1 **cup canola oil**
- ¾ **cup water**
- 2 **large eggs**
- ¼ **cup rum**
- 1 **cup drained crushed pineapple**

GLAZE
- 2 **cups confectioners' sugar, divided**
- 2 **tablespoons unsweetened pineapple juice**
- ¼ **cup cream of coconut**
- 1 **tablespoon rum**
- ¼ **cup flaked coconut**

1. Preheat oven to 350°. Grease and flour a 10-in. fluted tube pan.
2. In a large bowl, combine cake mix, pudding mix, oil, water, eggs and rum; beat on low speed for 30 seconds. Beat on medium for 2 minutes. Stir in pineapple. Transfer batter to prepared pan. Bake 45-50 minutes or until a toothpick inserted in center comes out clean. Cool in pan 15 minutes before removing to a wire rack.
3. In a small bowl, mix 1 cup of the confectioners' sugar and the pineapple juice; brush over warm cake. Cool cake completely.
4. In another bowl, mix cream of coconut, rum and the remaining confectioners' sugar; drizzle over cake. Sprinkle with flaked coconut.

BLACKBERRY BRANDY SLUSH

PREP: 10 MIN. + FREEZING
MAKES: 28 SERVINGS

We wanted a fun, grown-up twist on a favorite slushy, so we spiked it with blackberry brandy. The deep red color makes it very merry.
—Lindsey Spinler, Sobieski, WI

- 8 **cups water**
- 2 **cups sugar**
- 3 **cups blackberry brandy**
- 1 **can (12 ounces) frozen lemonade concentrate, thawed**
- 1 **can (12 ounces) frozen grape juice concentrate, thawed**
- 14 **cups lemon-lime soda, chilled**

1. In a large bowl, stir water and sugar until sugar is dissolved. Stir in brandy and juice concentrates. Transfer to freezer containers; freeze overnight.
2. To serve, place about ½ cup of the brandy mixture in each glass; top with ½ cup soda.

Holiday Helper
Don't splurge on top-shelf liquor for frozen cocktails; the flavors of the drink will mostly be determined by the fruit and juices you use, and the icy cold won't let the nuances of expensive flavors through.

"It's a soothing finish at the end of a big spread."
—DEBRA KEIL

Seafood Dinner

White Seafood Lasagna, p. 53

Insalata Caprese, p. 53

Rustic Tuscan
Pepper Bruschetta, p. 54

Calabrian Holiday Soup, p. 54

Antipasto Marinated
Vegetables, p. 55

Pepper Parmesan Beans, p. 56

Spumoni Torte, p. 56

WHITE SEAFOOD LASAGNA

PREP: 1 HOUR
BAKE: 40 MIN. + STANDING
MAKES: 12 SERVINGS

We make lasagna with shrimp and scallops as part of a traditional Italian holiday dinner. Every bite delivers a tasty jewel from the sea.
—Joe Colamonico, North Charleston, SC

- 9 uncooked lasagna noodles
- 1 tablespoon butter
- 1 pound uncooked shrimp (31-40 per pound), peeled and deveined
- 1 pound bay scallops
- 5 garlic cloves, minced
- ¼ cup white wine
- 1 tablespoon lemon juice
- 1 pound fresh crabmeat

CHEESE SAUCE
- ¼ cup butter, cubed
- ¼ cup all-purpose flour
- 3 cups 2% milk
- 1 cup shredded part-skim mozzarella cheese
- ½ cup grated Parmesan cheese
- ½ teaspoon salt
- ¼ teaspoon pepper
  Dash ground nutmeg

RICOTTA MIXTURE
- 1 carton (15 ounces) part-skim ricotta cheese
- 1 package (10 ounces) frozen chopped spinach, thawed and squeezed dry
- 1 cup shredded part-skim mozzarella cheese
- ½ cup grated Parmesan cheese
- ½ cup seasoned bread crumbs
- 1 large egg, lightly beaten

TOPPING
- 1 cup shredded part-skim mozzarella cheese
- ¼ cup grated Parmesan cheese
  Minced fresh parsley

1. Preheat oven to 350°. Cook lasagna noodles according to the package directions; drain.

2. In a large skillet, heat butter over medium heat. Add shrimp and scallops in batches; cook 2-4 minutes or until the shrimp turn pink and the scallops are firm and opaque. Remove from pan.

3. Add garlic to the same pan; cook for 1 minute. Add wine and lemon juice, stirring to loosen browned bits from pan. Bring to a boil; cook 1-2 minutes or until liquid is reduced by half. Add crab; heat through. Stir in shrimp and scallops.

4. For cheese sauce, melt butter over medium heat in a large saucepan. Stir in flour until smooth; gradually whisk in milk. Bring to a boil, stirring constantly; cook and stir for 1-2 minutes or until thickened. Remove from heat; stir in the remaining cheese sauce ingredients. In a large bowl, combine ricotta mixture ingredients; stir in 1 cup cheese sauce.

5. Spread ½ cup of the cheese sauce into a greased 13x9-in. baking dish. Layer with three noodles, half the ricotta mixture, half the seafood mixture and ⅔ cup of the cheese sauce. Repeat layers. Top with the remaining noodles and cheese sauce. Sprinkle with the remaining mozzarella cheese and Parmesan cheese.

6. Bake, uncovered, 40-50 minutes or until bubbly and top is golden brown. Let stand 10 minutes before serving. Sprinkle with parsley.

INSALATA CAPRESE

START TO FINISH: 25 MIN.
MAKES: 8 SERVINGS

A classic Caprese salad has colors that resemble the Italian flag. For extra zing, I add a splash of balsamic vinegar.
—Joe Colamonico, North Charleston, SC

- 2½ pounds plum tomatoes (about 10), cut into 1-inch pieces
- 1 carton (8 ounces) fresh mozzarella cheese pearls
- ½ cup pitted ripe olives
- 3 tablespoons olive oil
- ¼ cup thinly sliced fresh basil
- 2 teaspoons minced fresh oregano
- ½ teaspoon salt
- ¼ teaspoon pepper
  Balsamic vinegar, optional

In a large bowl, mix tomatoes, mozzarella cheese pearls and olives. Drizzle with oil. Sprinkle with basil, oregano, salt and pepper; toss to coat. Let stand for 10 minutes before serving. If desired, drizzle with vinegar.

1   teaspoon dried oregano
1   teaspoon dried basil
2½ teaspoons pepper, divided
1   pound lean ground
    beef (90% lean)
3   cups uncooked instant rice
1   package (10 ounces) frozen
    chopped spinach, thawed
    and squeezed dry
3   large eggs, beaten

1. Place chicken in a 6-qt. stockpot; add water to cover. Slowly bring to a boil. Reduce the heat; simmer, covered, for 2-3 hours. Meanwhile, in a large bowl, mix 1½ teaspoons salt, oregano, basil and 1 teaspoon pepper. Add beef; mix lightly but thoroughly. Shape into ½-in. balls.
2. Remove carcass from stockpot; cool. Return broth to a simmer; add meatballs. Cook, uncovered, 8-10 minutes or until meatballs are cooked through.
3. Remove meat from carcass; shred meat with two forks and return to pot. Discard the carcass and skin. Bring broth to a boil; stir in rice and spinach. Reduce heat; simmer, covered, for 5 minutes. Drizzle the beaten eggs into the soup, stirring constantly. Stir in remaining salt and pepper.

RUSTIC TUSCAN PEPPER BRUSCHETTA

START TO FINISH: 30 MIN.
MAKES: 4 DOZEN

If you love sweet red, yellow and orange peppers, pair them with fresh mint for a cold kitchen appetizer. Marinate for up to one hour before assembling.
—Noelle Myers, Grand Forks, ND

2   tablespoons olive oil
2   tablespoons balsamic vinegar
1   tablespoon honey
1   tablespoon minced fresh mint
1   each medium sweet yellow,
    orange and red pepper, cut
    into thin 1-inch strips
6   ounces fresh goat cheese
⅔   cup whipped cream cheese
48 assorted crackers

1. In a large bowl, whisk oil, vinegar, honey and mint. Add peppers; toss to coat. Let stand at least 15 minutes.
2. In a small bowl, beat goat cheese and cream cheese. Spread 1 rounded teaspoon on each cracker. Drain peppers well. Arrange the peppers on cheese-topped crackers.

CALABRIAN HOLIDAY SOUP

PREP: 15 MIN.
COOK: 3 HOURS
MAKES: 14 SERVINGS (3½ QUARTS)

My family is from the Italian region of Calabria; our version of Italian wedding soup has been handed down through the generations. We serve this soup with the Christmas meal as well as at weddings.
—Gwen Keefer, Sylvania, OH

1   broiler/fryer chicken
    (4 to 5 pounds)
3   teaspoons salt, divided

ANTIPASTO MARINATED VEGETABLES

PREP: 25 MIN.
COOK: 10 MIN. + CHILLING
MAKES: 10 SERVINGS

The colorful vegetables and the tart dressing make this a lively addition to a holiday table. As a side dish or a condiment, it's great either way. Three hours is enough to let the flavors blend.
—Barbara McCalley, Allison Park, PA

- 3 **celery ribs, sliced**
- 3 **large carrots, sliced**
- 1 **medium green pepper, julienned**
- 1 **can (14 ounces) water-packed artichoke hearts, rinsed, drained and quartered**
- 1 **jar (4½ ounces) whole mushrooms, drained**
- ¾ **cup sliced ripe olives**
- ¾ **cup olive oil**
- ⅓ **cup white wine vinegar**
- 2 **green onions (white parts only), thinly sliced**
- 2 **garlic cloves, minced**
- 1½ **teaspoons sugar**
- ¾ **teaspoon pepper**
- ¼ **teaspoon salt**
- 1 **jar (2 ounces) pimiento strips**
- 2 **tablespoons minced fresh parsley**

1. Place 1 in. of water, celery, carrots and green pepper in a large saucepan; bring to a boil. Reduce heat; simmer, covered, 5-7 minutes or until crisp-tender. Drain.

Transfer to a large bowl; add artichokes, mushrooms and olives.

2. In a small saucepan, whisk oil, vinegar, onions, garlic, sugar, pepper and salt; bring just to a boil. Pour over vegetables; toss to coat. Cool to room temperature. Stir in pimientos and parsley. Refrigerate until serving, 3 hours or more.

Holiday Helper

When a recipe calls for julienned bell peppers, start by holding the pepper by the stem and slicing from the top of the pepper down, using a chef's knife. Use this technique to slice around the seeds; then thinly slice the resulting pieces.

SPUMONI TORTE

PREP: 30 MIN.
BAKE: 25 MIN. + COOLING
MAKES: 16 SERVINGS

I made up this recipe to end a big Italian Christmas Eve dinner. I thought it would be nice and light after a heavy meal. The cake frosts the best when it's been stored in the freezer for a day.
—*Lynne Ogg, East Bethel, MN*

- 2 packages white cake mix (regular size)
- 1 teaspoon almond extract

FILLING

- 2¼ cups heavy whipping cream
- 1 cup confectioners' sugar, divided
- ½ cup 2% milk
- 1 package (3.4 ounces) instant pistachio pudding mix
- 6 tablespoons cream cheese, softened, divided
- ¼ cup baking cocoa
- 1 cup chopped maraschino cherries
- ½ teaspoon almond extract

1. Preheat oven to 350°. Line bottoms of three greased 9-in. round baking pans with parchment paper; grease paper. Prepare the cake mix batter according to the package directions, adding almond extract before mixing the batter. Transfer to prepared pans. Bake, 25-30 minutes or until a toothpick inserted in center comes out clean. Cool as the package directs.
2. In a small bowl, beat the cream until it begins to thicken. Add ⅔ cup of the confectioners' sugar; beat until soft peaks form. Place 1½ cups whipped cream in each of three bowls. In another bowl, whisk milk and pudding mix for 2 minutes. Let stand 2 minutes or until soft-set. Fold pudding into one bowl of whipped cream. In a second bowl of whipped cream, beat in 3 tablespoons cream cheese, cocoa and the remaining confectioners' sugar until combined. In the third bowl of cream, beat in maraschino cherries, almond extract and remaining cream cheese.
3. Place one cake layer on a serving plate; spread with the pistachio filling. Top with the second cake layer; spread with the maraschino filling. Top with the remaining cake layer; spread with the chocolate filling. Refrigerate until serving.

PEPPER PARMESAN BEANS

START TO FINISH: 15 MIN.
MAKES: 8 SERVINGS

A colorful mixture of peppers and green beans gets an Italian treatment with basil and Parmesan cheese in this delightful vegetable dish.
—*Marian Platt, Sequim, WA*

- 1 large sweet red pepper, diced
- 1 small green pepper, diced
- ¼ cup chopped onion
- 1 garlic clove, minced
- ¼ cup olive oil
- 1½ pounds fresh green beans, cut into 2-inch pieces
- 1 tablespoon minced fresh basil or 1 teaspoon dried basil
- 1 teaspoon salt
- ⅓ to ½ cup shredded Parmesan cheese

In a large skillet, saute the peppers, onion and garlic in oil until the vegetables are tender, about 3 minutes. Add the beans, basil and salt; toss to coat. Cover and cook over medium-low heat for 7-8 minutes or until the beans are crisp-tender. Stir in the cheese; serve immediately.

More Choices for Christmas Menus

When you're cooking a traditional family meal, everyone will have favorite dishes and must-have items. So feel free to depart from the menu and fill in with one of these delicious a la carte options.

ROASTED SAGE TURKEY WITH VEGETABLE GRAVY

PREP: 30 MIN. + CHILLING
BAKE: 2 HOURS 10 MIN. + STANDING
MAKES: 16 SERVINGS (3½ CUPS GRAVY)

There's no place like home-style when roasting the big bird. Instead of stuffing, fill this bird with fresh sage and sprigs of thyme.
—Beth Jacobson, Milwaukee, WI

- 1 **turkey (14 to 16 pounds)**
- 1 **tablespoon kosher salt**
- 1 **teaspoon ground sage**
- ½ **teaspoon garlic powder**
- 1 **large onion, chopped**
- 3 **celery ribs, chopped**
- 3 **medium carrots, chopped**
- 1¼ **cups water, divided**
- 3 **tablespoons canola oil**
- ½ **teaspoon freshly ground pepper**
- ¾ **cup white wine**
- 3 **fresh sage sprigs**
- 4 **fresh thyme sprigs**
GRAVY
- 1 **to 1½ cups reduced-sodium chicken broth or homemade chicken stock**
- ¼ **cup all-purpose flour**
- ¼ **teaspoon minced fresh sage**
- ¼ **teaspoon freshly ground pepper**

1. Remove giblets and neck from turkey. Reserve the turkey neck; refrigerate, covered, overnight. Place turkey in a 15x10-in. baking pan, breast side up. Secure skin to the underside of the neck cavity with toothpicks. Mix salt, sage and garlic powder. Tuck wings under turkey; tie drumsticks together. Pat turkey dry. Rub the outside of the turkey with the salt mixture. Refrigerate turkey, loosely covered, overnight.
2. Preheat oven to 475°. Place onion, celery, carrots and the reserved neck in bottom of a broiler pan; add ½ cup water. Place broiler pan rack over top; transfer turkey to rack. Rub the outside of turkey with oil; sprinkle with pepper. Pour wine and remaining water into turkey cavity; add sage and thyme sprigs.
3. Place turkey in the oven, legs facing toward back of oven. Roast, uncovered, 40 minutes.

4. Reduce oven setting to 350°. Cover breast tightly with a double thickness of foil. Roast 1½-2 hours longer or until a thermometer inserted in thickest part of thigh reads 170°-175°. (Thermometer should not touch bone or fat.)
5. Remove turkey from oven. Let stand, uncovered, 20 minutes before carving. Using a turkey baster, remove liquid from the turkey cavity to a large measuring cup. Line a strainer or colander with cheesecloth; place over measuring cup. With a slotted spoon, remove vegetables from bottom of broiler pan, reserving 1¼ cups. Discard neck. Strain cooking liquid into a measuring cup. Skim fat, reserving ¼ cup. Add enough broth to the cooking liquid to measure 2 cups.
6. In a large saucepan, mix flour and the reserved fat until smooth; gradually whisk in the broth mixture. Bring to a boil over medium-high heat, stirring constantly; cook and stir 1-2 minutes or until thickened. Add half the reserved vegetables. Puree the gravy using an immersion blender; or, cool gravy slightly and puree in a blender. Stir in the sage, pepper and remaining vegetables; heat through. Serve with turkey.

CRANBERRY EGGNOG SALAD

PREP: 15 MIN. + CHILLING
MAKES: 12 SERVINGS

For a bright salad with a holiday feel, stack a layer of raspberry gelatin and cranberry sauce over pineapple and eggnog.
—Nancy Foust, Stoneboro, PA

- 2½ **cups boiling water**
- 2 **packages (3 ounces each) cranberry or raspberry gelatin**
- 1 **can (14 ounces) whole-berry cranberry sauce**
- 1 **can (20 ounces) crushed pineapple, undrained**
- 2 **envelopes unflavored gelatin**
- 1½ **cups eggnog**
- 2 **tablespoons lime juice**

1. In a large bowl, add boiling water to cranberry gelatin; stir 2 minutes to completely dissolve. Refrigerate

40-50 minutes or until slightly thickened.
2. Place cranberry sauce in a small bowl; stir to break up. Fold into the gelatin mixture. Pour into an 8-cup ring mold coated with cooking spray; refrigerate 15-20 minutes longer or until set but not firm.
3. Meanwhile, drain crushed pineapple well, reserving juice in a small saucepan. Sprinkle unflavored gelatin over the pineapple juice; let stand 1 minute. Heat and stir over low heat until gelatin is completely dissolved. Stir in eggnog and lime juice. Refrigerate 12-15 minutes or until slightly thickened.
4. Fold the pineapple into the eggnog mixture. Carefully pour over the gelatin in the mold. Refrigerate until firm. Unmold onto a platter.

Holiday Helper
If I have trouble unmolding my favorite gelatin salad, I turn it over onto a serving platter and drape the mold with a hot damp towel for a minute. This loosens the gelatin and it comes right out.
—Alice Debus, Colville, WA

CHICKEN MARSALA BAKE

PREP: 45 MIN.
BAKE: 15 MIN.
MAKES: 8 SERVINGS

My Marsala bake is a little different from the "normal" potluck dish, so it's a nice change of pace to take to dinners. The best part: I serve it with fried polenta slices, so it's completely gluten-free and perfect for my husband, who has celiac disease.
—Deborah Stevens, Goodyear, AZ

- 1 **teaspoon salt**
- 1 **teaspoon dried oregano**
- 1 **teaspoon dried parsley flakes**
- 1 **teaspoon dried thyme**
- ½ **teaspoon garlic powder**
- ½ **teaspoon dried marjoram**
- ½ **teaspoon pepper**
- 8 **boneless skinless chicken breast halves (6 ounces each), cut in half**
- ¼ **cup olive oil**

SAUCE

- ½ **cup butter, cubed**
- 1 **pound sliced fresh mushrooms**
- 1 **shallot, chopped**
- 4 **thin slices prosciutto, chopped**
- 3 **garlic cloves, minced**
- 2 **cups reduced-sodium chicken broth**
- ¾ **cup Marsala wine**
- 2 **teaspoons minced fresh parsley or ½ teaspoon dried parsley flakes**
- ½ **teaspoon coarsely ground pepper**
- 2 **tablespoons cornstarch**
- ¼ **cup heavy whipping cream**
- ⅔ **cup grated Parmesan and Romano cheese blend**

1. Preheat oven to 375°. In a small bowl, mix the first seven ingredients; rub over chicken. In a large skillet, heat oil over medium-high heat. Brown chicken in batches on both sides. Transfer chicken to a greased 13x9-in. baking dish and a greased 8-in. square baking dish.
2. In a large skillet, heat butter over medium-high heat. Add mushrooms and shallot; cook and stir until tender. Add prosciutto and garlic; cook for 2 minutes longer.
3. Stir in broth, wine, parsley and pepper; bring to a boil. In a small bowl, mix the cornstarch and cream until smooth; stir

into the sauce. Return to a boil; cook and stir 1-2 minutes or until thickened.
4. Pour sauce over chicken; sprinkle with cheese. Bake, uncovered, 15-20 minutes or until a thermometer inserted in the chicken reads 165°.

ROASTED ACORN SQUASH & BRUSSELS SPROUTS

PREP: 15 MIN.
BAKE: 30 MIN.
MAKES: 8 SERVINGS

I love creating dishes with a few ingredients and easy steps, like this one! Maple syrup adds a slight sweetness, and pecans give a toasty crunch.
—Angela Lemoine, Howell, NJ

- 1 **medium acorn squash**
- 1 **pound fresh Brussels sprouts**
- 2 **tablespoons olive oil**
- ½ **teaspoon salt**
- ¼ **teaspoon pepper**
- 1¾ **cups pecan halves**
- ¼ **cup maple syrup**
- 3 **tablespoons butter**

1. Preheat oven to 375°. Cut squash lengthwise into quarters; remove and discard seeds. Cut each quarter crosswise into ½-in. slices; discard ends. Trim and halve Brussels sprouts.
2. Place squash and Brussels sprouts in a large bowl. Drizzle with oil; sprinkle with salt and pepper and toss to coat. Transfer to two foil-lined 15x10x1-in. baking pans. Roast 30-35 minutes or until vegetables are tender, stirring occasionally.
3. Meanwhile, in a large, dry skillet, toast the pecans over medium-low heat for 6-8 minutes or until lightly browned, stirring frequently. Add syrup and butter; cook and stir until the butter is melted.
4. Sprinkle vegetables with the pecan mixture; gently toss to combine.

GARLIC-HERB SMASHED SPUDS

START TO FINISH: 30 MIN.
MAKES: 16 SERVINGS

This is my most requested side dish whenever we're serving steak; it pairs beautifully with other meats, too. The garlic flavor is subtle and the texture is firm. If you like your potatoes a bit creamier, add a splash or two of milk.
—*Heather Burris, Kingsland, GA*

- 5 pounds small red potatoes
- 1½ cups 2% milk
- 1 package (6½ ounces) garlic-herb spreadable cheese
- ¾ cup butter, cubed
- ½ cup shredded cheddar cheese
- ¼ cup grated Parmesan cheese
- ¼ cup sour cream
- 2 tablespoons minced chives
- 2 teaspoons salt

Place potatoes in a Dutch oven; add water to cover. Bring to a boil. Reduce heat; cook, uncovered, 15-20 minutes or until tender. Drain; return to pan. Mash potatoes, gradually adding milk, spreadable cheese, butter, cheeses, sour cream, chives and salt.

HOLIDAY BEEF BOURGUIGNON

PREP: 40 MIN.
BAKE: 2½ HOURS
MAKES: 12 SERVINGS (3 QUARTS)

When we married four decades ago, I found this bourguignon recipe in a French cookbook. My husband and I still serve it for very special occasions.
—*Lyn Robitaille, East Hartland, CT*

- ⅔ cup all-purpose flour
- 1½ teaspoons salt, divided
- 1 boneless beef chuck roast (about 4 pounds), cut into 1-inch cubes
- 4 tablespoons olive oil, divided
- 2 garlic cloves, minced
- 2½ cups Burgundy wine or beef broth
- 3 cups beef broth

- ¼ cup minced fresh parsley or 4 teaspoons dried parsley flakes
- 2 bay leaves
- 1 package (14.4 ounces) frozen pearl onions
- 3 bacon strips, chopped
- 8 fresh thyme sprigs
- 2 tablespoons tomato paste
- ½ teaspoon pepper
- 3 tablespoons butter
- 1 pound medium fresh mushrooms, stems removed
  Hot cooked egg noodles

1. Preheat oven to 325°. In a shallow bowl, mix flour and 1 teaspoon salt. Add beef, a few pieces at a time, and toss to coat; shake off excess.
2. In an ovenproof Dutch oven, heat 2 tablespoons oil over medium heat. Brown beef in batches, adding oil as necessary. Remove with a slotted spoon.

3. Add garlic; cook 1 minute longer. Add wine, stirring to loosen browned bits from pan. Stir in broth, parsley, bay leaves and remaining salt. Return beef to the pan. Bring to a boil. Bake, covered, 2 hours.
4. Meanwhile, in a large skillet, cook onions and bacon over medium-high heat 10-12 minutes or until bacon is crisp, stirring occasionally.
5. Remove stew from the oven. Using a slotted spoon, transfer onion mixture to stew; stir in thyme, tomato paste and pepper. Return to oven; bake, covered, 30-45 minutes longer or until the beef and onions are tender.
6. In a large skillet, heat butter over medium-high heat. Add mushrooms; cook and stir 6-8 minutes or until tender.
7. Remove bay leaves and thyme sprigs from the stew. Stir in the mushrooms. Serve stew with hot egg noodles.

PORTOBELLO WELLINGTONS WITH SPINACH PISTACHIO PESTO

PREP: 45 MIN.
BAKE: 15 MIN.
MAKES: 6 SERVINGS
(ABOUT 1 CUP PESTO)

These tasty and elegant mushrooms take their cue from the classic beef Wellington; simply omit the ham/prosciutto to make this a completely meatless meal.
—TerryAnn Moore, Vineland, NJ

- 1 **tablespoon olive oil**
- 1 **shallot, finely chopped**
- 1¾ **cups water**
- 1 **package (6.2 ounces) fast-cooking long grain and wild rice mix**
- 1 **package (3½ ounces) fresh enoki mushrooms, trimmed**
- 4 **thin slices prosciutto or deli ham, cut into strips**
- 1 **tablespoon minced fresh cilantro**

- 6 **large portobello mushrooms (4-inch diameter), stems removed**
- ¼ **cup Vidalia onion salad dressing**
- 1 **package (17.3 ounces) frozen puff pastry, thawed**
- 1 **large egg, lightly beaten**
- 3 **tablespoons chopped pistachios**

PESTO
- 2 **cups fresh baby spinach**
- ⅔ **cup pistachios**
- ⅓ **cup grated Parmesan cheese**
- 2 **garlic cloves**
- 2 **teaspoons lemon juice**
- ½ **teaspoon grated lemon peel**
- ½ **teaspoon coarsely ground pepper**
- ½ **cup olive oil**

1. Preheat oven to 400°. In a large saucepan, heat oil over medium-high heat. Add shallot; cook and stir until tender. Add water, rice mix, contents of seasoning packet, enoki mushrooms, prosciutto and cilantro. Bring to a boil. Reduce heat; simmer, covered, for 5 minutes. Remove from heat; let stand 5 minutes. Fluff with a fork.

2. Brush portobello mushrooms with salad dressing. Grill the mushrooms, covered, over medium heat or broil 4 in. from heat 6-8 minutes on each side or until tender.

3. On a lightly floured surface, unfold puff pastry. Roll each pastry sheet into a 15x10x1-in. rectangle. Cut out six 5-in. circles from each rectangle. Place a mushroom in the center of each of six circles. Spoon ½ cup rice mixture over each mushroom. Top with the remaining circles. Press edges to seal. Set aside any remaining filling.

4. Place mushrooms 1 in. apart on a greased baking sheet. Brush pastry with egg; sprinkle with pistachios. Bake 15-18 minutes or until golden brown.

5. Meanwhile, for pesto, place spinach, pistachios, cheese, garlic, lemon juice, lemon peel and pepper in a food processor; cover and process until the ingredients are blended. While processing, gradually add oil in a steady stream. Serve with mushrooms and the remaining filling.

ROASTED SWEET POTATOES WITH BALSAMIC VINEGAR & ROSEMARY

PREP: 10 MIN.
BAKE: 30 MIN.
MAKES: 8 SERVINGS

This is classic comfort food that tastes great and makes your house smell welcoming on a Sunday afternoon. It accompanies so many things, and can be easily doubled to feed a crowd.
—Jessica Gerschitz, Jericho, NY

- 3 pounds sweet potatoes (about 3 large), peeled and cut into 1-inch cubes
- 4 teaspoons olive oil
- 1 to 2 tablespoons minced fresh rosemary or 1 to 2 teaspoons dried rosemary, crushed
- ¾ teaspoon salt
- ¼ teaspoon pepper
- 2 tablespoons balsamic vinegar
- ½ cup grated Parmesan cheese

1. Preheat the oven to 400°. In a large bowl, toss the sweet potatoes with oil, rosemary, salt and pepper; transfer to two 15x10x1-in. baking pans.
2. Roast 15-18 minutes or until tender and lightly browned, stirring occasionally. Toss with vinegar and cheese.

Holiday Helper
There's quite a range in price for balsamic vinegars, as the grapes, processing and aging method, and time all help determine the cost. Save higher-priced balsamics for drizzling over cooked foods as a finishing touch; go with a lower-cost brand when using it during the cooking process. You can substitute cider vinegar or a mild red wine vinegar. White wine vinegar is much stronger and sharper and should be used sparingly if it's your only substitute.

GRAPEFRUIT & FENNEL SALAD WITH MINT VINAIGRETTE

START TO FINISH: 15 MIN.
MAKES: 4 SERVINGS

My dad has a red grapefruit tree and shares his crop with me. I toss the grapefruit with onion, fennel and mint for a fresh, fabulous salad.
—Catherine Wilkinson, Dewey, AZ

- 1 medium red grapefruit
- 1 medium fennel bulb, halved and thinly sliced
- ¼ cup thinly sliced red onion

VINAIGRETTE
- 3 tablespoons fresh mint leaves
- 2 tablespoons sherry vinegar
- 1½ teaspoons honey
- ⅛ teaspoon salt
- ⅛ teaspoon coarsely ground pepper
- 2 tablespoons olive oil

1. Cut a thin slice from the top and bottom of the grapefruit; stand the grapefruit upright on a cutting board. With a knife, cut off the peel and outer membrane from the grapefruit. Cut along the membrane of each segment to remove fruit. Arrange the fennel, grapefruit and onion on a serving platter.
2. Place the mint, vinegar, honey, salt and pepper in a small food processor; cover and process until mint is finely chopped. While processing, gradually add oil in a steady stream. Drizzle over the salad.

CREME DE MENTHE SQUARES

PREP: 30 MIN. + CHILLING
MAKES: 9 SERVINGS

This layered bar hits all the sweet spots: It's airy, creamy, crunchy and the perfect mix of cool mint and rich chocolate. It has a old-fashioned appeal that no one in our family can resist.
—Marilyn Blankschien, Clintonville, WI

- 1¼ cups finely crushed Oreo cookies (about 14 cookies)
- 2 tablespoons butter, melted
- 1 teaspoon unflavored gelatin
- 1¾ cups cold 2% milk, divided
- 20 large marshmallows
- 3 tablespoons green creme de menthe
- 3 ounces cream cheese, softened
- 1 package (3.9 ounces) instant chocolate pudding mix
- 1 cup heavy whipping cream

1. In a small bowl, mix crushed cookies and melted butter. Reserve 3 tablespoons for topping. Press the remaining mixture onto bottom of a greased 8-in. square baking dish. Refrigerate 30 minutes.

2. In a large microwave-safe bowl, sprinkle gelatin over ½ cup cold milk; let stand 1 minute. Microwave on high for 30-40 seconds. Stir until gelatin is completely dissolved. Add marshmallows; cook 1-2 minutes longer or until marshmallows are puffed; stir until smooth. Stir in creme de menthe. Refrigerate 15-20 minutes or until cold but not set, stirring often.

3. Meanwhile, in a small bowl, gradually beat cream cheese until smooth. In another bowl, whisk pudding mix and the remaining cold milk. Gradually beat into the cream cheese.

4. In a large bowl, beat cream until soft peaks form; fold into the marshmallow mixture. Spoon half of the mixture over the prepared crust; refrigerate for 10 minutes. Layer with the pudding mixture and the remaining marshmallow mixture; top with the reserved crumbs. Refrigerate 2 hours or until set.

RICH RUM CAKE

PREP: 35 MIN.
BAKE: 25 MIN. + COOLING
MAKES: 12 SERVINGS

We like a touch of rum for the holidays, and this orangey rum cake is decadent alone or with swoops of whipped cream.
—Nancy Heishman, Las Vegas, NV

- 4 large eggs, separated
- 2½ cups confectioners' sugar
- ¾ cup orange juice
- ¼ cup butter, cubed
- ¾ cup rum
- 1 cup all-purpose flour
- 1 teaspoon baking powder
- ½ teaspoon ground cinnamon
- ¼ teaspoon salt
- ¼ teaspoon ground nutmeg
- ½ cup packed brown sugar, divided
- 1 teaspoon vanilla extract
- ¾ cup butter, melted
  Whipped cream and finely chopped glazed pecans, optional

1. Place egg whites in a large bowl; let stand at room temperature 30 minutes. For sauce, in a saucepan, combine confectioners' sugar, juice and cubed butter; cook and stir over medium-low heat until the sugar is dissolved. Remove from heat; stir in rum. Reserve ¾ cup for serving.

2. Preheat oven to 375°. Grease and flour a 10-in. tube pan. Sift flour, baking powder, cinnamon, salt and nutmeg together twice; set aside.

3. In a bowl, beat egg whites on medium until soft peaks form. Gradually add ¼ cup of the brown sugar, 1 tablespoon at a time, beating on high after each addition until the sugar is dissolved. Continue beating until stiff peaks form.

4. In another bowl, beat egg yolks until slightly thickened. Gradually add ¼ cup brown sugar and the vanilla, beating on high speed until thick. Fold a fourth of the egg whites into the batter. Alternately fold in the flour mixture and the remaining whites. Fold in melted butter.

5. Transfer to prepared pan. Bake on lowest oven rack for 25-30 minutes or until the top springs back when lightly touched. Immediately poke holes in cake with a fork; slowly pour remaining sauce over the cake, allowing sauce to absorb into the cake. Cool completely in pan on a wire rack. Invert onto a serving plate. Serve with the reserved sauce and, if desired, whipped cream and candied pecans.

"This layered bar hits all the sweet spots."
—MARILYN BLANKSCHIEN

MERRY
CRANBERRIES

Their festive color and tangy, tasty flavor make cranberries a perfect match for the holiday season. And you can pair them with anything—from cocktails to roasts!

CRANBERRY-ORANGE ROAST DUCKLINGS

PREP: 20 MIN.
BAKE: 3 HOURS + STANDING
MAKES: 10 SERVINGS

I came up with this recipe a few years ago. The first time I served it, there wasn't a speck of food left on the platter and I knew I had a winning recipe.
—Gloria Warczak, Cedarburg, WI

- 2 **domestic ducklings (4 to 5 pounds each)**
- 2 **medium navel oranges, quartered**
- 2 **sprigs fresh rosemary**
- 1½ **cups fresh or frozen cranberries, divided**
- 4 **cups orange juice**
- 1 **cup chicken broth**
- ¼ **cup soy sauce**
- 2 **teaspoons sugar**
- 2 **garlic cloves, minced**
- 1 **teaspoon grated fresh gingerroot**
- ⅔ **cup orange marmalade**

1. Preheat oven to 350°. Pierce duckling skin all over with a fork. Place four orange quarters, one sprig of rosemary and ¼ cup cranberries in each duckling cavity; tie drumsticks together. Place on a rack in a roasting pan, breast side up.
2. In a bowl, mix orange juice, chicken broth, soy sauce, sugar, garlic and ginger. Reserve and refrigerate ½ cup for glaze. Pour 1 cup over the ducklings; sprinkle with the remaining cranberries. Cover and bake 1 hour. Uncover and bake 1½ hours longer, basting frequently with the remaining orange juice mixture. (Drain fat from pan as it accumulates.)
3. For the glaze, mix marmalade and the reserved orange juice mixture; spread over the ducklings. Bake, uncovered, until a thermometer inserted in a thigh reads 180°, 30-40 minutes. Discard the oranges, rosemary and cranberries from the cavities. Let ducklings stand 10 minutes before carving.

CRANBERRY BOURBON

PREP: 10 MIN. + STANDING
MAKES: 10-13 SERVINGS
(2½ CUPS/20 OUNCES BOURBON)

The subtle tang of cranberry and warm winter spices make this bourbon just right for holiday toasts—neat, on the rocks or in a cocktail.
—James Schend, Pleasant Prairie, WI

- 3 **cups bourbon**
- 1 **cup dried cranberries**
- 1 **cinnamon stick (3 inches)**
- 4 **orange peel strips (3 inches)**

In an airtight glass container, combine bourbon, cranberries, cinnamon stick and orange peel. Store in a cool dry place 2-4 weeks. Strain to remove cranberries, cinnamon and orange peel; return to glass container. Store in a cool, dry place.
CRANBERRY MANHATTAN Fill a shaker three-fourths full with ice. Add 2 ounces Cranberry Bourbon, ¾ ounce sweet vermouth and a dash of bitters; cover and shake until cold. Strain into a cocktail glass and serve.
CRANBERRY OLD-FASHIONED In a rocks glass, muddle an orange slice, four dried cranberries and 2 dashes of bitters. Add ice. Pour in 1½ ounces of Cranberry Bourbon, 3 ounces of lemon-lime soda and 1 teaspoon orange juice.

*"Morning, afternoon or evening,
this is always a treat!"*
—MARY WEST

CRAN-ALMOND LOAF

PREP: 15 MIN.
BAKE: 1 HOUR + COOLING
MAKES: 1 LOAF (16 SLICES)

My delicious quick bread is comforting in the afternoon with a cup of tea, served toasted in the morning for breakfast, or as a midnight snack. Morning, afternoon or evening, this is always a treat!
—Mary West, Marstons Mills, MA

- 2 **cups all-purpose flour**
- 1 **cup sugar**
- 1 **teaspoon salt**
- ½ **teaspoon baking soda**
- ½ **teaspoon baking powder**
- ½ **teaspoon ground nutmeg**
- 2 **large eggs**
- 1 **cup buttermilk**
- ⅓ **cup canola oil**
- ¼ **teaspoon almond extract**
- 1 **cup dried cranberries, chopped**

1. Preheat oven to 350°. Whisk together the first six ingredients. In another bowl, whisk together eggs, buttermilk, oil and extract. Add to the flour mixture; stir just until moistened. Fold in cranberries.
2. Transfer the batter to a greased 9x5-in. loaf pan. Bake until a toothpick inserted in the center comes out clean, 60-65 minutes. Cool in pan 10 minutes before removing to a wire rack to cool completely.

Holiday Helper

As a substitute for 1 cup of buttermilk in baking, use 1 tablespoon of white vinegar or lemon juice plus enough milk to measure 1 cup. Stir, then let stand for 5 minutes. You can also use 1 cup of plain yogurt, or 1¾ teaspoons cream of tartar plus 1 cup milk.

CRANBERRY AMARETTO BREAD PUDDING

PREP: 15 MIN. + STANDING
BAKE: 50 MIN.
MAKES: 12 SERVINGS (1 CUP SAUCE)

This is an update to a recipe that's been in our family for three generations. The combination of white chocolate and amaretto mingled with seasonal cranberry is a favorite way to end any celebration's meal.
—Jennifer Evans DaCastello, Virginia Beach, VA

- 3 **large eggs**
- 4 **cups 2% milk**
- 1 **cup packed brown sugar**
- ¼ **cup butter, melted**
- 3 **teaspoons vanilla extract**
- 2 **tablespoons ground cinnamon**
- 3 **teaspoons ground nutmeg**
- 1 **teaspoon ground cloves**
- ½ **cup dried cranberries**
- ½ **cup toasted chopped pecans, optional**
- 6 **cups cubed day-old French bread**

SAUCE
- 1 **cup white baking chips**
- ¼ **cup butter, cubed**
- ¼ **cup amaretto**

1. Preheat oven to 350°. Whisk together eggs, milk, brown sugar, melted butter, vanilla and spices. Stir in cranberries and, if desired, pecans. Gently stir in bread; let stand until the bread is softened, about 15 minutes.
2. Transfer to a greased 13x9-in. baking dish. Bake until puffed and golden and a knife inserted near the center comes out clean, 50-55 minutes.
3. In a small heavy saucepan, heat baking chips and butter over low heat until melted and smooth, stirring constantly. Remove from heat; stir in amaretto. Serve with warm bread pudding.
NOTE To toast nuts, bake in a shallow pan in a 350° oven for 5-10 minutes or cook in a skillet over low heat until lightly browned, stirring occasionally.

½ cup plus 2 tablespoons
water, divided
1 envelope onion soup mix
3 tablespoons cornstarch

1. Place turkey breasts in a 5-qt. slow cooker. In a bowl, mix cranberry sauce, ½ cup water and soup mix. Pour half over the turkey. Cook, covered, on low until a thermometer reads 165°, 4-6 hours. Remove the turkey. Transfer cooking juices and the remaining cranberry mixture to a large saucepan.

2. When the turkey is cool enough to handle, shred it with two forks. Return the meat to the slow cooker; keep warm. Meanwhile, bring the cooking juices and the cranberry mixture to a boil. Mix cornstarch and the remaining water until smooth; gradually stir into the cranberry mixture. Cook and stir until thickened, about 2 minutes. Serve with turkey.

CRANBERRY-BERRY SAUCE

PREP: 10 MIN.
COOK: 20 MIN. + CHILLING
MAKES: 5½ CUPS

I've made this sauce every year I've cooked for my family. Recently I found a delightful mix that will surely become a tradition. You can use almost any seasonal fruit in this recipe.
—Michael Whalen, Baltimore, MD

2 packages (12 ounces each) fresh
or frozen cranberries, thawed
1½ cups fresh raspberries, divided
1½ cups fresh blueberries, divided
1¾ to 2 cups sugar
1 cup water
2 teaspoons minced
fresh gingerroot

1. In a 6-qt. stockpot, combine the cranberries, ¾ cup raspberries, ¾ cup blueberries, sugar, water and ginger. Bring to a boil, stirring to dissolve sugar. Reduce the heat to medium-low; cook, uncovered, until thickened, for 10-15 minutes, stirring occasionally. Stir in remaining raspberries and blueberries.

2. Transfer to a bowl; cool slightly. Refrigerate, covered, until cold.

SLOW-COOKED TURKEY BREASTS WITH CRANBERRY SAUCE

PREP: 15 MIN.
COOK: 4 HOURS
MAKES: 10 SERVINGS

This is a tasty and easy way to prepare a turkey breast in the slow cooker. Ideal for holiday potlucks, the sweet cranberry sauce complements the turkey nicely.
—Marie Ramsden, Fairgrove, MI

2 boneless skinless turkey breast
halves (2 pounds each)
1 can (14 ounces) jellied
cranberry sauce

"This is the best turkey sandwich ever!"
—CLEO GONSKE

TURKEY-CRANBERRY MONTE CRISTO

START TO FINISH: 30 MIN.
MAKES: 4 SERVINGS

Every year, my husband and I look forward to Thanksgiving leftovers just so we can make this sandwich. Once you try it, I'm sure you'll agree that this is the best turkey sandwich ever!
—Cleo Gonske, Redding, CA

- 8 slices egg bread
- 3 tablespoons Dijon mustard
- 10 ounces thinly sliced cooked turkey
- 6 ounces smoked Gouda cheese, thinly sliced
- ½ cup whole-berry cranberry sauce
- 3 large eggs
- ⅓ cup 2% milk
- ¼ teaspoon salt
- ¼ teaspoon pepper
- 3 teaspoons butter, divided
- 3 teaspoons canola oil, divided

1. Preheat oven to 350°. Spread mustard on four slices of bread. Layer with turkey and cheese. Spread cranberry sauce on the remaining bread slices; place on top of other sandwich halves.

2. In a shallow bowl, whisk eggs, milk, salt and pepper. In a large skillet, heat 1½ teaspoons each butter and oil over medium heat until the butter is melted. Dip two sandwiches in the egg mixture and place in the skillet. Cook until golden brown, 2-3 minutes per side. Repeat with the remaining butter, oil and sandwiches.

3. Transfer the sandwiches to a baking sheet. Bake until the cheese is melted, 4-5 minutes.

PEAR & PECAN SALAD WITH CRANBERRY VINAIGRETTE

START TO FINISH: 20 MIN.
MAKES: 12 SERVINGS

A tart cranberry dressing balances beautifully with sweet, juicy pears in this salad that's sure to impress. This recipe is light on carbs and quick to make—and it's oh so good!
—Jerry Gulley, Pleasant Prairie, WI

- 2 **tablespoons champagne or rice vinegar**
- ¾ **cup dried cranberries, divided**
- 2 **tablespoons thinly sliced shallot**
- 1½ **teaspoons Dijon mustard**
- 1½ **teaspoons honey**
- ¼ **teaspoon salt**
- ⅛ **teaspoon pepper**
- ⅓ **cup canola oil**
- 10 **cups Boston lettuce**
- 2 **medium pears, thinly sliced**
- ½ **cup chopped pecans, toasted**

1. Process champagne, ¼ cup of the cranberries, shallot, mustard, honey, salt and pepper in a small food processor until blended. While processing, add oil gradually in a steady stream.

2. In a bowl, combine lettuce and pears. Pour the dressing over the salad; toss to coat. Sprinkle with pecans and the remaining cranberries.

HONEY-GLAZED CARROTS WITH CRANBERRIES

PREP: 10 MIN.
COOK: 30 MIN.
MAKES: 8 SERVINGS

Stovetop sides are a smart way to free up oven space when making a holiday dinner. For a little more color, sprinkle the carrots with parsley before serving.
—Daniel Anderson, Kenosha, WI

- 2 **tablespoons butter**
- 2 **pounds carrots, thinly sliced diagonally**
- 1 **cup water**
- ½ **cup dried cranberries**
- ¼ **cup honey**
- ¾ **teaspoon salt**
- ⅛ **teaspoon pepper**

1. In a Dutch oven, heat butter over medium-high heat. Add carrots; cook and stir until crisp-tender, 8-10 minutes.

2. Stir in the remaining ingredients. Bring to a boil. Reduce heat; simmer, uncovered, until the carrots are tender and glazed, 18-20 minutes.

CRANBERRY APPLE-NUT PIE

PREP: 20 MIN.
BAKE: 45 MIN. + COOLING
MAKES: 8 SERVINGS

Wedges of this scrumptious ruby-red pie are a feast for the eyes and the taste buds. It's a stunning dessert to present when you want to impress dinner guests.
—Peggy Burdick, Burlington, MI

- 2 **cups fresh or frozen cranberries, chopped**
- 1¾ **cups sliced peeled tart apples**
- ½ **cup slivered almonds, toasted**
- 1 **tablespoon grated orange peel**
- 1¾ **cups sugar**
- ¼ **cup all-purpose flour**
- ½ **teaspoon ground cinnamon**
- ½ **teaspoon ground nutmeg**
- ⅛ **teaspoon salt**
  Pastry for double-crust pie (9 inches)
- 2 **tablespoons butter, melted**

1. Preheat oven to 400°. Combine cranberries, apples, almonds and orange peel. In another bowl, mix sugar, flour, cinnamon, nutmeg and salt; add to the fruit mixture and toss gently.

2. On a lightly floured surface, roll one half of the pastry dough to a ⅛-in.-thick circle; transfer to a 9-in. pie plate. Trim pastry even with rim. Add filling. Drizzle with butter. Roll remaining pastry to a ⅛-in.-thick circle. Place over the filling. Trim, seal and flute edge. Cut slits in top.

3. Bake until the crust is golden brown and the filling is bubbly, 45-50 minutes. Cool on a wire rack.

PASTRY FOR DOUBLE-CRUST PIE (9 INCHES) Combine 2½ cups all-purpose flour and ½ teaspoon salt; cut in 1 cup cold butter until crumbly. Gradually add ⅓-⅔ cup ice water, tossing with a fork until the dough holds together when pressed. Divide dough in half. Shape each half into a disk; wrap in plastic wrap. Refrigerate 1 hour or overnight.

"*A stunning dessert to present when you want to impress dinner guests.*"
—PEGGY BURDICK

"*So refreshing and cool—perfect with a big holiday meal!*"
—JULIE CURRINGTON

FROZEN PINEAPPLE-CRANBERRY SALAD

PREP: 10 MIN. + FREEZING
MAKES: 8 SERVINGS

Everyone in our family enjoys this cranberry salad at holiday gatherings. It is so refreshing and cool—perfect with a big holiday meal!
—Julie Currington, Gahanna, OH

- 12 **ounces cream cheese, softened**
- ¼ **cup sugar**
- ¼ **cup mayonnaise**
- 2 **cans (8 ounces each) crushed pineapple, drained**
- 1 **can (14 ounces) whole-berry cranberry sauce**
- 2 **cups whipped topping**

Beat the cream cheese, sugar and mayonnaise until smooth. Fold in the remaining ingredients; spoon into a foil-lined 8x4-in. loaf pan. Cover and freeze 8 hours or overnight. Remove from freezer 5 minutes before slicing.

CRANBERRY GREEN BEANS

PREP: 10 MIN.
BAKE: 25 MIN.
MAKES: 4 SERVINGS

Green beans are one of my family's favorite vegetables, so I'm always looking for new ways to serve them.
—Noelle Myers, Grand Forks, ND

- 1 **package (16 ounces) frozen French-style green beans, thawed and drained**
- ½ **cup dried cranberries**
- 2 **tablespoons olive oil**
- 1 **tablespoon brown sugar**
- 1 **tablespoon balsamic vinegar**
- 1 **teaspoon dried thyme**
- ¼ **cup sliced almonds, toasted**

1. Combine beans and cranberries in an ungreased 8-in. square baking dish. Mix oil, brown sugar, vinegar and thyme. Drizzle over bean mixture; toss to coat.
2. Bake, uncovered, at 350° for 20 minutes. Stir; bake until beans are tender, 5-10 minutes. Sprinkle with almonds.

CRANBERRY CAKE WITH CARAMEL SAUCE

PREP: 15 MIN.
BAKE: 30 MIN. + COOLING
MAKES: 15 SERVINGS (2 CUPS SAUCE)

This sweet and tangy cake, loaded with bits of cranberries and topped with warm caramel sauce, is even better served warm with a scoop of ice cream.
—Darlene Brenden, Salem, OR

- 2 **cups all-purpose flour**
- 1 **cup sugar**
- 2 **teaspoons baking powder**
- ¼ **teaspoon salt**
- 1 **cup heavy whipping cream**
- 1 **tablespoon butter, melted**
- 2 **cups fresh or frozen cranberries, halved**

SAUCE
- ½ **cup butter, cubed**
- 1 **cup heavy whipping cream**
- ½ **cup sugar**
- ½ **cup packed brown sugar**
- 1 **teaspoon vanilla extract**

1. Preheat oven to 350°. Grease a 13x9-in. baking dish.
2. Whisk together flour, sugar, baking powder and salt. Stir in cream and butter just until moistened. Fold in cranberries. Transfer to prepared pan. Bake until golden brown, 30-35 minutes. Cool in pan on a wire rack 10 minutes.
3. In a small saucepan, melt butter; stir in cream, sugar and brown sugar. Bring to a boil over medium heat, stirring constantly. Remove from heat; stir in vanilla. Serve with warm cake.

CRANBERRY SHORT RIBS

PREP: 20 MIN.
BAKE: 1½ HOURS
MAKES: 2 SERVINGS

We live in the Yukon bush, so I pick wild cranberries for this incredibly tender comfort food. When it's available, I'll sometimes substitute moose for the beef.
—Cathy Wylie, Dawson City, YT

- 1½ pounds bone-in beef short ribs
- ½ teaspoon salt, divided
- ¼ teaspoon pepper
- 1 tablespoon all-purpose flour
- 1 tablespoon brown sugar
- ⅛ teaspoon ground mustard
  Dash ground cloves
- ¾ cup water
- 2 teaspoons cider vinegar
- ½ cup fresh or frozen cranberries
- 1½ to 2 teaspoons grated lemon peel
- ½ teaspoon browning sauce, optional

1. Preheat oven to 350°. Place ribs in a greased 8-in. square baking dish; sprinkle with ¼ teaspoon salt and the pepper. Bake, covered, until tender, 1¼-1½ hours.
2. In a small saucepan, combine flour, brown sugar, mustard, cloves and the remaining salt; gradually whisk in water and vinegar until smooth. Stir in cranberries, lemon peel and, if desired, browning sauce; bring to a boil. Cook and stir until thickened, about 2 minutes.
3. Drain ribs. Pour the cranberry mixture over the ribs. Bake, uncovered, 15 minutes longer.

CRAN-MARNIER TRUFFLES

PREP: 45 MIN. + CHILLING
MAKES: 5 DOZEN

Silky smooth chocolate is studded with bits of dried cranberries in these luscious truffles. They're an exquisite ending for your Thanksgiving or Christmas celebration.
—Gerry Cofta, Milwaukee, WI

- 1½ cups sugar
- 1 can (5 ounces) evaporated milk
- ½ cup butter, cubed
- 8 ounces 53% cacao dark baking chocolate, chopped
- 2 cups miniature marshmallows
- 1 tablespoon Grand Marnier
- 2 teaspoons grated orange peel
- ½ cup dried cranberries, chopped
- 12 ounces semisweet chocolate, chopped
- 2 tablespoons shortening
  Baking cocoa, optional

1. In a heavy saucepan, combine sugar, milk and butter. Bring to a boil over medium heat. Cook, stirring constantly, until a candy thermometer reads 234° (soft-ball stage).
2. Remove from heat; stir in dark chocolate until melted. Stir in marshmallows, Grand Marnier and orange peel until blended. Stir in cranberries. Transfer to a bowl. Refrigerate until easy to handle, about 1½ hours.
3. Shape into 1-in. balls; place on waxed paper-lined baking sheets. Refrigerate, covered, until firm, about 1 hour.
4. In a microwave, melt semisweet chocolate and shortening; stir until smooth. Dip truffles in chocolate; allow excess to drip off. Return to lined baking sheets; refrigerate until set. Or, if desired, roll undipped truffles in cocoa. Store in an airtight container in the refrigerator.
NOTE We recommend that you test your candy thermometer before each use by bringing water to a boil; the thermometer should read 212°. Adjust your recipe temperature up or down based on your test.

CRANBERRY-ORANGE CAKE WITH LEMON GLAZE

PREP: 55 MIN. + COOLING
BAKE: 45 MIN. + COOLING
MAKES: 12 SERVINGS

After using cranberries for decorations in a wedding, I created this super moist cake to use up the surplus.
—S. Jade Klope, Paducah, KY

- 1 package (12 ounces) fresh or frozen cranberries
- 1½ cups sugar
- ½ cup butter, softened
- 1½ cups packed brown sugar
- 3 large eggs
- ⅓ cup unsweetened applesauce
- 1¾ cups all-purpose flour
- 3 teaspoons baking powder
- ½ teaspoon cream of tartar
- ¼ teaspoon salt
- ⅔ cup orange juice

GLAZE
- ⅔ cup confectioners' sugar
- 2 tablespoons butter, melted
- 4 teaspoons lemon juice

SUGARED CRANBERRIES
- 2 tablespoons water
- 2 tablespoons egg substitute
- 1 package (12 ounces) fresh or frozen cranberries
- ½ cup coarse sugar
- ½ cup superfine sugar

1. Preheat oven to 350°. Place the cranberries in a 15x10-in. baking pan; sprinkle with sugar. Bake until soft and bubbly, 35-45 minutes, stirring occasionally. Cool to room temperature.
2. Grease and flour a 10-in. fluted tube pan. Beat butter and brown sugar until crumbly. Add eggs, one at a time; beat after each addition. Beat in applesauce. In another bowl, whisk flour, baking powder, cream of tartar and salt; add to creamed mixture alternately with orange juice, beating well after each addition. Stir in cooled cranberries.
3. Transfer to prepared pan. Bake until a toothpick inserted in center comes out with moist crumbs, 45-55 minutes. Cool 15 minutes, then invert onto a serving plate. Mix confectioners' sugar, butter and lemon juice until smooth. Brush over cake. Let cake cool completely.
4. Meanwhile, in a large bowl, mix water and egg substitute. Add the cranberries; toss to coat. Place on a baking sheet and sprinkle with sugars. Transfer cranberries to a wire rack and let stand at room temperature 2 hours or until dry. Top cake with sugared cranberries to serve.
NOTE Use solid shortening to grease plain and fluted tube pans.

CRANBERRY CARAMELS

PREP: 1 HOUR + STANDING
MAKES: 1¼ POUNDS

When I make holiday goodies, my sister always asks when I'm sending the cranberry caramels!
—Jan Rinker, Craig, CO

- 1 teaspoon plus ¼ cup butter
- 1 cup sugar
- 1 cup chopped fresh cranberries
- 1 cup light corn syrup
- ½ cup heavy whipping cream
- ⅛ teaspoon salt

1. Line an 8-in. square pan with foil; grease foil with 1 teaspoon butter.
2. In a large heavy saucepan, combine sugar, cranberries, corn syrup, cream, salt and remaining butter. Cook and stir over medium heat until mixture comes to a boil. Dip a pastry brush in water and wash down the sides of the pan to eliminate sugar crystals. Cook, without stirring, until a candy thermometer reads 248° (firm-ball stage).
3. Remove from heat. Immediately pour into prepared pan (do not scrape the saucepan). Let stand until firm, about 5 hours or overnight.
4. Using foil, lift candy out of pan; remove foil. Using a buttered knife, cut into 1-in. squares. Wrap each in waxed paper.

½ cup red raspberry preserves
6 ounces cream cheese, softened
3 large eggs
½ cup 2% milk
2 teaspoons pumpkin pie spice

1. Preheat oven to 350°. For topping, in a bowl, combine ¾ cup cake mix, butter and water; stir in pecans. For filling, in a second bowl, combine cranberries, sugar, preserves and 2 tablespoons of the cake mix.
2. In a third bowl, combine cream cheese, eggs, milk, pie spice and the remaining cake mix; beat on low 30 seconds. Beat on medium 2 minutes. Transfer batter to a greased 13x9-in. pan. Spoon cranberry filling over top to within ½ in. of edges. Sprinkle with topping to edges of pan.
3. Bake until a toothpick inserted in center comes out clean, 55-60 minutes. Cool in pan on a wire rack.

CRANBERRY BEEF BRISKET

PREP: 15 MIN.
BAKE: 3 HOURS
MAKES: 12 SERVINGS

My mother-in-law gave me the recipe for this tender brisket. It yields a lot, so the leftovers can be used in many recipes that call for cooked beef.
—Annette Bartle, Lees Summit, MO

2 tablespoons canola oil
1 fresh beef brisket (4 to 5 pounds)
1 can (14 ounces) whole-berry cranberry sauce
½ cup beef broth
½ cup red wine or additional beef broth
1 envelope onion soup mix

1. Preheat oven to 350°. In a large skillet, heat oil over medium heat. Brown brisket on both sides. Transfer to a greased roasting pan. Combine the remaining ingredients; pour over the beef.
2. Roast, covered, until meat is tender, 3-4 hours. Cut diagonally across the grain into thin slices. If desired, strain the cooking juices and serve with the brisket.
NOTE This is a fresh beef brisket, not corned beef.

Holiday Helper
If you don't have boxed cake mix, you can make your own. To equal one box of white cake mix, combine 2½ cups all-purpose flour, 2 cups sugar, ½ cup powdered milk or dry buttermilk, 1 teaspoon baking powder and ½ teaspoon baking soda. Sift all ingredients together and store in a cool, dry place.

SPICED CRANBERRY CRISP CAKE

PREP: 25 MIN.
BAKE: 55 MIN. + COOLING
MAKES: 15 SERVINGS

This cake is a cross between a fruit crisp and a moist cake. We love the festive cranberry filling with its sweet-tangy flavor and the combination of soft cake, tender fruit and crunchy topping.
—Priscilla Yee, Concord, CA

1 package white cake mix (regular size), divided
2 tablespoons butter, melted
1 teaspoon water
½ cup chopped pecans, toasted
1 package (12 ounces) fresh or frozen cranberries
½ cup sugar

APPLE-CRANBERRY BREAKFAST RISOTTO

PREP: 15 MIN.
COOK: 3 HOURS
MAKES: 10 SERVINGS

Cranberries and apples are tart enough to balance the sweetness in this hearty dish that's fun for an after-presents breakfast on Christmas morning.
—Betsy King, Duluth, MN

- ¼ cup butter, cubed
- 1½ cups uncooked arborio rice
- 2 medium apples, peeled and chopped
- ⅓ cup packed brown sugar
- ¼ teaspoon kosher salt
- 1½ teaspoons ground cinnamon
- ⅛ teaspoon ground nutmeg
- ⅛ teaspoon ground cloves
- 3 cups 2% milk
- 2 cups unsweetened apple juice
- 1 cup dried cranberries

1. Heat butter in a 4-qt. slow cooker set on high until melted. Add rice; stir to coat. Add apples, brown sugar, salt and spices. Stir in milk and apple juice.
2. Set slow cooker to low. Cook, covered, until rice is tender, 3-4 hours, stirring halfway. Stir in cranberries during the last 15 minutes of cooking.

PORK TENDERLOIN WITH CRANBERRY APPLE CHUTNEY

PREP: 15 MIN.
BAKE: 20 MIN.
MAKES: 4 SERVINGS (1 CUP CHUTNEY)

The zingy-sweet fruit compote complements the spices in the rub in this juicy pork roast that can be your holiday headliner.
—Teresa Ralston, New Albany, OH

- 1 tablespoon brown sugar
- 1 teaspoon salt
- 1 teaspoon ancho chili powder
- ½ teaspoon ground mustard
- ½ teaspoon pepper
- 1 pork tenderloin (1 pound)

CHUTNEY

- 3 tablespoons butter
- ½ cup finely chopped sweet onion
- 2 medium apples, peeled and diced
- ½ cup dried cranberries
- 3 tablespoons maple syrup
- 1½ teaspoons Worcestershire sauce
- ½ teaspoon ground cinnamon
- ⅛ teaspoon ground cloves

1. Preheat oven to 425°. Mix the first five ingredients; rub over pork. Place on a rack in a shallow roasting pan. Roast until a thermometer reads 145°, 20-30 minutes. Remove roast from oven; tent with foil. Let stand 5 minutes before slicing.
2. In a large skillet, heat butter over medium-high heat. Add onion; saute until tender. Add the remaining ingredients; cook and stir until apples are tender. Serve with pork.

CORIANDER-CRUSTED BEEF WITH SPICY CRANBERRY RELISH

PREP: 25 MIN. + CHILLING
COOK: 1¾ HOURS + STANDING
MAKES: 8 SERVINGS (6 CUPS RELISH)

Jalapeno gives cranberries an extra jolt in this rich, savory roast.
—Donna Thomas, Dallas, TX

- 1½ **cups orange juice**
- 6 **cups fresh or frozen cranberries**
- 1½ **cups sugar**
- ½ **cup olive oil**
- 1 **to 2 jalapeno peppers, seeded and finely chopped**
- 5 **garlic cloves, minced**
- 1 **tablespoon red wine vinegar**
- ½ **teaspoon ground cumin**
- ¼ **teaspoon salt**

RUB

- 4 **shallots, finely chopped**
- ¾ **cup kosher salt**
- 6 **tablespoons packed brown sugar**
- ¼ **cup coriander seeds, ground**
- ¼ **cup whole peppercorns, ground**
- 4 **garlic cloves, minced**
- 1 **beef ribeye roast (3 to 4 pounds)**

1. Bring orange juice to a boil. Cook until reduced by half, about 15 minutes. Pulse cranberries with sugar in a food processor until coarsely chopped.
2. In a large skillet, heat oil over medium heat. Add jalapeno; saute until tender, 1-2 minutes. Add garlic; cook 1 minute longer. Stir in cranberry mixture, orange juice, vinegar, cumin and salt.
3. For the rub, mix shallots, kosher salt, brown sugar, coriander, peppercorns and garlic; rub over roast. Refrigerate, covered, 8 hours or overnight.
4. Preheat oven to 350°. Remove and discard rub from roast; place roast on a rack in a shallow roasting pan, fat side up. Roast until meat reaches desired doneness (for medium-rare, a thermometer should read 145°; medium, 160°; well-done, 170°), 1¾-2¼ hours. Remove roast from oven; tent with foil. Let stand 15 minutes. Slice and serve with relish.
NOTE Wear disposable gloves when cutting hot peppers; the oils can burn skin. Avoid touching your face.

CHICKEN-CRANBERRY HOT DISH

PREP: 30 MIN.
COOK: 4 HOURS
MAKES: 4 SERVINGS (2 CUPS SAUCE)

In my family, we never eat chicken without cranberry sauce! This chicken is fall-off-the-bone tender; the sauce is divine with mashed potatoes.
—Lorraine Caland, Shuniah, ON

- 2 **tablespoons canola oil**
- 1 **broiler/fryer chicken (4 pounds), cut up**
- ½ **teaspoon salt**
- ¼ **teaspoon pepper**
- 1 **medium onion, chopped**
- 1 **celery rib, chopped**
- 1 **cup whole-berry cranberry sauce**
- ½ **cup chili sauce**
- 2 **tablespoons brown sugar**
- 1 **tablespoon grated lemon peel**
- 1 **tablespoon balsamic vinegar**
- 1 **tablespoon A.1. steak sauce**
- 1 **tablespoon Dijon mustard**

1. In a large skillet, heat oil over medium-high heat. Brown chicken on both sides in batches; sprinkle with salt and pepper. Transfer to a 4-qt. slow cooker.
2. Add onion and celery to the skillet; saute over medium-high heat until tender, 3-4 minutes. Stir in the remaining ingredients. Pour over the chicken.
3. Cook, covered, on low until the chicken is tender, 4-5 hours. Skim fat from cooking juices; serve with chicken.

CHRISTMAS COMFORT FOOD

Old favorites that deliver the warmth and closeness of family history celebrated and shared, these dishes are truly a source of comfort and joy.

3¼ cups dried currants
2⅔ cups raisins
1 cup chopped walnuts
⅔ cup chopped candied citron
   or candied lemon peel
4 cups all-purpose flour, divided
1 cup butter, softened
2 cups packed brown sugar
4 large eggs
1 cup molasses
1 teaspoon baking soda
1 teaspoon each ground
   cinnamon, nutmeg and cloves
1 cup strong brewed coffee

1. Preheat oven to 300°. Grease and flour three 9x5-in. loaf pans. Line the bottom of each pan with waxed paper; grease and flour the paper. Combine currants, raisins, walnuts, candied citron and ¼ cup flour. Toss to coat; set aside.

2. Cream butter and brown sugar until light and fluffy. Add eggs, one at a time, beating well after each addition. Beat in molasses. In another bowl, whisk baking soda, cinnamon, nutmeg, cloves and the remaining flour; add to the creamed mixture alternately with coffee. Stir into the currant mixture and mix well.

3. Transfer to prepared pans. Bake until a toothpick inserted in center comes out clean, 1¼-1½ hours. Cool in pans for 10 minutes before removing to wire racks to cool completely. Wrap tightly and store in the refrigerator for at least 2 days to blend the flavors. Slice and bring to room temperature before serving. Refrigerate leftovers.

ALCOHOL-SOAKED FRUITCAKES
Using a toothpick, poke holes on all sides of fruitcakes until they are well perforated. Pour about 1 cup of selected alcohol (such as brandy, rum or whiskey) into a bowl. Brush some alcohol over all sides of the fruitcakes. Cut three 36x17-in. pieces of cheesecloth. Let each piece soak in the bowl of alcohol; gently squeeze out some of the excess. Place each fruitcake on a piece of the cheesecloth and tightly wrap cheesecloth around fruitcake. Wrap each loaf tightly in foil and place in the refrigerator. Remove foil and brush each cheesecloth-covered loaf with 2-3 additional tablespoons of alcohol once a week for up to 1 month.

GRANDMA'S MOLASSES FRUITCAKE

PREP: 25 MIN. + CHILLING
BAKE: 1¼ HOURS + COOLING
MAKES: 3 LOAVES (16 SLICES EACH)

This dense, dark, moist fruitcake was my grandmother's recipe. The flavor just gets better and better as it sits in the fridge, so be sure to make it ahead!
—Debbie Harmon, Lavina, MT

SUGAR COOKIES

PREP: 30 MIN.
BAKE: 10 MIN./BATCH
MAKES: 5 DOZEN

This dates back to a Swedish woman born in 1877 who mixed her cookies by feel and taste. Her daughter, Esther Davis, came up with the precise measurements and shared the recipe with me. These are my favorite cookies, and I hope they'll become yours as well.
—*Helen Wallis, Vancouver, WA*

- ½ **cup butter, softened**
- ½ **cup shortening**
- 1 **cup sugar**
- 1 **large egg**
- 1 **teaspoon vanilla extract**
- 2¼ **cups all-purpose flour**
- ½ **teaspoon baking powder**
- ½ **teaspoon baking soda**
  Additional sugar

1. Preheat oven to 350°. Cream butter, shortening and sugar until light and fluffy. Beat in egg and vanilla. In another bowl, whisk flour, baking powder and baking soda; gradually beat into the creamed mixture.
2. Shape into 1-in. balls. Roll in the additional sugar. Place on greased baking sheets; flatten with a glass. Bake until set, 10-12 minutes. Remove to wire racks to cool.

CHEESY SCALLOPED POTATOES & HAM

PREP: 45 MIN.
BAKE: 1¾ HOURS
MAKES: 2 CASSEROLES
(8 SERVINGS EACH)

Creamy, cheesy and easy to make, this casserole is the definition of comfort food. This makes two casseroles, so it's great for a crowd; it freezes nicely, too.
—*Salina Bontrager, Kalona, IA*

- 2 **cans (10¾ ounces each) condensed cream of chicken soup, undiluted**
- 2 **cups sour cream**
- ⅔ **cup butter, melted**
- 1 **teaspoon garlic powder**
- 1 **teaspoon pepper**
- 6½ **pounds potatoes, peeled and cut into ¼-inch slices**
- 6 **cups cubed fully cooked ham (about 2½ pounds)**
- 1 **package (16 ounces) process cheese (Velveeta), cubed**

1. Preheat oven to 350°. Mix the first five ingredients. Stir in potatoes, ham and cheese. Transfer to two greased 13x9-in. baking dishes.
2. Bake, covered, for 1 hour. Bake, uncovered, until potatoes are tender, 45-55 minutes longer.
FREEZE OPTION Cover and freeze unbaked casseroles. To use, partially thaw in refrigerator overnight. Remove from refrigerator 30 minutes before baking. Preheat oven to 350°. Bake casseroles as directed, increasing time as necessary to heat through and for a thermometer inserted in center to read 165°.

3 pounds baby red potatoes, halved
6 medium carrots, halved lengthwise and cut into 1-inch pieces
4 fresh thyme sprigs
4 fresh dill sprigs
2 fresh rosemary sprigs
1 medium lemon
1 small navel orange
1 teaspoon salt
½ teaspoon pepper
3 cups chicken broth, warmed
6 green onions, cut into 2-inch pieces

1. Preheat oven to 350°. Peel and cut garlic cloves into quarters. Place chicken on a cutting board. Tuck wings under chicken. With a sharp paring knife, cut 24 small slits in breasts, drumsticks and thighs. Insert a piece of garlic in each slit. Tie drumsticks together.
2. Place potatoes and carrots in a shallow roasting pan; top with herbs. Place chicken, breast side up, over the vegetables and herbs. Cut lemon and orange in half; gently squeeze juices over chicken and vegetables. Place squeezed fruits inside the chicken cavity. Sprinkle chicken with salt and pepper. Pour broth around chicken.
3. Roast until a thermometer inserted in the thickest part of a thigh reads 170°-175°, 2-2½ hours. Sprinkle green onions over the vegetables during the last 20 minutes. (Cover loosely with foil if the chicken browns too quickly.)
4. Remove chicken from oven; tent with foil. Let stand 15 minutes before carving. Discard herbs. If desired, skim fat and thicken pan drippings for gravy. Serve with chicken and vegetables.

OLD-FASHIONED SCALLOPED PINEAPPLE

PREP: 10 MIN.
BAKE: 30 MIN. + STANDING
MAKES: 6 SERVINGS

My deliciously different dressing goes well with turkey or ham. It's also good for dessert with a little cream poured over the top!
—Nancy Brown, Dahinda, IL

3 large eggs, beaten
2 cups sugar
1 can (8 ounces) crushed pineapple, undrained
½ cup butter, melted
¼ cup milk
4 cups cubed bread

Preheat oven to 350°. Combine eggs, sugar, pineapple, butter and milk; add bread cubes and toss to coat. Transfer to a greased 8-in. square baking dish. Bake, uncovered, until a thermometer reads 160°, 30-35 minutes. Let stand 10 minutes. Refrigerate leftovers.

CITRUS-HERB ROAST CHICKEN

PREP: 25 MIN.
BAKE: 2 HOURS + STANDING
MAKES: 8 SERVINGS

This dish is one of my all-time favorites. The flavorful, juicy chicken has the aromas of spring: fresh herbs, lemon and spring onions. It's the perfect one-pot meal. I make the gravy right in the pan.
—Megan Fordyce, Fairchance, PA

6 garlic cloves
1 roasting chicken (6 to 7 pounds)

Holiday Helper
To make the gravy for this chicken, heat the roasting pan on the stovetop over low heat. Add a couple of tablespoons of flour and stir with a whisk until the gravy thickens. Season with salt, pepper and fresh parsley, and serve with the chicken.

"*The flavorful, juicy chicken has the aromas of spring.*" —MEGAN FORDYCE

CINNAMON ROLL CREAM CHEESE COFFEE CAKE

PREP: 35 MIN.
BAKE: 70 MIN. + COOLING
MAKES: 16 SERVINGS

Cheesecake, coffee cake and cinnamon rolls—all rolled into one!
—Deanna Smith, Meridian, ID

½ cup butter, softened
1 cup sugar
1 large egg
2 teaspoons vanilla extract
2¼ cups all-purpose flour
2 teaspoons baking powder
1 teaspoon ground cinnamon
½ teaspoon salt
¾ cup 2% milk

CHEESECAKE FILLING
2 packages (8 ounces each) cream cheese, softened
½ cup sugar
2 tablespoons all-purpose flour
3 teaspoons vanilla extract
2 large eggs, lightly beaten

CINNAMON FILLING
1 cup packed brown sugar
⅓ cup butter, melted
2 tablespoons ground cinnamon

1. Preheat oven to 350°. Cream butter and sugar until light and fluffy. Beat in egg and vanilla. In another bowl, whisk flour, baking powder, cinnamon and salt; add to the creamed mixture alternately with milk, beating well after each addition. Spread three-fourths of the batter into a greased 9-in. springform pan (batter will be thick). Set the remaining batter aside.

2. In another bowl, beat cream cheese, sugar and flour until smooth. Beat in vanilla. Add eggs; beat on low speed just until combined. Pour over batter.

3. Mix cinnamon filling ingredients. Drop by tablespoonfuls over the cream cheese mixture. Cut through cream cheese filling with a knife to swirl the cinnamon filling. Drop reserved batter by tablespoonfuls over filling. Place pan on a baking sheet.

4. Bake until center is almost set, 70-80 minutes. Cover loosely with foil during the last 30 minutes if needed to prevent overbrowning. Cool on a wire rack 10 minutes. Carefully run a knife around the edge of the pan to loosen. Cool 1 hour; remove the sides of the pan. Serve warm. Refrigerate leftovers.

CREAMY ORANGE GELATIN

PREP: 20 MIN. + CHILLING
MAKES: 12 SERVINGS

After two graduation celebrations in less than a year, it was clear that this recipe was everyone's favorite.
—Sue Gronholz, Beaver Dam, WI

  4 **cups boiling water**
  4 **packages (3 ounces each) orange gelatin**
  1 **quart vanilla ice cream, softened**
1½ **cups orange juice**
  2 **cans (11 ounces each) mandarin oranges, drained**
    Orange slices, optional

1. Add boiling water to gelatin; stir for 2 minutes to completely dissolve. Stir in ice cream and orange juice until blended. Refrigerate until partially set.
2. Fold in oranges. Pour into two 6-cup ring molds coated with cooking spray. Refrigerate overnight or until firm. Unmold onto a serving plate. If desired, serve with orange slices.

PUMPKIN SPICE LOAVES

PREP: 20 MIN.
BAKE: 50 MIN. + COOLING
MAKES: 2 LOAVES (12 SLICES EACH)

I've loved baking all my life, but when my mom made the choice to be vegan, I had to find new recipes. This one's a keeper!
—Marisa Holt, Los Angeles, CA

  2 **cups all-purpose flour**
1½ **cups white whole wheat flour**
1½ **cups packed brown sugar**
⅓ **cup sugar**
  2 **teaspoons baking soda**
  1 **teaspoon salt**
  1 **teaspoon ground cinnamon**
½ **teaspoon ground nutmeg**
½ **teaspoon ground allspice**
¼ **teaspoon ground cloves**
  1 **can (15 ounces) solid-pack pumpkin**
½ **cup canola oil**
½ **cup unsweetened applesauce**
⅓ **cup maple syrup**
⅓ **cup water**

1. Preheat oven to 350°. Whisk flours, sugars, baking soda, salt and spices. In a second bowl, whisk pumpkin, oil, applesauce, maple syrup and water. Add to flour mixture; stir just until moistened.
2. Transfer to two 8x4-in. loaf pans coated with cooking spray. Bake until a toothpick inserted in the center comes out clean, 50-60 minutes.
3. Cool 10 minutes in pans before removing to wire racks to cool.
FOR LARGER LOAVES Prepare the recipe as directed above, using two 9x5-in. loaf pans. Bake in a preheated 350° oven until a toothpick inserted in the center comes out clean, 35-40 minutes.

SLOW COOKER MUSHROOM BEEF STROGANOFF

PREP: 15 MIN.
COOK: 6 HOURS
MAKES: 8 SERVINGS

I love making this for my husband and me to have on a cold night. It warms you right up! Greek yogurt can be substituted for sour cream.
—Meg Hilton, Atlanta, GA

- 2 **pounds boneless beef chuck steak**
- 1 **pound sliced fresh mushrooms**
- 2 **medium onions, chopped**
- 1 **can (10¾ ounces) condensed golden mushroom soup, undiluted**
- 2 **tablespoons reduced-sodium soy sauce**
- 2 **tablespoons Dijon mustard**
- 1 **tablespoon Worcestershire sauce**
- 3 **garlic cloves, minced**
- ¾ **teaspoon salt**
- ½ **teaspoon pepper**
- 2 **tablespoons cornstarch**
- 2 **tablespoons water**
- 1 **cup sour cream**
  Hot cooked egg noodles
  Minced fresh parsley, optional

1. Cut steak into 3x½-in. strips. In a 5- or 6-qt. slow cooker, combine the next nine ingredients. Stir in the steak strips. Cook, covered, on low until the meat is tender, 6-8 hours.
2. Transfer steak to a serving dish; keep warm. Skim fat from cooking juices. Mix cornstarch and water until smooth; stir into cooking juices. Cook, covered, on high until thickened, 10-15 minutes. Stir in sour cream; pour over beef. Serve with noodles and, if desired, minced parsley.

Holiday Helper

When a recipe instructs you to slice uncooked beef, try putting the meat in the freezer until it's partially frozen before cutting it. Meat that is firm (but not frozen rock-solid!) is easier to cut into strips.

AUNT NANCY'S CREAM OF CRAB SOUP

PREP: 10 MIN.
COOK: 25 MIN.
MAKES: 6 SERVINGS

My sister, Nancy, is one of the best cooks I know. When my daughter was getting married, I put together a cookbook of her favorite family recipes—Nancy's soup was a must-have. Our family often had this with a salad before Christmas Eve services.
—Lynne German, Woodland Hills, CA

- ¼ **cup butter, cubed**
- 1 **teaspoon chicken bouillon granules**
- 2 **tablespoons finely grated onion**
- ¼ **cup cornstarch**
- 4 **cups half-and-half cream**
- 1 **pound jumbo lump crabmeat, drained**
- 1 **tablespoon grated Parmesan cheese**
- 2 **teaspoons seafood seasoning**
- ¼ **teaspoon salt**
- ¼ **teaspoon ground nutmeg**
- ⅛ **teaspoon pepper**
- 3 **tablespoons sherry**

1. In a large saucepan, heat butter and bouillon over medium heat. Add onion; cook and stir until tender, 1-2 minutes. Stir in cornstarch until blended; gradually whisk in cream. Bring just to a boil, stirring constantly. Stir in crab, cheese and seasonings. Reduce heat; simmer, uncovered, to allow flavors to blend, about 20 minutes, stirring occasionally.
2. Stir in sherry; heat 1-2 minutes longer. Sprinkle with more nutmeg and serve.

FOUR-CHEESE SAUSAGE RIGATONI

PREP: 35 MIN.
BAKE: 30 MIN.
MAKES: 12 SERVINGS

Everyone loves this tasty blend of sausage, creamy tomato sauce and four different cheeses. You can swap turkey sausage for pork sausage, if desired.
—Teresa Ralston, New Albany, OH

- 1 **package (16 ounces) rigatoni pasta**
- 1 **pound bulk Italian sausage**
- 1 **medium sweet red pepper, chopped**
- 1 **small onion, chopped**
- 2 **garlic cloves, minced**
- ¾ **cup heavy whipping cream**
- 1 **can (28 ounces) crushed tomatoes in puree**
- 1 **can (6 ounces) tomato paste**
- 2 **teaspoons Italian seasoning**
- ½ **teaspoon crushed red pepper flakes**
- 1 **carton (15 ounces) whole-milk ricotta cheese**
- 1 **cup shredded Parmesan cheese, divided**
- 1 **log (4 ounces) fresh goat cheese, softened**
- 1 **large egg, lightly beaten**
- 1 **teaspoon salt**
- ½ **teaspoon pepper**
- 8 **ounces fresh mozzarella cheese, cubed**
   Torn fresh basil, optional

1. Preheat oven to 350°. In a 6-qt. stockpot, cook rigatoni according to package directions. Drain; transfer to a bowl.

2. In same stockpot, cook and crumble sausage with red pepper and onion over medium heat until meat is no longer pink. Add garlic; cook 1 minute longer. Drain. Add cream; cook 5 minutes, stirring occasionally. Stir in tomatoes, tomato paste, Italian seasoning and pepper flakes. Cook, uncovered, over medium-low heat until the sauce thickens slightly, 5-8 minutes. Meanwhile, combine ricotta, ½ cup of the Parmesan, the goat cheese, egg and seasonings.

3. Stir rigatoni into the meat sauce.

Spread 3 cups into each of two greased 11x7-in. baking dishes. Top each with half of the cheese mixture, then half of the remaining pasta mixture.

4. Bake, covered, 25 minutes. Sprinkle with mozzarella and the remaining Parmesan cheese. Bake, uncovered, until cheeses are melted, about 5 minutes. If desired, sprinkle with basil.

FREEZE OPTION Prepare casseroles without mozzarella and the remaining ½ cup Parmesan cheese; freeze cheeses separately in resealable plastic freezer bags. Cover and freeze unbaked casseroles. To use, partially thaw in refrigerator overnight. Remove from refrigerator 30 minutes before baking. Bake casseroles as directed, increasing time as necessary to heat through and for a thermometer inserted in center to read 165°. If desired, sprinkle with basil.

SMOKY PINEAPPLE CHEESE BALL

PREP: 15 MIN. + CHILLING
MAKES: 2¾ CUPS

Smoky paprika balances sweet pineapple in this distinctively different cheese ball. This is my family's all-time favorite holiday appetizer.
—Debra Keil, Owasso, OK

- 2 **packages (8 ounces each) reduced-fat cream cheese**
- 1 **small green pepper, finely chopped**
- ½ **cup crushed pineapple, drained**
- 1 **teaspoon dried minced onion**
- 1 **teaspoon seasoned salt**
- ½ **teaspoon smoked paprika**
- 1½ **cups chopped pecans, divided**
   Assorted crackers

1. Beat cream cheese until smooth. Beat in pepper, pineapple, onion, seasoned salt and paprika. Stir in ½ cup pecans. Refrigerate, covered, at least 1 hour.

2. Spread remaining pecans on a large piece of plastic. Shape cheese mixture into a ball; roll in pecans to coat evenly. Wrap in plastic; refrigerate at least 1 hour.

3. Serve with crackers.

GINGERBREAD MEN COOKIES

PREP: 40 MIN. + CHILLING
BAKE: 10 MIN./BATCH + COOLING
MAKES: ABOUT 2 DOZEN

No holiday cookie platter would be complete without gingerbread men! This is a tried-and-true recipe I'm happy to share.
—Mitzi Sentiff, Annapolis, MD

- ½ cup butter, softened
- ¾ cup packed dark brown sugar
- ⅓ cup molasses
- 1 large egg
- 2 tablespoons water
- 2⅔ cups all-purpose flour
- 1 teaspoon baking soda
- ½ teaspoon salt
- 2 teaspoons ground ginger
- ½ teaspoon ground cinnamon
- ½ teaspoon ground nutmeg
- ½ teaspoon ground allspice
  Frosting of choice

1. Cream butter and brown sugar until light and fluffy. Beat in molasses, egg and water. In a second bowl, whisk together the remaining ingredients minus frosting; gradually beat into creamed mixture. Divide the dough in half. Shape each half into a disk; wrap disks in plastic. Refrigerate until easy to handle, about 30 minutes.
2. Preheat oven to 350°. On a lightly floured surface, roll each disk of dough to a ⅛-in. thickness. Cut with a floured 4-in. gingerbread man cookie cutter. Place cutouts 2 in. apart on greased baking sheets.
3. Bake until edges are firm, 8-10 minutes. Remove to wire racks to cool completely. Frost as desired.

Holiday Helper

Light and dark molasses can be used interchangeably in baking recipes, but use blackstrap molasses with caution in cooking or baking. Made from the third boiling of sugar syrup, blackstrap molasses is darker and more bitter than light or dark, and the intense flavor can be overwhelming.

EGGNOG POUND CAKE

PREP: 15 MIN.
BAKE: 40 MIN. + COOLING
MAKES: 20 SERVINGS

When you're having company, this cake—served with a custard sauce and a dash of nutmeg—inspires oohs and aahs!
—Audrey Kaalaas, Kirkland, IL

- 1 **package yellow cake mix (regular size)**
- 1¼ **cups eggnog**
- 3 **large eggs**
- ¼ **cup butter, softened**
- 2 **teaspoons ground nutmeg**
- ½ **to 1 teaspoon vanilla extract**

CREAMY CUSTARD SAUCE
- ¼ **cup sugar**
- 1 **tablespoon cornstarch**
- ¼ **teaspoon salt**
- 1 **cup whole milk**
- 1 **large egg yolk, beaten**
- 1 **teaspoon butter**
- ¼ **teaspoon vanilla extract**
- ½ **cup heavy whipping cream, whipped**
  Additional nutmeg, optional

1. Preheat oven to 350°. Grease and flour a 10-in. fluted tube pan. Combine the first six ingredients; beat on low speed for 30 seconds. Beat on medium speed for 2 minutes.
2. Transfer to prepared pan. Bake until a toothpick inserted in the center comes out clean, 40-45 minutes. Cool in the pan 10 minutes before removing to a wire rack to cool completely.
3. For sauce, in a heavy saucepan, mix sugar, cornstarch and salt. Whisk in milk. Cook and stir over medium heat until thickened and bubbly. Reduce heat to low; cook and stir 1-2 minutes longer. Remove from heat.
4. In a bowl, whisk a small amount of hot mixture into egg yolk; return all to pan, whisking constantly. Bring to a gentle boil; cook and stir 2 minutes. Remove from heat; stir in butter and vanilla. Cool completely. Fold in whipped cream; refrigerate until cold. Serve sauce with cake; if desired, sprinkle with nutmeg.
NOTE This recipe was tested with commercially prepared eggnog.

SLOW-COOKED BIG BREAKFAST

PREP: 30 MIN.
COOK: 3 HOURS
MAKES: 12 SERVINGS

We make this during holidays or on mornings when we know we're going to have a busy day. You can set this to cook overnight on low for an early breakfast, or for three hours on high for a leisurely brunch.
—Delisha Paris, Elizabeth Cty, NC

- 1 **pound bulk pork sausage**
- 2 **pounds potatoes (about 4 medium), peeled and cut into ½-in. cubes**
- ¼ **cup water**
- 1 **large onion, finely chopped**
- 1 **medium sweet red pepper, chopped**
- 2 **cups fresh spinach**
- 1 **cup chopped fresh mushrooms**
- 1 **pound cubed deli ham**
- 1 **cup shredded cheddar cheese**
- 12 **large eggs**
- ½ **cup 2% milk**
- 1 **teaspoon garlic powder**
- 1 **teaspoon pepper**
- ½ **teaspoon salt**

1. In a large skillet, cook and crumble sausage over medium heat until no longer pink, 5-7 minutes; drain.
2. Meanwhile, place the potatoes and water in a large microwave-safe dish and microwave, covered, on high until the potatoes are tender, 6 minutes, stirring halfway. Drain and add to the sausage.
3. Stir in onion, red pepper, spinach, mushrooms, ham and cheese. Transfer to a greased 6-qt. slow cooker.
4. Whisk together the remaining ingredients until blended; pour over the sausage mixture. Cook, covered, on low until the eggs are set, 3-4 hours. Let stand, uncovered, for 10 minutes before serving.

"This cake inspires oohs and aahs!"
—AUDREY KAALAAS

2. Bake pie on a lower oven rack 10 minutes. Reduce oven setting to 325°; bake until a knife inserted near the center comes out clean, 45-50 minutes. Cool on a wire rack; serve or refrigerate within 2 hours. If desired, top with sweetened whipped cream and additional ground nutmeg.

MOCHA PUNCH

PREP: 15 MIN. + CHILLING
MAKES: 25 SERVINGS

I first tried this smooth, creamy punch at a friend's Christmas open house. It was so special and distinctive I didn't leave until I had the recipe. Having a frosty glass of this chocolate punch is almost like sipping a chocolate shake.
—*Yvonne Hatfield, Norman, OK*

  6 **cups water**
  ½ **cup sugar**
  ½ **cup instant chocolate drink mix**
  ¼ **cup instant coffee granules**
  ½ **gallon vanilla ice cream**
  ½ **gallon chocolate ice cream**
  1 **cup heavy whipping cream, whipped**

1. In a large saucepan, bring water to a boil. Remove from heat. Add sugar, drink mix and instant coffee granules; stir until dissolved. Refrigerate, covered, 4 hours or overnight.
2. About 30 minutes before serving, pour mixture into a large punch bowl. Add scoops of ice cream; stir until partially melted. Top servings with whipped cream.

HUBBARD SQUASH PIE

PREP: 15 MIN.
BAKE: 55 MIN.
MAKES: 8 SERVINGS

My mom made this pie—never pumpkin—each Thanksgiving, and everyone looked forward to it. I have fond memories of my dad cutting up this hulking big blue hubbard squash on the kitchen counter and cooking it for her to make the pies. A more manageable butternut squash will deliver an equally delicate-tasting pie!
—*Patti Ann Christian, Ararat, NC*

  1   **sheet refrigerated pie pastry**
  1   **large egg**
  1½ **cups mashed cooked Hubbard or butternut squash**
  1   **can (12 ounces) evaporated milk**
  1   **cup sugar**
  2   **tablespoons molasses**
  1   **tablespoon cornstarch**
  ½   **teaspoon salt**
  ¼   **teaspoon ground nutmeg**
       Sweetened whipped cream and
          additional nutmeg, optional

1. Preheat oven to 400°. Unroll pastry sheet into a 9-in. pie plate; flute the edge. In a large bowl, whisk together egg, squash, milk, sugar, molasses, cornstarch and salt. Pour into pastry shell; sprinkle with nutmeg.

MIXED NUT CLUSTERS

PREP: 30 MIN. + CHILLING
MAKES: 6 DOZEN

Serve these with hot chocolate to keep everyone happy and warm. They also make great gifts—box them up with each cluster in a foil or paper candy cup.
—Ida Tuey, South Lyon, MI

- 2 **cups semisweet chocolate chips**
- 1 **can (14 ounces) sweetened condensed milk**
- 1 **tablespoon honey**
- 1 **tablespoon vanilla extract**
- 1 **cup each chopped walnuts, cashews, pecans and almonds**

1. In a large heavy saucepan, melt chocolate chips, milk and honey over low heat; stir until blended. Remove from heat. Stir in vanilla; add nuts.
2. Drop by rounded tablespoonfuls onto baking sheets lined with parchment paper. Refrigerate until firm. Store in refrigerator.

CRANBERRY-ORANGE RICE PUDDING

PREP: 30 MIN.
COOK: 20 MIN.
MAKES: 5 SERVINGS

Velvety custard and sweet-tart fruit make a delightful combination. Serve it as part of a Yuletide brunch, too.
—Anne Ashdown, Salt Lake City, UT

- 1 **cup fresh or frozen cranberries**
- ⅓ **cup plus ½ cup sugar, divided**
- ½ **cup orange juice**
- 4 **teaspoons grated orange peel**
- 2 **cups 2% milk, divided**
- 2 **cups cooked rice**
- 2 **large eggs**
- ¼ **teaspoon orange extract**

1. In a small saucepan, combine cranberries, ⅓ cup sugar, orange juice and peel. Cook over medium heat until berries pop, about 10-12 minutes, stirring occasionally. Keep warm.
2. In a large saucepan, combine 1½ cups milk, rice and the remaining sugar; bring to a boil over medium heat. Cook until

"Serve these with hot chocolate to keep everyone happy and warm."
—IDA TUEY

thick and creamy, about 15 minutes, stirring occasionally. Whisk together eggs and remaining milk. Stir into rice mixture. Cook and stir until mixture reaches 160°, about 2 minutes.
3. Remove from heat; stir in extract. Serve warm with cranberry topping. Refrigerate leftovers.

WASSAIL BOWL

START TO FINISH: 25 MIN.
MAKES: 12 SERVINGS

We served this at my family's open house on Christmas Eve—to welcome anyone who came a-wassailing!
—Sharon Tipton, Casselberry, FL

- 2 **cinnamon sticks (3 inches)**
- 16 **whole cloves**
- 6 **cups apple cider or juice**
- 2 **cups cranberry juice**
- 1 **cup orange juice**
- ¼ **cup sugar**
- 1 **teaspoon angostura bitters**
- 1 **medium orange, quartered and sliced**
- 1 **to 2 cups rum**

Place cinnamon and cloves on a double thickness of cheesecloth. Gather the corners of the cloth to enclose the seasonings; tie securely with string. Place apple cider, juices, sugar and bitters in a large saucepan. Add orange slices and the spice bag. Bring to a boil. Reduce heat; simmer, uncovered, 10-12 minutes or until the punch reaches desired temperature. Discard the spice bag. Stir in rum.

FLUFFED FRUIT SALAD

START TO FINISH: 10 MIN.
MAKES: 14 SERVINGS

I like this recipe because I can prepare it in advance when entertaining, and it never disappoints. Even people who don't care for cranberries like this treat.
—*Christine Halandras, Meeker, CO*

- 1 can (20 ounces) unsweetened pineapple tidbits, drained
- 1 can (14 ounces) whole-berry cranberry sauce
- 1 can (11 ounces) mandarin oranges, drained
- 1 carton (8 ounces) frozen whipped topping, thawed
- ½ to 1 teaspoon grated orange peel
- Lettuce leaves, optional
- ½ cup pecan halves, toasted

Combine pineapple, cranberry sauce and oranges. Fold in whipped topping and orange peel. Serve on lettuce if desired. Just before serving, sprinkle with pecans.

AUNT ROSE'S FANTASTIC BUTTER TOFFEE

PREP: 25 MIN.
COOK: 15 MIN.
MAKES: ABOUT 2 LBS

I love everything about the country... especially good old-fashioned home cooking. This toffee is a family favorite!
—*Kathy Dorman, Snover, MI*

- 2 cups unblanched whole almonds
- 11 ounces milk chocolate, chopped
- 1 cup butter, cubed
- 1 cup sugar
- 3 tablespoons cold water

1. Preheat oven to 350°. In a shallow baking pan, toast almonds until golden brown, 5-10 minutes; stir occasionally. Cool. Pulse chocolate in a food processor until finely ground (do not overprocess); transfer to a bowl. Pulse almonds until coarsely chopped. Sprinkle 1 cup almonds into a greased 15x10-in. pan. Sprinkle with 1 cup chocolate.
2. In a heavy saucepan, combine butter, sugar and water. Cook over medium heat until a candy thermometer reads 290° (soft-crack stage), stirring occasionally.
3. Immediately pour mixture over almonds and chocolate in pan. Sprinkle with remaining chocolate and almonds. Refrigerate until set; break into pieces.
NOTE Test your candy thermometer before each use by bringing water to a boil; the thermometer should read 212°. Adjust your recipe temperature up or down based on your test.

HOMEMADE PEANUT BUTTER CUPS

PREP: 20 MIN. + CHILLING
MAKES: 3 DOZEN

I choose pretty mini muffin liners and colored sprinkles to coordinate with the holiday we're celebrating. These irresistible candies with gooey peanut butter centers are so easy to make!
—LaVonne Hegland, St. Michael, MN

 1 **cup creamy peanut butter, divided**
 ½ **cup confectioners' sugar**
 4½ **teaspoons butter, softened**
 ½ **teaspoon salt**

 2 **cups semisweet chocolate chips**
 4 **milk chocolate candy bars (1.55 ounces each), coarsely chopped**
 Colored sprinkles, optional

1. Combine ½ cup of the peanut butter, the confectioners' sugar, butter and salt until smooth.

2. In a microwave, melt chocolate chips, candy bars and the remaining peanut butter; stir until smooth.

3. Drop teaspoonfuls of the chocolate mixture into paper-lined miniature muffin cups. Drop a scant teaspoonful of the peanut butter mixture into each cup;

top with another teaspoonful of the chocolate mixture. If desired, decorate with sprinkles. Refrigerate until set. Store in an airtight container.

Holiday Helper
It is important to chop chocolate before it's melted. Chopping ensures more even melting, since chocolate may burn before large pieces melt.

SEASONAL
GET-TOGETHERS

The holiday season brings all kinds of gatherings, from brunches to cocktail parties and everything in between. Turn here to create just the right menu for your event.

Christmas Morning Breakfast

Whether it's a family breakfast after the presents are
opened or a brunch with friends, this special day
deserves a special breakfast. Go sweet or
savory or both—it's all delicious!

PEAR-STUFFED FRENCH TOAST WITH BRIE, CRANBERRIES & PECANS

PREP: 35 MIN. + CHILLING
BAKE: 35 MIN. + STANDING
MAKES: 10 SERVINGS

This French toast is stuffed with fresh pears, dried cranberries, pecans, Brie and cream cheese. It's an easy overnight recipe that is so elegant and rich, it also makes an indulgent dessert!
—Lindsay Sprunk, Noblesville, IN

- 2 tablespoons butter
- 4 medium pears, peeled and thinly sliced
- 3 tablespoons packed brown sugar, divided
- 1 package (8 ounces) cream cheese, softened
- ½ cup dried cranberries
- ⅓ cup chopped pecans, toasted
- 20 slices French bread (½ inch thick)
- 1 round (8 ounces) Brie cheese, rind removed and thinly sliced
- 3 large eggs
- 2 cups 2% milk
- 3 teaspoons vanilla extract
- ½ teaspoon ground cinnamon
- ¼ teaspoon salt
  Maple syrup, optional

1. In a large skillet, heat the butter over medium heat. Add pears and 2 tablespoons brown sugar; cook and stir until the pears are tender, 4-6 minutes. In a bowl, mix cream cheese, cranberries and pecans.
2. Place half the bread slices in a greased 13x9-in. baking dish. Layer with the cream cheese mixture, pear mixture and Brie. Top with the remaining bread slices. Whisk together the next five ingredients and the remaining brown sugar. Pour over the bread. Refrigerate, covered, overnight.
3. Preheat oven to 375°. Remove French toast from refrigerator while the oven heats. Bake, uncovered, until the top is golden brown, 35-40 minutes. Let stand for 10 minutes before serving. If desired, serve with syrup.

SPARKLING ORANGES

PREP: 35 MIN. + CHILLING
MAKES: 8 SERVINGS

We were living in Texas when I found the recipe for this simple yet elegant salad. I was thrilled— this was a great way to use our surplus of fresh oranges! Since it's prepared ahead, there's no last-minute fuss.
—Janie Bush, Weskan, KS

- ½ cup sugar
- ½ cup orange marmalade
- 1 cup white grape juice
- ½ cup lemon-lime soda
- 8 large oranges, peeled and sectioned
- 3 tablespoons slivered almonds, toasted
- 3 tablespoons flaked coconut, toasted

1. In a small saucepan over medium heat, combine sugar and marmalade; cook and stir until the sugar is dissolved. Remove from heat. Stir in grape juice and soda. Pour over orange sections; toss to coat. Refrigerate, covered, overnight.
2. Using a slotted spoon, remove the oranges to a serving dish. Sprinkle with almonds and coconut.
NOTE To toast nuts and coconut, bake in separate shallow pans in a 350° oven for 5-10 minutes or until golden brown, stirring occasionally.

EGGNOG PANCAKES

START TO FINISH: 20 MIN.
MAKES: 12 PANCAKES

My family loves it when mornings start with a platter piled high with featherlight flapjacks. Pancakes made from a mix just can't compare to these homemade delights.
—Marilyn Mueller, Fayetteville, AR

- 2 **cups all-purpose flour**
- 4 **teaspoons baking powder**
- ½ **teaspoon salt**
- ¼ **teaspoon ground nutmeg, optional**
- 2 **large eggs**
- 1½ **cups eggnog**
- 2 **tablespoons butter, melted**

1. Mix flour, baking powder, salt and, if desired, nutmeg. In a second bowl, whisk eggs, eggnog and butter; stir into the dry ingredients just until moistened.
2. Preheat griddle over medium heat. Lightly grease the griddle. Pour batter by ¼ cupfuls onto the griddle; cook until the bubbles on top begin to pop and the bottoms are golden brown. Turn; cook until the second side is golden brown.
NOTE This recipe was tested with commercially prepared eggnog.

CANADIAN BACON WITH APPLES

START TO FINISH: 20 MIN.
MAKES: 6 SERVINGS

At the holidays, I'd rather spend time with family than in the kitchen, so I rely on easy-to-fix recipes like this. No one can resist Canadian bacon and apples coated with a brown sugar glaze.
—Paula Marchesi, Lenhartsville, PA

- ½ **cup packed brown sugar**
- 1 **tablespoon lemon juice**
- ⅛ **teaspoon pepper**
- 1 **large unpeeled red apple**
- 1 **large unpeeled green apple**
- 1 **pound sliced Canadian bacon**

1. In a large skillet, mix brown sugar, lemon juice and pepper. Cook and stir over medium heat until the sugar is dissolved. Cut each apple into 16 wedges; add to the brown sugar mixture. Cook over medium heat until the apples are tender, 5-7 minutes, stirring occasionally. Remove the apples to a platter with a slotted spoon; keep warm.
2. Add bacon to the skillet; cook over medium heat, turning once, until heated through, about 3 minutes. Transfer to the platter. Pour the remaining brown sugar mixture over apples and bacon.

Holiday Helper

To make whipped butter like some restaurants serve with their pancakes, let the butter soften at room temperature, then beat it with an electric mixer until light and fluffy. Some restaurants mix in a little honey, confectioners' sugar or orange peel for added flavor.

CINNAMON-APPLE CIDER MONKEY BREAD

PREP: 20 MIN.
BAKE: 45 MIN. + STANDING
MAKES: 16 SERVINGS

I use the cold-weather staples cinnamon and apple cider to turn plain cinnamon rolls into monkey bread. It's a hit with my boys, who love the sticky sweetness.
—Kelly Walsh, Aviston, IL

- **5 envelopes (.74 ounce each) instant spiced cider mix**
- **3 tubes (12.4 ounces each) refrigerated cinnamon rolls with icing**
- **2 medium Granny Smith apples, peeled and chopped**
- **1 cup chopped pecans or walnuts**
- **6 tablespoons butter, melted**
- **2 teaspoons ground cinnamon**

1. Preheat oven to 350°. Combine cider mixes. Separate cinnamon rolls, setting aside icings; cut each roll into quarters. Add to the cider mixture; toss to coat.
2. Arrange a third of the dough pieces in a well-greased 10-in. fluted tube pan; top with half the apples and half the pecans. Repeat layers once. Top with the remaining dough.
3. Mix melted butter, cinnamon and the icing from one container until blended.

Drizzle over the rolls. Bake until golden brown, 45-50 minutes. (If needed, cover loosely with foil during the last 5 minutes to prevent overbrowning.)
4. Immediately invert monkey bread onto a serving plate; keep pan inverted for 10 minutes, allowing the bread to release from the pan. Remove the pan. Meanwhile, microwave the remaining icing, uncovered, until softened, about 10 seconds. Drizzle over the monkey bread. Serve warm.

"Mini marshmallows bring out the youngster in anyone!"
—MINDIE HILTON

FOUR-CHEESE BAKED EGGS

PREP: 15 MIN.
BAKE: 25 MIN. + STANDING
MAKES: 12 SERVINGS

When I created this dish, I was thrilled that my husband enjoyed it so much. He normally prefers omelets for brunch, but he devoured his first helping of these eggs, then asked for more.
—Lisa Speer, Palm Beach, FL

- 1 **cup whole-milk ricotta cheese**
- 3 **ounces cream cheese, softened**
- 7 **large eggs**
- 6 **tablespoons butter, melted**
- ½ **teaspoon salt**
- ¼ **teaspoon pepper**
- 3 **tablespoons all-purpose flour**
- ½ **teaspoon baking powder**
- 3 **cups grated Gruyere or Swiss cheese**
- 2 **tablespoons minced chives or chopped green onions**
- ¼ **cup shredded Parmesan cheese**

1. Preheat oven to 350°. Beat ricotta and cream cheeses until smooth. Add eggs, butter, salt and pepper; beat until blended. In another bowl, whisk flour with baking powder; add to the egg mixture. Stir in Gruyere cheese and chives. Pour into a greased 13x9-in. baking dish. Sprinkle with Parmesan.
2. Bake, uncovered, until a knife inserted in the center comes out clean, 25-30 minutes. Let stand 10 minutes before cutting.

MOCHA MINT COFFEE

PREP: 10 MIN.
COOK: 2 HOURS
MAKES: 8 SERVINGS

This doctored-up coffee benefits from hints of mint, cocoa and cinnamon. And the mini marshmallows bring out the youngster in anyone!
—Mindie Hilton, Susanville, CA

- 6 **cups hot brewed coffee**
- 2 **packets instant hot cocoa mix**
- ½ **cup dulce de leche**
- ¼ **cup peppermint crunch baking chips or mint chocolate chips**
- 4 **teaspoons sugar**
- 1 **cup miniature marshmallows**
- ½ **teaspoon ground cinnamon**
  Chocolate sauce, optional

1. In a 3-qt. slow cooker, combine first five ingredients. Cook, covered, on low until hot, 2-3 hours.
2. Ladle coffee into mugs. Top with marshmallows; sprinkle with cinnamon. Drizzle with chocolate sauce if desired.
NOTE This recipe was tested with Nestle La Lechera dulce de leche. If using Eagle Brand dulce de leche (caramel flavored sauce), thicken according to package directions before using.

Holiday Helper
By law, cheese can be called Gruyere only if it comes from a specific region of Switzerland. Swiss cheese is a common substitute, if not quite as flavorful. French Gruyere-style cheeses include Comté and Beaufort.

Cookie-Decorating Party

Little ones love helping in the kitchen, so make it a party!
Let tiny bakers create their own works of cookie art while enjoying
a spread of kid-friendly foods. Grab a plastic tablecloth and
some sprinkles and frosting, and let the fun begin.

NEVER FAIL CUTOUT COOKIES

PREP: 45 MIN. + CHILLING
BAKE: 10 MIN./BATCH + COOLING
MAKES: ABOUT 5 DOZEN

I have tried many recipes for cutout cookies over the years—this one is foolproof. My daughter and my granddaughter love making these for holidays and social events. Most of all, we enjoy decorating them. You can try almond flavoring or another flavoring of choice. This recipe is easily doubled.
—Irene Palm, Mansfield, OH

- 2 **cups butter, softened**
- 1 **package (8 ounces) cream cheese, softened**
- 2 **cups granulated sugar**
- 2 **large egg yolks**
- 2 **teaspoons vanilla extract**
- 5 **cups all-purpose flour**

FROSTING
- 3½ **cups confectioners' sugar**
- 3 **tablespoons butter, softened**
- 1 **tablespoon shortening**
- 1 **teaspoon vanilla extract**
- 4 **to 5 tablespoons 2% milk**
  Food coloring of choice, optional
  Assorted sprinkles or candies, optional

1. Beat butter, cream cheese and sugar until light and fluffy. Beat in egg yolks and vanilla. Gradually beat in flour. Divide the dough into four portions; shape each into a disk. Wrap each disk in plastic; refrigerate until firm enough to roll, about 30 minutes.
2. Preheat oven to 350°. On a lightly floured surface, roll each disk of dough to ¼-in. thickness. Cut with floured 3-in. holiday cookie cutters. Place 1 in. apart on ungreased baking sheets.
3. Bake until the edges are light golden, 12-14 minutes. Cool on pans 5 minutes. Remove to wire racks to cool completely.
4. For the frosting, beat confectioners' sugar, butter, shortening, vanilla and enough milk to reach the desired consistency. If desired, tint with food coloring. Spread or pipe over cookies. Decorate as desired.

DECORATING TIPS

Shake different colors of sanding sugar, sugar crystals, nonpareils, jimmies and pearls into separate cups of a muffin tin. Set it out for the kids to scoop up the items they want to decorate with.

EASY PARMESAN BISCUITS

START TO FINISH: 15 MIN.
MAKES: 5 BISCUITS

This recipe is simple but so good. Children love to dip the biscuits in butter and coat them with the cheese. Warm from the oven, one biscuit per person usually isn't enough.
—Linda Becker, Olympia, WA

- 1 **tube (6 ounces) refrigerated buttermilk biscuits, separated into 5 biscuits**
- 3 **tablespoons butter, melted**
- ½ **cup grated Parmesan cheese**

Preheat oven to 400°. Dip both sides of biscuits into melted butter, then into cheese. Place 1 in. apart in a well-greased 9-in. round pan. Bake until golden brown, 8-11 minutes. Serve warm.

"Much-loved meatball subs are even better as a casserole."
—RICK FRIEDMAN

MEATBALL SUBMARINE CASSEROLE

START TO FINISH: 30 MIN.
MAKES: 4 SERVINGS

We were hosting a bunch of friends, and after a comedy of errors, I had to come up with a Plan B for dinner. Much-loved meatball subs are even better as a casserole—so delicious!
—*Rick Friedman, Palm Springs, CA*

1 **package (12 ounces) frozen fully cooked Italian meatballs**

4 **slices sourdough bread**
1½ **teaspoons olive oil**
1 **garlic clove, halved**
1½ **cups pasta sauce with mushrooms**
½ **cup shredded part-skim mozzarella cheese, divided**
½ **cup grated Parmesan cheese, divided**

1. Preheat broiler. Microwave meatballs, covered, on high until heated through, 4-6 minutes. Meanwhile, place bread on an ungreased baking sheet; brush one side of the bread with oil. Broil 4-6 in. from the heat until golden brown, 1-2 minutes. Rub the bread with the cut surface of the garlic; discard garlic. Tear the bread into bite-sized pieces; transfer to a greased 11x7-in. baking dish. Reduce oven setting to 350°.
2. Add pasta sauce, ¼ cup mozzarella cheese and ¼ cup Parmesan cheese to the meatballs; toss to combine. Pour the mixture over the bread pieces; sprinkle with the remaining cheeses. Bake, uncovered, until the cheeses are melted, 15-18 minutes.

CHICKEN & BACON ROLL-UPS

PREP: 20 MIN. + CHILLING
MAKES: 4 DOZEN

My children like these so much that they ask for them every day for lunch during the summer. Whenever I have leftover chicken or turkey breast, this is a delicious way to use it up.
—*Patricia Nieh, Portola Valley, CA*

- 1 **can (9¾ ounces) chunk white chicken, drained**
- 1 **carton (8 ounces) spreadable garden vegetable cream cheese**
- 1 **cup salsa, divided**
- 4 **pieces ready-to-serve fully cooked bacon, crumbled**
- 6 **flour tortillas (8 inches), room temperature**

Mix chicken, cream cheese, ½ cup salsa and bacon; spread over tortillas. Roll up tightly; wrap in plastic. Refrigerate at least 1 hour. Just before serving, unwrap and cut tortillas into 1-in. slices. Serve with remaining salsa.

RAMEN NOODLE SALAD

START TO FINISH: 25 MIN.
MAKES: 16 SERVINGS

With added crunch from ramen noodles and sunflower seeds, plus a sweet, glossy dressing, this lively salad is a definite crowd pleaser!
—*Beverly Sprague, Baltimore, MD*

- ½ **cup sugar**
- ½ **cup canola oil**
- ¼ **cup cider vinegar**
- 1½ **teaspoons soy sauce**
- ¼ **teaspoon salt**
- 2 **packages (3 ounces each) ramen noodles**
- 2 **tablespoons butter**
- 1 **bunch romaine, torn (7 cups)**
- 1 **bunch broccoli, cut into florets (4 cups)**
- 6 **green onions, chopped**
- ½ **cup sunflower kernels**

1. Whisk together the first five ingredients. Refrigerate, covered, until serving.
2. Discard the seasoning packet from noodles (or save for another use). Break the noodles into small pieces. In a large skillet, heat butter over medium-high heat. Add the noodles; saute until golden brown.
3. Combine romaine, broccoli, onions, sunflower kernels and noodles. Just before serving, whisk the dressing and pour over the salad; toss to coat.

APPLE CINNAMON CAKE

PREP: 15 MIN.
BAKE: 40 MIN. + COOLING
MAKES: 12 SERVINGS

This cake is equally good for breakfast or dessert, so be sure not to eat all of it after dinner! Easy to make, it's super moist on the inside and it has a crispy, cinnamon-rich crunch on the outside.
—Marideane Maxwell, Albany, GA

 1 **package yellow cake mix (regular size)**
 1 **can (21 ounces) apple pie filling**
 4 **large eggs**
 ⅔ **cup canola oil**
 6 **tablespoons cinnamon sugar, divided**
GLAZE
 1 **cup confectioners' sugar**
 ¼ **teaspoon ground cinnamon**
 1 **to 2 tablespoons water**

1. Preheat oven to 350°. Grease and flour a 10-in. fluted tube pan. Combine the cake mix, pie filling, eggs and oil; beat on low speed for 30 seconds. Beat on medium speed for 2 minutes. Pour half of the batter into the prepared pan. Sprinkle with 3 tablespoons cinnamon sugar. Add the remaining batter; top with the remaining cinnamon sugar.
2. Bake until a toothpick inserted in the center comes out clean, 40-45 minutes. Cool in pan 10 minutes before removing to a wire rack to cool completely. Mix confectioners' sugar, cinnamon and enough water to reach the desired consistency. Spoon glaze over cake, allowing some to flow over the sides.
NOTE For easier removal of cakes, use solid shortening to grease plain and fluted tube pans.

Holiday Helper

Removing a cake from a fluted tube pan too soon can cause it to crack, break or stick to the pan. Leaving a cake in the pan too long, however, can cause moisture to form between the cake and the pan. Give the cake a couple of hours to cool, then see if it comes out of the pan easily.

CHEWY CARAMEL-COATED POPCORN

START TO FINISH: 25 MIN.
MAKES: ABOUT 6 QUARTS

When I was a kid, my mom made this recipe often. I've adapted it to make it more chewy and gooey than her crunchy, nut-loaded version. I get requests to make this for every event that I host, and never have a single leftover!
—Shannon Dobos, Calgary, AB

 1½ **cups butter, cubed**
 2⅔ **cups packed light brown sugar**
 1 **cup golden syrup**
 1 **teaspoon vanilla extract**
 24 **cups popped popcorn**

1. Line two 15x10x1-in. pans with parchment paper. In a large heavy saucepan, melt butter over medium-high heat. Add brown sugar and syrup, stirring to dissolve the brown sugar. Bring to a full rolling boil. Boil and stir for 1 minute. Remove from heat and quickly stir in vanilla.
2. Pour the caramel mixture over popcorn; stir lightly to coat. Using a rubber spatula, press the popcorn into the prepared pans. Cool. Pull apart into pieces. Store in airtight containers.

Holiday Open House Buffet

Open your door to family and friends this year with a casual yet festive Christmas party. A beautiful buffet of delicious food is sure to welcome all visitors and help make spirits bright.

PEPPER-STUFFED PORK TENDERLOIN

PREP: 40 MIN.
BAKE: 45 MIN. + STANDING
MAKES: 8 SERVINGS

Spicy stuffing balances the delicate flavor of pork in this flavorful dish that looks great on the plate—and tastes even better!
—Margaret Allen, Abingdon, VA

- 2 **tablespoons canola oil**
- 3 **small sweet red peppers, finely chopped**
- 1 **large onion, finely chopped**
- 2 **small celery ribs, finely chopped**
- 1½ **teaspoons dried thyme**
- ¾ **teaspoon garlic salt**
- ¾ **teaspoon paprika**
- ½ **teaspoon cayenne pepper**
- 3 **pork tenderloins (¾ pound each)**
- 4 **teaspoons lemon-pepper seasoning**
- 4 **teaspoons fennel seed, crushed**

1. Preheat oven to 325°. In a large skillet, heat oil over medium-high heat. Add red peppers, onion and celery; saute until tender, 3-4 minutes. Add thyme, garlic salt, paprika and cayenne; saute 1 minute longer. Remove from heat; set aside.

2. Make a lengthwise slit down the center of each tenderloin to within ½ in. of the bottom. Open the tenderloins so they lie flat; cover with plastic wrap and flatten to ½-in. thickness. Remove plastic wrap from the tenderloins; fill with vegetable stuffing mixture. Close the tenderloins; tie at 2-in. intervals with kitchen string, securing ends with toothpicks.

3. Place on a rack in a shallow baking pan coated with cooking spray. Combine lemon-pepper and fennel; rub over the tenderloins.

4. Bake until a thermometer inserted into pork reads 145°, 45-55 minutes. Remove tenderloins from oven; let stand 5 minutes. Discard toothpicks and string. Cut each tenderloin into eight slices.

GINGER-APRICOT TOSSED SALAD

PREP: 25 MIN.
COOK: 10 MIN.
MAKES: 6 SERVINGS (¾ CUP DRESSING)

This dish is a nice change from an ordinary green salad and is elegant enough for company. The dressing is one of my favorites. Its sweetness complements the crisp greens and crunchy green beans.
—Trisha Kruse, Eagle, ID

- 1 **can (16 ounces) apricot halves, drained**
- ¼ **cup rice vinegar**
- 1 **teaspoon sugar**
- ½ **teaspoon minced fresh gingerroot**
- 1 **garlic clove, minced**
- ¼ **teaspoon salt**
- ¼ **teaspoon pepper**
- 1½ **pounds fresh green beans, trimmed and cut into 2-inch pieces**
- 5 **cups torn mixed salad greens**
- 1 **medium mango, peeled and cubed**
- 3 **tablespoons coarsely chopped dry roasted peanuts**

1. Process the first seven ingredients in a blender until smooth. Fill a 6-qt. stockpot two-thirds full with water. Add beans; cook, uncovered, until crisp-tender, 8-10 minutes.

2. Remove the beans and immediately drop them into ice water. Drain and pat dry. In a salad bowl, combine salad greens, mango and beans. Sprinkle with peanuts. Serve with dressing.

MAKE-AHEAD MARINATED SHRIMP

PREP: 15 MIN. + MARINATING
MAKES: 6 CUPS

Dress up your holiday buffet table with this tasty shrimp recipe. It's an appetizer that's so easy, you'll have plenty of time to enjoy your party.
—Phyllis Schmalz, Kansas City, KS

- ¾ cup water
- ½ cup red wine vinegar
- ¼ cup olive oil
- ¾ teaspoon salt
- ¾ teaspoon minced fresh oregano or ¼ teaspoon dried oregano
- ¾ teaspoon minced fresh thyme or ¼ teaspoon dried thyme
- 1 garlic clove, minced
- ¼ teaspoon pepper
- 1½ pounds peeled and deveined cooked shrimp (16-20 per pound)
- 1 can (14 ounces) water-packed artichoke hearts, rinsed, drained and halved
- ½ pound small fresh mushrooms, halved

In a large resealable plastic bag, combine the first eight ingredients. Add shrimp, artichokes and mushrooms; seal and turn to coat. Refrigerate 8 hours or overnight, turning occasionally.

APRICOT HAM BALLS

PREP: 20 MIN.
BAKE: 45 MIN.
MAKES: 2 DOZEN

My family always requests these flavorful ham balls for our annual open house. I usually have to double the recipe to make sure I have enough for the guests!
—Loretta Walker, Great Falls, MT

- 3 large eggs
- 1¾ cups apricot nectar, divided
- 1 cup dry bread crumbs
- ¼ cup chopped onion
- 1½ pounds ground fully cooked ham
- 1 pound bulk pork sausage
- 1 cup packed brown sugar
- ¼ cup vinegar
- 2 tablespoons all-purpose flour
- 1 teaspoon ground mustard
- ½ teaspoon ground allspice
- ½ teaspoon Worcestershire sauce

1. Preheat oven to 325°. Whisk eggs with ¾ cup of the apricot nectar. Stir in bread crumbs and onion. Add ham and sausage; mix lightly but thoroughly. Shape into 2-in. balls. Place in an ungreased 13x9-in. baking dish.
2. In another bowl, mix the remaining ingredients and the remaining nectar. Pour over ham balls. Bake, uncovered, until meat is no longer pink, 45-50 minutes.

HASH BROWN BROCCOLI BAKE

PREP: 25 MIN.
BAKE: 50 MIN.
MAKES: 14 SERVINGS

Here's a perfect dish for a potluck or holiday buffet. It goes well with fish, poultry, pork or beef. Cheddar cheese can be substituted for Swiss. I'll often double the recipe to serve a crowd.
—Jeanette Volker, Walton, NE

- 4 **tablespoons butter, divided**
- 2 **tablespoons all-purpose flour**
- 1 **teaspoon salt**
- ⅛ **teaspoon ground nutmeg**
- ⅛ **teaspoon pepper**
- 2 **cups 2% milk**
- 1 **package (8 ounces) cream cheese, cubed**
- 2 **cups shredded Swiss cheese**
- 6 **cups frozen shredded hash brown potatoes (about 20 ounces), thawed**
- 1 **package (16 ounces) frozen chopped broccoli, thawed**
- ½ **cup dry bread crumbs**

1. Preheat oven to 350°. In a large saucepan, melt 2 tablespoons butter. Stir in flour, salt, nutmeg and pepper until smooth; gradually add milk. Bring to a boil; cook and stir until thickened, about 2 minutes. Remove from heat. Add cheeses; stir until melted. Stir in hash browns.

2. Spoon half of the potato mixture into a greased 2-qt. baking dish. Top with broccoli and the remaining potato mixture. Bake, covered, for 35 minutes.

3. Melt the remaining butter; toss with bread crumbs. Sprinkle over casserole. Bake, covered, until heated through and topping is golden, 15-20 minutes.

NAPOLEON CREMES

PREP: 15 MIN. + CHILLING
MAKES: 4 DOZEN

For our annual holiday party, I set out a buffet with lots of food and candies, including these lovely layered treats. They're so creamy...and with a layer of green pistachio pudding peeking out, they're very merry!
—Gloria Jesswein, Niles, MI

- 2 cups finely crushed graham cracker crumbs
- 1 cup flaked coconut
- ¼ cup granulated sugar
- ¼ cup baking cocoa
- ½ cup plus 2 tablespoons butter, melted
- 1 teaspoon vanilla extract

FILLING
- ½ cup butter, softened
- 2 cups confectioners' sugar
- 1 package (3.4 ounces) instant pistachio or lemon pudding mix
- 3 tablespoons milk

TOPPING
- 1 cup (6 ounces) semisweet chocolate chips
- 3 tablespoons butter

1. Combine graham cracker crumbs, coconut, sugar and cocoa. Stir in melted butter and vanilla. Press onto bottom of a greased 9-in. square baking dish. Refrigerate 30 minutes.

2. For filling, beat softened butter until smooth. Add confectioners' sugar, pudding mix and milk; beat until fluffy. Spread over the crust. Refrigerate until firm, 1½-2 hours.

3. For topping, microwave chocolate chips and butter on high, stirring every 30 seconds, until melted and smooth. Cool. Spread over the pudding layer. Refrigerate until set. Cut into bars.

ULTIMATE CHOCOLATE BREAD PUDDING

PREP: 30 MIN.
BAKE: 45 MIN.
MAKES: 12 SERVINGS

When I really want to impress guests, I serve this decadent bread pudding. With just a few staple ingredients, I can turn out this masterpiece in no time!
—Erin Chilcoat, Central Islip, NY

- 1 tablespoon plus ½ cup butter, divided
- 2 cups (12 ounces) semisweet chocolate chips
- 1 cup packed light brown sugar
- 3 large eggs
- 2 cups whole milk
- 1 tablespoon vanilla extract
- 2 teaspoons instant espresso powder
- ½ teaspoon salt
- 1 pound egg bread or challah, cubed

SAUCE
- ½ cup heavy whipping cream
- 1 large egg yolk
- ½ cup packed light brown sugar
- ⅛ teaspoon salt
- 2 tablespoons butter
- ¼ cup chopped pecans, toasted
- ¼ cup flaked coconut, toasted
- 2 to 3 teaspoons brandy, optional

SWEETENED WHIPPED CREAM
- ¾ cup heavy whipping cream
- 2 tablespoons confectioners' sugar
- 1 to 2 tablespoons brandy, optional

1. Preheat oven to 350°. Grease a 9-in. springform pan with 1 tablespoon butter. Cube the remaining butter; place in a small saucepan. Add chocolate chips and brown sugar. Cook and stir over medium heat until the sugar is dissolved. Remove from the heat.

2. In a large bowl, whisk the eggs, milk, vanilla, espresso powder and salt. Gently stir in bread; let stand until the bread is softened, about 15 minutes. Fold in the chocolate mixture. Transfer to prepared pan. Bake pudding, uncovered, until a knife inserted in the center comes out clean, 45-55 minutes. Cool on a wire rack for 15 minutes.

3. Meanwhile, for sauce, heat cream in a small heavy saucepan until bubbles form around the sides. In a small bowl, whisk together egg yolk, brown sugar and salt. Whisk a small amount of hot cream into the egg mixture; return all to pan, stirring constantly. Cook and stir until mixture is thickened and coats the back of a spoon. Stir in butter. Fold in pecans and coconut. If desired, stir in brandy. Cool.

4. For whipped cream, beat cream until it begins to thicken. Add confectioners' sugar and, if desired, brandy; beat until soft peaks form.

5. Carefully run a knife around the edge of the springform pan to loosen; remove rim from pan. Serve pudding warm with sauce and whipped cream.

NOTE To toast nuts and coconut, bake in separate shallow pans in a 350° oven for 5-10 minutes or until golden brown, stirring occasionally.

"When I really want to impress guests, I serve this!"

—ERIN CHILCOAT

MAKE-AHEAD ENTERTAINING

Want to deliver a beautiful spread with delectable dishes, but don't want to neglect your guests? These recipes help get you out of the kitchen and into the party.

MAPLE-PECAN PORK CHOPS

START TO FINISH: 30 MIN.
MAKES: 4 SERVINGS (1¼ CUPS SAUCE)

For a standout supper, start with these sweet and savory chops—the combination of apple juice, sweet maple syrup and crunchy pecans is guaranteed to make any occasion special.
—Taste of Home *Test Kitchen*

 2 tablespoons spicy brown mustard
 ½ teaspoon pepper
 ½ cup maple syrup, divided
 4 bone-in pork loin chops
   (¾ inch thick and 8 ounces each)
 1 tablespoon butter
 ½ cup unsweetened apple juice
 1 cup pecan halves

1. Mix mustard, pepper and 2 teaspoons maple syrup. Lightly drizzle over both sides of pork chops.
2. In a large nonstick skillet, heat butter over medium heat. Brown pork chops 2-3 minutes on each side. Add apple juice. Reduce heat; simmer, covered, until a thermometer reads 145°, 15-20 minutes. Remove chops; let stand 5 minutes, keeping them warm.

3. Add pecans and the remaining syrup to the skillet; cook and stir until blended, 1-2 minutes. Serve with pork chops.
FREEZE OPTION Cool pork chops. Prepare the maple sauce, but do not add the pecans. Freeze pecans and pork chops with sauce in separate freezer containers. To use, thaw pecans; partially thaw pork chops with sauce in refrigerator overnight. Heat slowly in a covered skillet, turning occasionally, until a thermometer inserted in the pork reads 165°. Remove chops to a platter. Add pecans to sauce; serve with chops.

HOISIN MEATBALLS

PREP: 15 MIN.
COOK: 2½ HOURS
MAKES: ABOUT 2 DOZEN

These meatballs are braised in hoisin sauce and cabernet sauvignon for a delicious, rich sauce. If you prefer not to use wine, substitute beef broth.
—Lisa de Perio, Dallas, TX

 1 cup dry red wine or beef broth
 3 tablespoons hoisin sauce
 2 tablespoons soy sauce
 1 large egg
 4 green onions, chopped
 ¼ cup finely chopped onion
 ¼ cup minced fresh cilantro
 2 garlic cloves, minced
 ½ teaspoon salt
 ½ teaspoon pepper
 1 pound ground beef
 1 pound ground pork
   Sesame seeds

1. Preheat broiler. In a 3-qt. slow cooker, whisk together wine, hoisin and soy sauces. Cook, covered, on high for 30 minutes. Meanwhile, combine the next seven ingredients. Add beef and pork; mix lightly but thoroughly. Shape into 1½-in. meatballs; place on a rack in a broiler pan. Broil 3-4 in. from heat until browned, 3-4 minutes.
2. Add meatballs to slow cooker. Cook, covered, on low, stirring halfway through, until the meatballs are cooked through, 2-3 hours. Sprinkle with sesame seeds.
FREEZE OPTION Freeze cooled meatball mixture in freezer containers. To use, partially thaw in refrigerator overnight. Microwave, covered, on high until heated through, about 8 minutes, gently stirring halfway through.

LOUISIANA JAMBALAYA

PREP: 10 MIN.
COOK: 30 MIN.
MAKES: 12 SERVINGS

My husband helped add a little spice to my life. He grew up on spicy Cajun cooking, while I'd eaten mostly meat-and-potato meals. The flavors have been a revelation!
—Sandi Pichon, Memphis, TN

- ¼ cup canola oil
- ½ pound smoked sausage, halved and sliced
- 2 cups cubed fully cooked ham
- 2 celery ribs, chopped
- 1 large onion, chopped
- 1 medium green pepper, chopped
- 5 green onions, thinly sliced
- 2 garlic cloves, minced
- 1 can (14½ ounces) diced tomatoes, undrained
- 1 teaspoon dried thyme
- 1 teaspoon salt
- ½ teaspoon pepper
- ¼ teaspoon cayenne pepper
- 2 cans (14½ ounces each) chicken broth
- 1 cup uncooked long grain rice
- ⅓ cup water
- 4½ teaspoons Worcestershire sauce
- 2 pounds peeled and deveined cooked shrimp (31-40 per pound)

1. In a Dutch oven, heat oil over medium-high heat. Add sausage and ham; saute until lightly browned. Remove and keep warm. In drippings, saute celery, onion, green pepper and green onions until tender. Add garlic; cook and stir for 1 minute longer. Stir in tomatoes, thyme, salt, pepper and cayenne; cook 5 minutes longer.

2. Stir in broth, rice, water and Worcestershire sauce. Bring to a boil. Reduce heat; simmer, covered, until rice is tender, about 20 minutes. Stir in the sausage mixture and shrimp; heat through.

FREEZE OPTION Prepare jambalaya as directed, omitting rice and shrimp. Freeze shrimp and the cooled jambalaya in separate freezer containers. Store the rice in an airtight container at room temperature. To use, partially thaw the jambalaya in the refrigerator overnight. Place the jambalaya in a 6-qt. stockpot; heat through. Add the rice; cook, covered, about 10 minutes. Add the frozen shrimp; continue cooking until the shrimp are heated through and the rice is tender, 5-7 minutes.

"Such a great appetizer to have waiting in the freezer!"
—CARLA MENDRES

CRISPY SRIRACHA SPRING ROLLS

PREP: 50 MIN.
COOK: 10 MIN./BATCH
MAKES: ABOUT 2 DOZEN

While in the Bahamas, friends suggested a restaurant that served amazing chicken spring rolls. When I got home, I created my own version. Such a great appetizer to have waiting in the freezer!
—Carla Mendres, Winnipeg, MB

- 3 **cups coleslaw mix (about 7 ounces)**
- 3 **green onions, chopped**
- 1 **tablespoon soy sauce**
- 1 **teaspoon sesame oil**
- 1 **pound boneless skinless chicken breasts**
- 1 **teaspoon seasoned salt**
- 2 **packages (8 ounces each) cream cheese, softened**
- 2 **tablespoons Sriracha Asian hot chili sauce**
- 1 **package (24 to 28 each) spring roll wrappers, thawed**
  Oil for deep-fat frying
  Sweet chili sauce, optional

1. Toss coleslaw mix, onions, soy sauce and sesame oil; let stand while cooking chicken. In a saucepan, bring 4 cups of water to a boil. Reduce heat to maintain a simmer. Add the chicken; cook, covered, until a thermometer inserted in chicken reads 165°, 15-20 minutes. Remove chicken; cool slightly. Finely chop chicken; toss with seasoned salt.

2. In a large bowl, mix cream cheese and chili sauce; stir in chicken and coleslaw mixture. With one corner of a spring roll wrapper facing you, place about 2 tablespoons of filling just below the center of the wrapper. (Cover remaining wrappers with a damp paper towel until ready to use.) Fold bottom corner over filling; moisten remaining edges with water. Fold side corners toward center over filling; roll up tightly, pressing tip to seal. Repeat.

3. In an electric skillet or deep-fat fryer, heat oil to 375°. Fry spring rolls, a few at a time, until golden brown, 6-8 minutes, turning occasionally. Drain on paper towels. If desired, serve with sweet chili sauce.

FREEZE OPTION Freeze uncooked rolls in freezer containers, spaced so they don't touch; separate the layers with waxed paper. To use, fry frozen spring rolls as directed, increasing time as necessary.

FAVORITE MARINATED BRISKET

PREP: 20 MIN. + MARINATING
BAKE: 2½ HOURS
MAKES: 8 SERVINGS

I've made this recipe for years. Words I hear whenever I serve it are "Yummy!" and "Pass the brisket, please!"
—Terri Singer, Ottawa, ON

- 3 **garlic cloves, minced**
- 1 **tablespoon paprika**
- 1½ **teaspoons ground mustard**
- 1 **teaspoon salt**
- ½ **teaspoon pepper**
- 1 **fresh beef brisket (3 pounds)**
- 3 **cups water**
- 1 **bottle (12 ounces) chili sauce**
- ½ **cup soy sauce**
- ⅓ **cup maple syrup**
- 2 **medium onions, sliced**
- 6 **medium potatoes, peeled and cut into 2-in. pieces**

1. Mix the first five ingredients; rub over the brisket. Mix water, chili sauce, soy sauce and syrup; pour 2½ cups into a large resealable plastic bag. Add brisket; seal bag and turn to coat. Refrigerate at least 8 hours or overnight. Cover and refrigerate remaining marinade.

2. Preheat oven to 350°. Place onions in an ovenproof Dutch oven. Drain the brisket; discard the marinade left in the bag. Place the brisket over onions; arrange the potatoes around brisket. Pour the reserved marinade over top.

3. Bake, covered, until meat is tender, 2½-3 hours. Remove meat and potatoes to a serving plate. Skim fat from the cooking juices. Cut brisket diagonally across the grain into thin slices. Serve the brisket and potatoes with the cooking juices.

FREEZE OPTION Using a slotted spoon, remove the vegetables to a bowl to cool. Transfer the brisket and cooking juices to a greased 13x9-in. dish; cool completely. Add the vegetables. Cover and freeze. To use, partially thaw in refrigerator overnight. Remove from refrigerator 30 minutes before baking. Preheat oven to 350°. Reheat brisket and vegetables, covered, until a thermometer inserted in center reads 165°, about 1 hour. Thinly slice meat across the grain. Serve meat and potatoes with the cooking juices.

NOTE This is a fresh beef brisket, not corned beef.

MEDITERRANEAN PASTRY PINWHEELS

PREP: 20 MIN. + FREEZING
BAKE: 15 MIN.
MAKES: 16 APPETIZERS

These quick appetizers are irresistible on the plate, and the flavors of sun-dried tomatoes and pesto balance beautifully!
—*Kristen Heigl, Staten Island, NY*

- 1 sheet frozen puff pastry, thawed
- 1 package (8 ounces) cream cheese, softened
- ¼ cup prepared pesto
- ¾ cup shredded provolone cheese
- ½ cup chopped oil-packed sun-dried tomatoes
- ½ cup chopped ripe olives
- ¼ teaspoon pepper

1. Preheat oven to 400°. Unfold puff pastry; roll into a 10-in. square.
2. Beat cream cheese and pesto until smooth; stir in the remaining ingredients. Spread the cheese mixture to within ½ in. of pastry edges. Roll up jelly-roll style. Freeze 30 minutes. Cut crosswise into 16 slices.
3. Bake cut-side down on a parchment paper-lined baking sheet until golden brown, 12-15 minutes.
FREEZE OPTION Cover and freeze unbaked pastry slices on waxed paper-lined baking sheets until firm. Transfer to resealable plastic freezer bags; return to freezer. To use, preheat oven to 400°; bake pastries until golden brown, 15-20 minutes.

CHOCOLATE CHERRY CANDIES

PREP: 40 MIN. + CHILLING
MAKES: ABOUT 4½ DOZEN

I make these only at Christmastime for family and a few close friends; my family really looks forward to this special treat!
—*Melody Daugherty, Long Beach, CA*

- ⅔ cup creamy peanut butter
- ¼ cup butter, softened
- 2 cups confectioners' sugar
- 1 cup finely chopped walnuts
- 1 cup flaked coconut
- ¼ cup finely chopped maraschino cherries
- 1 tablespoon maraschino cherry juice
- 2 cups (12 ounces) semisweet chocolate chips
- 2 tablespoons shortening

1. Beat peanut butter, butter and confectioners' sugar until crumbly. Stir in walnuts, coconut, cherries and cherry juice. Refrigerate, covered, at least 1 hour. Shape rounded teaspoonfuls of filling into balls. Freeze 10 minutes.
2. In a microwave or heavy saucepan, melt chocolate chips and shortening; stir until smooth. Dip balls in chocolate, allowing excess to drip off; place on waxed paper. Refrigerate until chocolate is firm.
FREEZE OPTION Freeze candy in freezer containers, separating layers with waxed paper. To use, serve frozen or thaw in refrigerator before serving.

CREAMY CHOCOLATE FUDGE

PREP: 15 MIN. + CHILLING
COOK: 30 MIN.
MAKES: 5 POUNDS (150 PIECES)

Is there anything more decadent than chocolate fudge? You can make this treat and keep it in your freezer until the holidays. Be sure to use a stand mixer— I burnt out the motor of my hand mixer when I tried it on this recipe. Now that's thick and delicious fudge!
—Joan Airey, Rivers, MB

- 1 teaspoon plus 1 cup butter, divided
- 4 cups semisweet chocolate chips
- 1 jar (7 ounces) marshmallow creme
- 4½ cups sugar
- 1 can (12 ounces) evaporated milk
- 2 teaspoons vanilla extract
- 1 cup chopped walnuts, optional

1. Line a 15x10x1-in. pan with foil; grease foil with 1 teaspoon butter. Place chocolate chips, remaining butter and marshmallow creme in bowl of a stand mixer.
2. In a large heavy saucepan, combine sugar and milk. Bring to a rapid boil over medium heat, stirring constantly. Cook and stir for 8 minutes. Slowly add the sugar mixture to the chocolate mixture, beating on medium speed until the fudge begins to hold its shape, 3-5 minutes. Beat in vanilla. If desired, stir in walnuts. Spread into prepared pan. Refrigerate, covered, until firm, 1-2 hours.
3. Use the foil to lift fudge out of pan. Remove foil; cut fudge into 1-in. squares. Layer between waxed paper in an airtight container; refrigerate.
FREEZE OPTION Freeze fudge in freezer containers, separating layers with waxed paper. To use, thaw in the refrigerator before serving.

NEW ENGLAND LAMB BAKE

PREP: 25 MIN.
BAKE: 1½ HOURS
MAKES: 8 SERVINGS

This dish is hearty and perfect for warming up on a chilly winter evening. The aroma is almost as delightful as the dish itself.
—Frank Grady, Fort Kent, ME

- 1 tablespoon canola oil
- 2 pounds boneless leg of lamb, cut into 1-inch cubes
- 1 large onion, chopped
- ¼ cup all-purpose flour
- 3 cups chicken broth
- 2 large leeks (white portion only), cut into ½-inch slices
- 2 large carrots, sliced
- 2 tablespoons minced fresh parsley, divided
- ½ teaspoon dried rosemary, crushed
- ½ teaspoon salt
- ¼ teaspoon pepper
- ¼ teaspoon dried thyme
- 3 large potatoes, peeled and sliced
- 3 tablespoons butter, melted and divided

1. Preheat oven to 375°. In a Dutch oven, heat oil over medium heat. Add lamb and onion; cook and stir until the meat is no longer pink. Stir in flour until blended. Gradually add broth. Bring to a boil; cook until thickened, 1-2 minutes, stirring to loosen browned bits from pan. Add leeks, carrots, 1 tablespoon parsley, rosemary, salt, pepper and thyme.
2. Spoon into a greased 13x9-in. or 3-qt. baking dish. Cover with potato slices; brush with 2 tablespoons melted butter. Bake 1 hour; brush potatoes with the remaining butter. Return to oven; bake until meat is tender and potatoes are golden, 30 minutes to 1 hour more. Cool briefly; sprinkle with remaining parsley.
FREEZE OPTION Remove baking dish from oven; cool completely. Before adding remaining parsley, cover dish and freeze. Freeze parsley separately. To use, partially thaw lamb in refrigerator overnight. Remove from refrigerator 30 minutes before baking; thaw the remaining parsley. Preheat oven to 350°. Reheat, covered, until a thermometer reads 165°, about 1 hour. Sprinkle with the remaining parsley.

CHICKEN & BLUE CHEESE PIZZA

PREP: 25 MIN.
BAKE: 20 MIN.
MAKES: 2 DOZEN PIECES

The blue cheese in place of the expected mozzarella gives this pizza a surprising and sophisticated taste. It's excellent as an entree or appetizer—it can be prepared in a round pizza pan as well.
—Beverly Lynch, Sugar Grove, IL

- 1 **tablespoon butter**
- 4 **tablespoons olive oil, divided**
- 2½ **cups sliced baby portobello mushrooms**
- 1 **medium onion, halved and sliced**
- 3 **garlic cloves, minced**
- 4 **cups fresh baby spinach**
- 2 **cups coarsely chopped cooked chicken breast**
- ¼ **teaspoon salt**
- ¼ **teaspoon pepper**
- 1 **tube (13.8 ounces) refrigerated pizza crust**
- ¾ **cup crumbled blue cheese**
- 6 **bacon strips, cooked and crumbled**

1. Preheat oven to 450°. In a large skillet, heat butter and 1 tablespoon oil over medium heat. Add mushrooms and onion; cook and stir until tender, 4-6 minutes. Add garlic; cook 1 minute longer. Add spinach; cook and stir over medium-high heat until wilted, 1-2 minutes.
2. Stir in the chicken, salt and pepper. Unroll and press dough onto bottom of a greased 15x10x1-in. pan. Spoon the chicken mixture over the dough. Bake until the crust is lightly browned, 14-16 minutes.
3. Sprinkle with cheese and bacon; drizzle with the remaining oil. Bake until heated through, 3-5 minutes.
FREEZE OPTION Prepare pizza as directed, decreasing bake time to 10 minutes. Top with cheese and bacon; drizzle with remaining oil. Cool. Securely wrap and freeze partially baked pizza. To use, unwrap pizza; bake until crust is lightly browned and the toppings are heated through, 15-20 minutes.

SMOKY BRAISED CHUCK ROAST

PREP: 15 MIN. + MARINATING
BAKE: 2½ HOURS
MAKES: 8 SERVINGS

After tiring of the same sauces, I began experimenting with spices and flavors, coming up with this concoction. It's excellent with steak, London broil or a roast, and delivers the flavor of a summer cookout all year long!
—Karen Brown, Tunkhannock, PA

- 4 **teaspoons beef bouillon granules**
- ¼ **cup hot water**
- 1¾ **cups water**
- 2 **tablespoons brown sugar**
- 1 **teaspoon dried rosemary, crushed**
- 1 **teaspoon dried basil**
- ¾ **teaspoon dried tarragon**
- ½ **teaspoon garlic powder**
- ¼ **teaspoon dried oregano**
  Dash pepper
- ½ **teaspoon liquid smoke, optional**
- 1 **beef chuck roast (3 to 4 pounds)**

1. Dissolve bouillon in hot water; stir in water, brown sugar, seasonings and, if desired, liquid smoke. Pour marinade into a large resealable plastic bag. Add beef; seal bag and turn to coat. Refrigerate overnight.
2. Preheat oven to 325°. Transfer roast to a Dutch oven; pour remaining marinade over top. Bake, covered, until tender, 2½-3 hours.
FREEZE OPTION Place sliced chuck roast in freezer containers; top with cooking juices. Cool and freeze. To use, partially thaw in refrigerator overnight. Microwave, covered, on high, stirring gently and adding a little broth if necessary, until heated through.

Holiday Helper
I make a great variation of the Smoky Braised Chuck Roast marinade, which I use on boneless chicken breasts. Substitute chicken bouillon for the beef, omit the oregano and liquid smoke and add ¼ teaspoon of poultry seasoning.
—Karen Brown, Tunkhannock, PA

4. Preheat oven to 350°. Combine ricotta cheese, spinach, Italian cheese blend, ¾ cup Parmesan cheese, eggs and the remaining Italian seasoning. Spread 1 cup of the chicken mixture into a greased 13x9-in. baking dish. Layer with three noodles, about ¾ cup of the chicken mixture and about 1 cup of the ricotta mixture. Repeat layers three times.

5. Bake, covered, 40 minutes. Sprinkle with remaining Parmesan cheese. Bake, uncovered, until bubbly and cheese is melted, 10-15 minutes. Let stand 10 minutes before cutting.

FREEZE OPTION Cool unbaked lasagna; cover and freeze. To use, partially thaw in refrigerator overnight. Remove from refrigerator 30 minutes before baking. Preheat oven to 350°. Cover the lasagna with foil; bake as directed until heated through and a thermometer inserted into the center reads 165°, increasing time to 45-50 minutes. Sprinkle with the remaining Parmesan cheese. Bake, uncovered, until bubbly and cheese is melted, 10-15 minutes. Let stand 10 minutes before cutting.

CHICKEN MARSALA LASAGNA

PREP: 50 MIN.
BAKE: 50 MIN. + STANDING
MAKES: 12 SERVINGS

I love chicken Marsala, but it's hard to feed to a crowd. This recipe is my solution. I grew up with turkey ham, and keep small blocks of it in the freezer and shave some off when needed for recipes.
—Debbie Shannon, Ringgold, GA

- 12 **lasagna noodles**
- 4 **teaspoons Italian seasoning, divided**
- 1 **teaspoon salt**
- ¾ **pound boneless skinless chicken breasts, cubed**
- 1 **tablespoon olive oil**
- ¼ **cup finely chopped onion**
- ½ **cup butter, cubed**
- ½ **pound sliced baby portobello mushrooms**
- 12 **garlic cloves, minced**
- 1½ **cups beef broth**
- ¾ **cup Marsala wine, divided**
- ¼ **teaspoon coarsely ground pepper**
- 3 **tablespoons cornstarch**
- ½ **cup finely chopped fully cooked ham**
- 1 **carton (15 ounces) ricotta cheese**
- 1 **package (10 ounces) frozen chopped spinach, thawed and squeezed dry**
- 2 **cups shredded Italian cheese blend**
- 1 **cup grated Parmesan cheese, divided**
- 2 **large eggs, lightly beaten**

1. Cook noodles according to package directions; drain. Mix 2 teaspoons Italian seasoning and salt; sprinkle over chicken breasts. In a large skillet, heat oil over medium-high heat. Add the chicken; saute until no longer pink. Remove and keep warm.

2. In the same skillet, cook onion in butter over medium heat for 2 minutes. Stir in mushrooms; cook until tender, 4-5 minutes longer. Add garlic; cook and stir 2 minutes.

3. Stir in broth, ½ cup of wine and the pepper; bring to a boil. Mix cornstarch and the remaining wine until smooth; stir into pan. Bring to a boil; cook and stir until thickened, about 2 minutes. Stir in ham and chicken.

CAPPUCCINO PARTY PUNCH

PREP: 15 MIN. + CHILLING
MAKES: 32 SERVINGS

I first had this coffee-flavored punch at my baby shower, and it's been my favorite ever since. It rivals any coffeehouse variety.
—Angela Schwartz, Marietta, GA

- 3½ **quarts water**
- 2⅓ **cups sugar**
- ¾ **cup instant coffee granules**
- ½ **cup chocolate syrup**
- 1 **gallon vanilla ice cream**
- 1 **pint coffee ice cream**

1. In a 6-qt. stockpot, bring water to a boil. Remove from heat. Stir in sugar, coffee and chocolate syrup until the sugar is dissolved. Cool to room temperature. Transfer to four half-gallon containers. Refrigerate, covered, 4 hours or overnight.

2. Just before serving, pour the coffee mixture into a punch bowl. Add scoops of vanilla and coffee ice cream; stir until partially melted.

TEXAS GARLIC MASHED POTATOES

PREP: 20 MIN.
COOK: 30 MIN.
MAKES: 6 SERVINGS

These creamy mashed potatoes get their flavor burst from garlic and caramelized onions. They're great with any meal.
—Richard Markle, Midlothian, TX

- 1 **whole garlic bulb**
- 1 **teaspoon plus 1 tablespoon olive oil, divided**
- 1 **medium white onion, chopped**
- 4 **medium potatoes, peeled and quartered**
- ¼ **cup butter, softened**
- ¼ **cup sour cream**
- ¼ **cup grated Parmesan cheese**
- ¼ **cup 2% milk**
- ½ **teaspoon salt**
- ¼ **teaspoon pepper**

1. Preheat oven to 425°. Remove papery outer skin from garlic bulb, but do not peel or separate cloves. Cut top off of the garlic bulb, exposing individual cloves. Brush the cut cloves with 1 teaspoon oil. Wrap in foil. Bake until cloves are soft, 30-35 minutes.

2. Meanwhile, in a large skillet over low heat, heat remaining oil. Add onion; cook until golden brown, 15-20 minutes, stirring occasionally. Transfer to a food processor. Process until blended; set aside.

3. Place potatoes in a large saucepan; add water to cover. Bring to a boil. Reduce heat; cook, uncovered, until tender, 15-20 minutes. Drain; return to pan. Squeeze softened garlic onto potatoes; add butter, sour cream, cheese, milk, salt, pepper and onion. Beat until mashed.

FREEZE OPTION Place cooled mashed potato mixture in a freezer container and freeze. To use, partially thaw in refrigerator overnight. Microwave, covered, on high, stirring twice and adding a little milk if necessary, until heated through.

PEAR CHUTNEY CHICKEN

START TO FINISH: 30 MIN.
MAKES: 4 SERVINGS

With the distinctive combination of flavors in this recipe, dinner is sure to satisfy. My freezer is hardly ever without single servings of the dish my grandson calls "pear chix."
—Sheila O'Connell Berg, Lucas Valley, CA

- 1 **can (15¼ ounces) sliced pears**
- 4 **boneless skinless chicken breast halves (4 ounces each)**
- 2 **tablespoons all-purpose flour**
- ¼ **teaspoon pepper**
- 2 **tablespoons olive oil**
- ½ **cup chopped onion**
- ½ **cup mango chutney**
- 1 **to 2 tablespoons lemon juice**
- 1 **to 1½ teaspoons curry powder**

1. Drain pears, reserving ¼ cup juice; set pears and juice aside. Flatten chicken to ¼-in. thickness. In a large resealable bag, mix flour and pepper. Add the chicken in batches and shake to coat.

2. In a large skillet, heat oil over medium heat. Add the chicken; cook until no longer pink, 5-6 minutes on each side. Remove and keep warm.

3. In same skillet, combine onion, chutney, lemon juice, curry powder and reserved pear juice. Bring to a boil. Add chicken and pears. Reduce heat; simmer, uncovered, until heated through, 3-5 minutes.

FREEZE OPTION Cool the chicken mixture. Freeze in freezer containers. To use, partially thaw in refrigerator overnight. Microwave, covered, on high, stirring once, until heated through, 8-10 minutes.

MULLED WINE

PREP: 15 MIN.
COOK: 30 MIN. + CHILLING
MAKES: 5 SERVINGS

This mulled wine is soothing and satisfying with a delightful blend of spices warmed to perfection. Chilling the wine mixture overnight allows the flavors to blend, so don't omit this essential step.
—Taste of Home *Test Kitchen*

- 1 **bottle (750 milliliters) fruity red wine**
- 1 **cup brandy**
- 1 **medium orange, sliced**
- 1 **medium lemon, sliced**
- 1 **cup sugar**
- ⅛ **teaspoon ground nutmeg**
- 2 **cinnamon sticks (3 inches)**
- ½ **teaspoon whole allspice**
- ½ **teaspoon aniseed**
- ½ **teaspoon whole peppercorns**
- 3 **whole cloves**

GARNISH
   Cinnamon stick, star anise and orange twist

1. In a large saucepan, combine first six ingredients. Place remaining spices on a double thickness of cheesecloth. Gather the corners of the cloth to enclose the seasonings; tie securely with string. Add the spice bag to the wine mixture.
2. Bring to a boil, stirring occasionally. Reduce heat; simmer gently, covered, 20 minutes. Cool. Refrigerate, covered, overnight.
3. Strain; discard the fruit and the spice bag. Reheat the wine; serve warm in mugs. Top as desired.

SLOW COOKER BUTTERNUT SQUASH SOUP

PREP: 30 MIN.
COOK: 6 HOURS
MAKES: 12 SERVINGS (3 QUARTS)

Much of the work for this soup can be done in advance, and it keeps all day in the slow cooker. This can easily be doubled if you're feeding a crowd. Once you've tried it, try mixing it up—add sage or savory with the thyme or replace it with nutmeg. For a vegan version, replace the chicken broth with vegetable broth.
—Jennifer Machado, Alta, CA

- 1 **tablespoon olive oil**
- 1 **large onion, chopped**
- 2 **garlic cloves, minced**
- 1 **medium butternut squash (about 4 pounds), peeled and cut into 1-inch pieces**
- 1 **pound Yukon Gold potatoes (about 2 medium), cut into ¾-inch pieces**
- 2 **teaspoons minced fresh thyme or ¾ teaspoon dried thyme**
- 1½ **teaspoons salt**
- ¼ **teaspoon pepper**
- 5 **to 6 cups chicken or vegetable broth**
   Sour cream, optional

1. In a large skillet, heat oil over medium heat. Add onion; saute until tender, 4-5 minutes. Add garlic; cook 1 minute longer. Transfer to a 6-qt. slow cooker. Add the next five ingredients and 5 cups broth to slow cooker. Cook, covered, on low until the vegetables are soft, 6-8 hours.
2. Puree the soup using an immersion blender. Or, cool slightly and puree soup in batches in a blender; return to slow cooker. Stir in additional broth to reach desired consistency; heat through. If desired, top servings with sour cream.
FREEZE OPTION Freeze cooled soup in freezer containers. To use, partially thaw in refrigerator overnight. Heat through in a saucepan, stirring occasionally and adding a little broth if necessary.

BUTTER PECAN
ICE CREAM TORTE

PREP: 40 MIN. + COOLING
BAKE: 10 MIN. + FREEZING
MAKES: 12 SERVINGS

A simple nut crust and smooth caramel sauce are all the preparation required for this impressive dessert. Be sure to start making it at least 12 hours before serving. Wrapped tightly, it will keep in the freezer for one month.
—Judy Wilson, Sun City West, AZ

CARAMEL SAUCE
1½ cups packed brown sugar
¾ cup heavy whipping cream
6 tablespoons unsalted butter, cubed
⅛ teaspoon salt
½ teaspoon vanilla extract

CRUST
¼ cup unsalted butter, softened
⅓ cup packed brown sugar
1 teaspoon vanilla extract
⅔ cup all-purpose flour
⅔ cup chopped pecans, toasted

TOP LAYER
½ gallon butter pecan ice cream, softened if necessary
½ cup chopped pecans or pecan halves, toasted

1. Preheat oven to 350°. In a large saucepan, combine brown sugar, cream, butter and salt. Bring to a gentle boil; cook and stir 1 minute. Remove from heat; stir in vanilla. Cool completely.

2. Meanwhile, for the crust, cream butter, brown sugar and vanilla. Gradually add flour. Stir in chopped pecans. Press onto bottom and ½ in. up the sides of a greased 9-in. springform pan. Place the pan on a baking sheet.

3. Bake until lightly browned, 10-12 minutes. Cool slightly. Spread with ½ cup caramel sauce. Cool on a wire rack.

4. Spread ice cream over caramel layer. Freeze 15 minutes. Top with additional chopped pecans or pecan halves. Freeze, covered, several hours or overnight. Cover and refrigerate the remaining caramel sauce.

5. Loosen the sides from the pan with a knife; remove the rim from the pan. Heat the caramel sauce and serve with the torte.

LEMON SNOWBALL

PREP: 25 MIN. + CHILLING
MAKES: 20 SERVINGS

For a special occasion like a church supper, I make this beautiful dessert. Lemon and coconut go wonderfully together—and it just looks like Christmas!
—Lucy Rickers, Bonsall, CA

- 2 **envelopes unflavored gelatin**
- ¼ **cup cold water**
- 1 **cup boiling water**
- 1 **cup granulated sugar**
- 1 **can (12 ounces) frozen orange juice concentrate, thawed**
- 2 **tablespoons grated lemon peel**
- 2 **tablespoons lemon juice**
  Dash salt
- 3 **cups heavy whipping cream, divided**
- 1 **prepared angel food cake (8 to 10 ounces), cubed**
- ¼ **cup confectioners' sugar**
- ½ **cup flaked coconut**

1. Sprinkle gelatin over cold water. Let stand 5 minutes. Add boiling water; stir until gelatin is dissolved. Add the next five ingredients; mix well. Refrigerate, stirring occasionally, until the mixture begins to thicken, about 25 minutes.
2. In another bowl, beat 2 cups cream until stiff peaks form; fold into the lemon mixture. Line a 12-cup bowl with plastic wrap. Layer with 1 cup each lemon filling and cake cubes. Repeat layers five times; top with the remaining filling. Refrigerate, covered, 6 hours or up to 2 days.
3. To serve, invert the bowl onto a large serving platter. Remove the plastic wrap. Beat confectioners' sugar and the remaining cream until stiff peaks form; spread over cake. Sprinkle with coconut.

WHITE CHOCOLATE CRANBERRY ORANGE BARS

PREP: 10 MIN.
BAKE: 30 MIN. + COOLING
MAKES: 2 DOZEN

This is my take on my mother's recipe for chocolate chunk bars, which she made every Christmas Eve. Our family is scattered across the country now; making these reminds me of home. If you don't have a pastry cutter, you can use two sharp knives or a potato masher. My mom makes this with semisweet chocolate chunks.
—Erin Powell, Amarillo, TX

- 1½ **cups all-purpose flour**
- ½ **cup packed brown sugar**
- ½ **cup cold butter, cubed**

FILLING
- 1 **large egg**
- 1 **can (14 ounces) sweetened condensed milk**
- 1 **teaspoon grated orange peel**
- 1 **teaspoon orange extract**
- 1½ **cups white baking chips**
- 1 **cup dried cranberries**

1. Preheat oven to 350°. Line a 13x9-in. pan with foil, letting the ends extend up the sides of the pan; grease foil. In a bowl, mix flour and brown sugar; cut in butter with a pastry cutter until crumbly. Press onto the bottom of the prepared pan. Bake until light golden brown, 10-12 minutes. Cool bars on a wire rack.
2. For filling, whisk together egg, milk, orange peel and extract until blended; stir in baking chips and cranberries. Spread evenly over the crust. Bake until top is golden brown, 20-25 minutes longer. Cool 15 minutes in the pan on a wire rack. Lifting with foil, remove the bars from pan. Cut into bars. Refrigerate any leftovers.
FREEZE OPTION Freeze cooled bars in freezer containers, separating layers with waxed paper. To use, thaw before serving.

Holiday Helper
Before inverting a gelatin mold onto a serving plate, wet the surface of the serving dish. This allows the gelatin to slide and makes it easy to center on the plate.
—Elaine C., Louisville, KY

RED HOT
CHRISTMAS

Add some heat to your holiday season!
Whether you crave a meal cooked on the grill
or under the broiler, or just want some added spice,
this collection brings excitement to your menus.

GRILLED SWEET POTATO CASSEROLE

PREP: 20 MIN. • **GRILL:** 25 MIN.
MAKES: 6 SERVINGS

I absolutely love sweet potato casserole and can hardly wait until the holidays to begin baking it. This version can be done on the grill in less than 30 minutes! Large sweet potatoes may require more cinnamon-sugar topping ingredients. Add more mini marshmallows before serving if desired.
—Norma Conley, Richmond, KY

- 6 medium sweet potatoes (about 3¾ pounds)
- ½ cup butter
- ¾ teaspoon ground cinnamon
- 6 tablespoons packed brown sugar
- ¾ cup chopped pecans
- 1 cup miniature marshmallows

1. Peel and cut potatoes into ½-in. slices; transfer each potato to individual pieces of heavy-duty foil (12 in. square). Cut butter into thin slices; place between potato slices. Sprinkle with cinnamon, brown sugar and pecans. Fold foil around potatoes, sealing tightly. Grill, covered, over medium heat or broil 4 in. from heat until potatoes are tender, 18-22 minutes, turning occasionally.
2. Remove potatoes from grill; carefully open tops of foil. Sprinkle marshmallows over potatoes and return potatoes to grill rack (do not seal foil). Grill until marshmallows are softened, 3-4 minutes longer.

GRILLED BANANAS FOSTER

START TO FINISH: 25 MIN.
MAKES: 4 SERVINGS

Bananas Foster is my husband's favorite dessert, and this is one of the easiest recipes I have found. Not only is it delicious, it's a great way to use those bananas that are a little too ripe to just peel and eat.
—Rebecca Clark, Warrior, AL

- 4 small ripe bananas, unpeeled
- 3 tablespoons butter
- 2 tablespoons maple syrup
- 2 tablespoons hot caramel ice cream topping
- 2 cups vanilla ice cream
- 8 vanilla wafers, crushed

1. Trim ends and cut unpeeled bananas lengthwise; place on an oiled grill rack over medium heat. Grill, covered, until peel is dark brown and bananas are softened, 3-4 minutes on each side. Cool slightly.
2. Meanwhile, in a small cast-iron skillet or 9-in. disposable foil pie pan, combine butter, syrup and caramel topping; place on grill rack. Cook, uncovered, over medium heat until heated through, 4-5 minutes, stirring frequently. Remove from heat.
3. Remove peel from bananas; cut each piece in half crosswise. To serve, place ice cream in dessert dishes; top with bananas. Drizzle with sauce; sprinkle with crushed wafers.

BROILED GERMAN CHOCOLATE CAKE

PREP: 25 MIN.
BAKE: 30 MIN. + COOLING
MAKES: 15 SERVINGS

Traditional German chocolate cake gets a whole new spin with this inventive version that's finished off under the high heat of the broiler instead of being frosted in layers.
—Linda Schend, Kenosha, WI

- 1 cup quick-cooking oats
- ½ cup butter, cubed
- 4 ounces German sweet chocolate, chopped
- 1¼ cups boiling water
- 3 large eggs
- 1 cup packed light brown sugar
- 1½ cups all-purpose flour
- 1 cup sugar
- 1 teaspoon baking soda
- ½ teaspoon salt

TOPPING
- 1½ cups packed light brown sugar
- 1 cup flaked coconut
- 1 cup chopped pecans
- ¾ cup butter, melted
- ½ cup half-and-half cream

1. Preheat oven to 350°. Grease a 13x9-in. pan. In a bowl, combine oats, butter and chocolate; pour boiling water over top. Let stand 10 minutes.

2. Stir oatmeal mixture until combined; whisk in eggs and brown sugar. In another bowl, whisk together flour, sugar, baking soda and salt; stir into oatmeal mixture just until combined.

3. Transfer to prepared pan. Bake until a toothpick inserted in center comes out clean, 30-35 minutes. Remove from oven. Preheat broiler.

4. Combine topping ingredients; spread over warm cake. Broil 4 in. from heat until lightly browned, 3-4 minutes.

WASABI CRAB CAKES

PREP: 35 MIN.
BAKE: 15 MIN.
MAKES: 2 DOZEN (½ CUP SAUCE)

With wasabi in both the crab cakes and the dipping sauce, this festive appetizer brings its own heat to the holiday party.
—Marie Rizzio, Interlochen, MI

- 1 medium sweet red pepper, finely chopped
- 1 celery rib, finely chopped
- ⅓ cup plus ½ cup dry bread crumbs, divided
- 3 green onions, finely chopped
- 2 large egg whites
- 3 tablespoons fat-free mayonnaise
- ¼ teaspoon prepared wasabi
- 1½ cups lump crabmeat, drained
  Cooking spray

SAUCE
- 1 celery rib, finely chopped
- ⅓ cup fat-free mayonnaise
- 1 green onion, finely chopped
- 1 tablespoon sweet pickle relish
- ½ teaspoon prepared wasabi

1. Preheat oven to 425°. Combine the red pepper, celery, ⅓ cup bread crumbs, green onions, egg whites, mayonnaise and wasabi. Fold in crabmeat.

2. Place the remaining bread crumbs in a shallow bowl. Drop a heaping tablespoonful of the crab mixture into crumbs. Gently coat and shape into a ¾-in.-thick patty; place on a baking sheet coated with cooking spray. Repeat with remaining mixture.

3. Spritz crab cakes with cooking spray. Bake until golden brown, 15-18 minutes, turning once.

4. Meanwhile, combine the sauce ingredients. Serve with crab cakes.

NOTE Wear disposable gloves when cutting hot peppers; the oils can burn skin. Avoid touching your face.

GRILLED BRUSSELS SPROUTS
START TO FINISH: 25 MIN.
MAKES: 4 SERVINGS

During a beach vacation, in an effort to cook our entire meal outside on the grill, I made our not-so-simple veggie choice into a simple grilled side dish. For spicier sprouts, season with red pepper flakes.
—Tiffany Ihle, Bronx, NY

- 16 **fresh Brussels sprouts (about 1½-inch diameter), trimmed**
- 1 **medium sweet red pepper**
- 1 **medium onion**
- ½ **teaspoon salt**
- ½ **teaspoon garlic powder**
- ¼ **teaspoon coarsely ground pepper**
- 1 **tablespoon olive oil**

1. In a large saucepan, place a steamer basket over 1 in. of water; bring water to a boil. Place Brussels sprouts in basket. Reduce heat to maintain a simmer; steam, covered, until crisp-tender, 4-6 minutes. Cool slightly; cut each sprout in half.
2. Cut red pepper and onion into 1½-in. pieces. On four metal or soaked wooden skewers, alternately thread the Brussels sprouts, red pepper and onion pieces. Mix salt, garlic powder and pepper. Brush vegetables with oil, then sprinkle with the salt mixture. Grill, covered, over medium heat or broil 4 in. from heat until the vegetables are tender, 10-12 minutes, turning occasionally.

HOMEMADE SPICY HOT SAUCE
PREP: 45 MIN.
PROCESS: 10 MIN.
MAKES: 5 HALF-PINTS

I created this spicy recipe one day using what I had available from my garden—hot peppers, carrots, onion and garlic. The carrots made this recipe stand out.
—Carolyn Wheel, Fairfax, VT

- 20 **habanero peppers (4½ ounces)**
- 5 **serrano peppers (2½ ounces)**
- 15 **dried arbol chiles**
- 2 **large carrots (5½ ounces), peeled, halved lengthwise and quartered**
- 1 **large sweet onion (15 ounces), cut into eight wedges**
- 8 **garlic cloves, halved**
- 1 **cup water**
- ¾ **cup white vinegar (minimum 5% acetic acid)**
- ½ **cup fresh lime juice**
- 3 **teaspoons salt**
- 1 **teaspoon coarsely ground pepper**

1. Cut habanero and serrano peppers in half; discard stems and seeds. Place the arbol chiles in a bowl; add boiling water to cover. Let stand, covered, 10 minutes, then drain.
2. In a well-ventilated area, fill a 6-qt. stockpot three-quarters full of water; bring to a boil. Add carrots, onion and garlic. Return to a boil; cook until soft, 20-22 minutes. Remove with a slotted spoon to a bowl. Add peppers to the pot; return to a boil. Boil 1 minute; drain. Place water, vinegar, lime juice, salt and pepper in a blender. Add vegetables; cover and process until smooth. Return to stockpot; bring to a boil.
3. Carefully ladle mixture into five hot half-pint jars, leaving ½-in. headspace. Remove air bubbles and adjust the headspace, if necessary, by adding more hot mixture. Wipe rims. Center lids on jars and screw on the bands.
4. Place jars into canner with simmering water, ensuring they are covered with water. Bring to a boil; process for 10 minutes. Remove jars and cool.

2 quarts water
1 cup paprika
1 cup chili powder
2 packages (3 ounces each) crab boil in a bag
½ cup packed brown sugar
2 medium onions, quartered, divided
2 tablespoons dried rosemary, crushed
2 tablespoons dried thyme
10 garlic cloves, peeled and halved, divided
2 quarts cold water
2 turkey-size oven roasting bags
1 turkey (10-12 pounds)
¼ cup olive oil

RUB
3 tablespoons paprika
3 tablespoons chili powder
2 tablespoons garlic powder
2 tablespoons ground cumin

1. In a stockpot, combine water, paprika, chili powder, crab boil in bag, brown sugar, half of the onions, the rosemary, thyme and half of the garlic. Bring to a boil. Cook and stir for 5 minutes. Remove from heat. Add cold water to cool the brine to room temperature.

2. Place one oven roasting bag inside the other. Place the turkey inside both bags; pour in cooled brine. Seal bags, pressing out as much air as possible; turn to coat turkey. Place in a shallow roasting pan. Refrigerate for 18-24 hours, turning occasionally.

3. Remove turkey from brine, reserving the brine in the bag; rinse turkey and pat dry. Place the remaining onion and garlic in the turkey cavity. Drizzle oil over the turkey. Mix rub ingredients; rub over skin.

4. Prepare grill for indirect heat, placing a 13x9-in. disposable foil pan over coals. Carefully pour the reserved brine into the pan. Place turkey over pan on rack, breast side up. Grill, covered, over indirect medium heat for 1 hour. Tent turkey with foil; grill until a thermometer inserted in thickest part of thigh reads 170-175°, 1½-2 hours longer. Cover and let stand 20 minutes before carving.

Holiday Helper
You can find crab boil in a bag seasoning packets in the seafood or spice section of the grocery store. The spicy combination includes a host of ingredients: pickling spices, mustard seed, peppercorns, celery seeds, red pepper flakes and sea salt.

SPICED & GRILLED TURKEY

PREP: 30 MIN. + MARINATING
COOK: 2½ HOURS + STANDING
MAKES: 10 SERVINGS

My fiance loves to grill, so for the holidays we decided to grill our turkey instead of deep-frying it. It was the best thing we ever tasted! Having the brine in the pan under the turkey catches the drippings, but also keeps everything nice and moist. Start with the breast down, then flip to the other side.
—Sydney Botelho, Columbia, SC

SPICY SAUSAGE & APPLE OVERNIGHT CASSEROLE

PREP: 20 MIN. + CHILLING
BAKE: 55 MIN.
MAKES: 12 SERVINGS

For many years I've hosted Mother's Day brunch. One year I didn't make this delightfully spicy casserole and thought the family would toss me from my own house!
—Dawn Vance, Geneva, IL

 2 **pounds bulk pork sausage**
 3 **medium tart apples, peeled and cut into ¼-inch slices**
 12 **cups cubed Italian bread**
 1½ **cups shredded sharp cheddar cheese**
 9 **large eggs**
 3 **cups 2% milk**
 ¾ **teaspoon yellow mustard**

1. In a large skillet, cook and crumble sausage over medium heat until no longer pink, 6-8 minutes. Remove with a slotted spoon; drain on paper towels. Discard drippings, reserving 1 tablespoon. Add apples to drippings; cook and stir over medium heat until tender, 4-6 minutes.
2. In a bowl, combine sausage, apples, bread and cheese. Transfer to a greased 13x9-in. baking dish. In another bowl, whisk eggs, milk and mustard; pour over bread mixture. Refrigerate, covered, several hours or overnight.
3. Preheat oven to 350°. Remove casserole from refrigerator while oven heats. Bake, covered, until a knife inserted near the center comes out clean, about 45 minutes. Uncover; bake until golden brown, 10-15 minutes longer. Let stand 5-10 minutes before serving.

FREEZE OPTION Cover and freeze unbaked casserole. To use, partially thaw in refrigerator overnight. Remove from refrigerator 30 minutes before baking. Preheat oven to 350°. Bake as directed, increasing time as needed or until golden brown and a knife inserted near the center comes out clean.

ORANGE-CHILI CHOCOLATE COOKIES

PREP: 15 MIN.
BAKE: 10 MIN./BATCH
MAKES: 3 DOZEN

I love spicy chocolate so I came up with this recipe. Whenever I make it I always am asked for the recipe—and the fact that it starts with a packaged sugar cookie mix makes it super easy!
—Debbie Blunt, Wickenburg, AZ

 1 **package (17½ ounces) sugar cookie mix**
 ⅓ **cup baking cocoa**
 4 **teaspoons grated orange peel**
 ½ **teaspoon ground cinnamon**
 ¼ to ½ **teaspoon cayenne pepper**
 ½ **cup butter, softened**
 1 **large egg**
 1 **teaspoon vanilla extract**
 1 **teaspoon Triple Sec, optional**
 TOPPING
 2 **tablespoons sugar**
 1 **teaspoon ground cinnamon**

1. Preheat oven to 350°. Combine cookie mix, cocoa, orange peel, cinnamon and cayenne. Beat in butter, egg, vanilla and, if desired, Triple Sec.
2. Mix sugar and cinnamon. Roll dough into 1-in. balls; roll in sugar mixture. Place 2 in. apart on ungreased baking sheets. Bake until set, 8-10 minutes. Remove from pans to wire racks to cool.

"Whenever I want to make a special meal to celebrate with friends, I choose this."
—CINDI BREAZEALE

PEPPER-CRUSTED BEEF TENDERLOIN WITH MUSHROOMS

PREP: 10 MIN. + MARINATING
GRILL: 1¼ HOURS + STANDING
MAKES: 12 SERVINGS

My dad, an incredible person and cook, taught me to make this tenderloin. Whenever I want to make a special, memorable meal to celebrate with our friends, I choose this.
—Cindi Breazeale, Granbury, TX

- 1 **beef tenderloin roast (5-6 pounds)**
- ½ **cup Worcestershire sauce**
- 2 **tablespoons kosher salt**
- 2 **tablespoons Beau Monde seasoning**
- 2 **tablespoons lemon juice**
- 2 **tablespoons coarsely ground pepper**
- ¼ **cup butter, melted**

MUSHROOMS

- 2 **tablespoons butter**
- 1 **pound medium fresh mushrooms, quartered**
- ½ **teaspoon salt**
- ¼ **teaspoon pepper**
- 1 **tablespoon lemon juice**

1. Tuck the thin tail end of tenderloin under roast for even thickness; tie beef at 3-in. intervals with kitchen string. Place in a large resealable plastic bag. Add the Worcestershire sauce, salt, Beau Monde seasoning and lemon juice. Seal bag and turn to coat. Refrigerate 1 hour.
2. Drain beef, discarding the marinade. Sprinkle beef with pepper. Prepare grill for indirect heat, using a drip pan. Place beef over pan and grill, covered, over indirect medium heat for about 1¼ hours to desired doneness (for medium-rare, a thermometer should read 135°; medium, 140°; medium-well, 145°), turning and basting with ¼ cup melted butter. Remove roast from grill; tent with foil. Let stand 15 minutes before slicing.
3. Meanwhile, in a large skillet, heat 2 tablespoons butter over medium-high heat. Saute mushrooms with salt and pepper until tender, 8-10 minutes. Stir in lemon juice. Cut string and slice beef. Serve with mushrooms.

TO PREPARE IN OVEN Preheat oven to 425°. Prepare as directed; place on a rack in a shallow roasting pan. Roast until meat reaches desired doneness (for medium-rare, a thermometer should read 135°; medium, 140°; medium-well, 145°), about 50 minutes. Remove roast from oven; tent with foil. Let stand 15 minutes before slicing. Prepare the mushrooms as directed.

GRILLED CAULIFLOWER WEDGES

START TO FINISH: 30 MIN.
MAKES: 8 SERVINGS

This meal is incredibly easy, yet is packed with flavor and looks like a dish from a five-star restaurant. The grill leaves the cauliflower cooked but crisp, and the red pepper flakes add bite.
—Carmel Hall, San Francisco, CA

- 1 **large head cauliflower**
- 1 **teaspoon ground turmeric**
- ½ **teaspoon crushed red pepper flakes**
- 2 **tablespoons olive oil**
   Lemon juice, additional olive oil and pomegranate seeds, optional

1. Remove leaves and trim stem from cauliflower. Cut cauliflower into eight wedges. Mix turmeric and pepper flakes. Brush the wedges with oil, then sprinkle with the turmeric mixture.
2. Grill, covered, over medium-high heat or broil 4 in. from heat until the cauliflower is tender, 8-10 minutes on each side. If desired, drizzle with lemon juice and additional oil and serve with pomegranate seeds.

Holiday Helper
To remove pomegranate seeds without making a mess, score the fruit with a sharp knife from top to bottom in four places, then split it open over a bowl of water. Gently pull out the seeds under water; they'll fall to the bottom as the flesh floats to the top.

SPICE UP MY LIFE CHILI

PREP: 45 MIN.
COOK: 25 MIN.
MAKES: 18 SERVINGS (7 QUARTS)

My big-batch chili will spice things up and keep you warm on a crisp winter day. Serve with a side of cornbread, or spoon over pasta for a change of pace.
—Amy Hutchinson, Iowa Falls, IA

- 4 **pounds lean ground beef (90% lean)**
- 2 **medium onions, finely chopped**
- 2 **medium green peppers, finely chopped**
- 2 **jalapeno peppers, seeded and finely chopped**
- 4 **cans (16 ounces each) chili beans, undrained**
- 4 **cans (15 ounces each) tomato sauce**
- 4 **cans (10 ounces each) diced tomatoes and green chilies**
- 4 **cups tomato juice**
- 3 **tablespoons chili powder Shredded Colby-Monterey Jack cheese, optional**

1. In a stockpot, cook and crumble beef with onions and peppers in batches over medium heat until beef is no longer pink and vegetables are tender, 15-20 minutes; drain. Return the beef mixture to pot.
2. Stir in beans, tomato sauce, tomatoes, tomato juice and chili powder. Bring to a boil. Reduce heat; simmer, uncovered, to allow flavors to blend, 25-30 minutes. If desired, serve with cheese.
FREEZE OPTION Freeze cooled chili in freezer containers. To use, partially thaw in refrigerator overnight. Heat through in a saucepan, stirring occasionally.
NOTE Wear disposable gloves when cutting hot peppers; the oils can burn skin. Avoid touching your face.

CARAMEL CREME BRULEE

PREP: 20 MIN.
BAKE: 40 MIN. + CHILLING
MAKES: 14 SERVINGS

This recipe comes out perfect every time and it's always a crowd-pleaser! A torch works best to get the sugar caramelized while keeping the rest of the custard cool. You may want to use even more sugar to create a thicker, more even crust on top.
—Jenna Fleming, Lowville, NY

- 4½ **cups heavy whipping cream**
- 1½ **cups half-and-half cream**
- 15 **large egg yolks**
- 1⅓ **cups sugar, divided**
- 3 **teaspoons caramel extract**
- ¼ **teaspoon salt**
- ⅓ **cup packed brown sugar**

1. Preheat oven to 325°. In a large saucepan, combine whipping cream and cream; heat until bubbles form around the sides of the pan. Remove from heat.

In a bowl, whisk egg yolks, 1 cup sugar, extract and salt until blended but not foamy. Slowly stir in hot cream mixture.
2. Place an ungreased broiler-safe 13x9-in. baking dish in a larger baking pan big enough to hold it without touching. Pour egg mixture into dish. Place pan on oven rack; add very hot water to pan to within 1 in. of top of dish. Bake until center is just set and top appears dull, 40-50 minutes. Remove dish from water bath to a wire rack; cool 1 hour. Refrigerate until cold.
3. Mix brown sugar and remaining granulated sugar. Sprinkle sugar mixture evenly over custard.
4. Caramelize topping. To use a kitchen torch, hold torch flame about 2 in. above custard surface and rotate it slowly until sugar is evenly caramelized. Serve immediately or refrigerate up to 1 hour. To caramelize topping in a broiler, first let stand at room temperature 30 minutes. Preheat broiler. Broil 3-4 in. from heat until sugar is caramelized, 2-3 minutes. Serve immediately or refrigerate up to 1 hour.

STEAKS WITH CHERRY-CHIPOTLE GLAZE

PREP: 15 MIN. + MARINATING
GRILL: 10 MIN.
MAKES: 4 SERVINGS

The spicy glaze turns an inexpensive cut of meat into something special. My son, who claims to be a "meat-a-tarian," especially loves this and asks for it all year long.
—Cheryl Snavely, Hagerstown, MD

- ¼ cup sherry vinegar
- ¼ cup balsamic vinegar
- ¼ cup Worcestershire sauce
- ¼ cup olive oil
- 2 garlic cloves, minced
- 2 teaspoons Dijon mustard
- ¼ teaspoon salt
- ¼ teaspoon pepper
- 2 beef flat iron or top sirloin steaks (1 pound each)

GLAZE
- 2 tablespoons cherry preserves
- 1 tablespoon brown sugar
- 1 tablespoon olive oil
- 1 chipotle pepper in adobo sauce, minced

1. In a shallow bowl, combine the first eight ingredients. Add meat; turn to coat. Refrigerate at least 4 hours.
2. In a bowl, whisk the glaze ingredients. Drain beef, discarding the marinade. Grill, covered, over medium heat or broil 4 in. from heat until meat reaches desired doneness (for medium-rare, a thermometer should read 135°; medium, 140°; medium-well, 145°), about 4 minutes per side. Baste with glaze during the last 2 minutes of cooking. Cut steaks in half to serve.

GRILLED GORGONZOLA PEAR SALAD

START TO FINISH: 30 MIN.
MAKES: 4 SERVINGS

I served this at a recent dinner party. The contrast in flavors and textures and the beautiful presentation were a great way to start the evening.
—Jennifer Daskevich, Los Angeles, CA

- 5 tablespoons olive oil
- 2 tablespoons sherry vinegar
- 1 tablespoon honey
- 1 tablespoon stone-ground mustard
- 1 teaspoon Dijon mustard
- 1 teaspoon chopped shallot
- 1 small garlic clove, minced
- ¼ teaspoon salt
- ⅛ teaspoon pepper

SALAD
- ¼ cup crumbled Gorgonzola cheese
- ¼ cup chopped walnuts
- 1 tablespoon honey
- 2 medium pears, halved and cored
- 1 teaspoon olive oil
- 4 cups fresh arugula

1. Whisk the first nine ingredients. In another bowl, combine cheese, walnuts and honey until blended. Set aside the vinaigrette and the cheese mixture.
2. Brush pear halves with oil. Place pear halves, cut sides down, on an oiled grill rack over medium heat. Grill, covered, 4 minutes. Turn; fill with Gorgonzola mixture. Grill, covered, until pears are lightly browned, 4-6 minutes longer.
3. Drizzle vinaigrette over arugula; toss to coat. Divide between four salad plates; top with pear halves and serve.

"These cakes are a showstopper on a plate!"
—CAROLYN CROTSER

SLOW COOKER CHIPOTLE BEEF CARNITAS

PREP: 40 MIN. • **COOK:** 8 HOURS
MAKES: 16 SERVINGS PLUS ¼ CUP
LEFTOVER SPICE MIXTURE

I came up with this recipe while trying to figure out what I could do with a pot roast that had been in the freezer. Now I keep the rub in a plastic bag, ready and waiting in my cupboard, and I can get the roast into the slow cooker in less than 15 minutes.
—Ann Piscitelli, Nokomis, FL

- 2 **tablespoons kosher salt**
- 2 **tablespoons brown sugar**
- 1 **tablespoon ground cumin**
- 1 **tablespoon smoked paprika**
- 1 **tablespoon chili powder**
- 1 **teaspoon garlic powder**
- 1 **teaspoon ground mustard**
- 1 **teaspoon dried oregano**
- 1 **teaspoon cayenne pepper**
- 1 **boneless beef chuck roast (3 pounds)**
- 2 **large sweet onions, thinly sliced**
- 3 **poblano peppers, seeded and thinly sliced**
- 2 **chipotle peppers in adobo sauce, finely chopped**
- 3 **tablespoons canola oil**
- 1 **jar (16 ounces) salsa**
- 16 **flour tortillas (8 inches), warmed**
- 3 **cups crumbled queso fresco or shredded Monterey Jack cheese**
  Optional toppings: cubed avocado, sour cream and minced fresh cilantro

1. Mix the first nine ingredients. Cut roast in half; rub with ¼ cup spice mixture. Cover and store remaining spice mixture in a cool, dry place up to 1 year. Place onions and peppers in a 4-qt. slow cooker. In a large skillet, heat oil over medium heat. Brown roast on all sides. Transfer meat and drippings to slow cooker. Top with salsa. Cook, covered, on low until meat is tender, 8-10 hours.
2. Remove roast; shred with two forks. Skim fat from cooking juices. Return meat to slow cooker; heat through. Using a slotted spoon, place ½ cup meat mixture on each tortilla. Sprinkle with cheese. Add toppings of your choice.

PEPPERMINT LAVA CAKES

START TO FINISH: 30 MIN.
MAKES: 4 SERVINGS

It never ceases to amaze to see warm chocolate pudding ooze out of the center of this tender chocolate cake. These cakes are a showstopper on a plate!
—Carolyn Crotser, Colorado Springs, CO

- ⅔ **cup semisweet chocolate chips**
- ½ **cup butter, cubed**
- 1 **cup confectioners' sugar**
- 2 **large eggs**
- 2 **large egg yolks**
- 1 **teaspoon peppermint extract**
- 6 **tablespoons all-purpose flour**
- 2 **tablespoons crushed peppermint candies**

1. Preheat oven to 425°. In a microwave-safe bowl, melt chocolate chips and butter for 30 seconds; stir until smooth. Whisk in confectioners' sugar, eggs, egg yolks and extract until blended. Fold in flour.
2. Transfer to four generously greased 4-oz. ramekins. Bake on a baking sheet until a thermometer reads 160° and edges of cakes are set, 14-16 minutes.
3. Remove from the oven; let stand for 5 minutes. Run a knife around the sides of the ramekins; invert onto dessert plates. Sprinkle with crushed candies. Serve immediately.

ORANGE CHOCOLATE LAVA CAKES
Substitute ¾ teaspoon orange extract for the peppermint extract; substitute 1½ teaspoons orange peel mixed with 1 tablespoon coarse sugar for the peppermint candies.

COOKIE EXCHANGE

Christmas means lots and lots of cookies in all shapes, sizes and flavors. Cookies to gift, cookies to swap and cookies to share. Choose your favorites, and get baking!

CHOCOLATE-CHERRY THUMBPRINT COOKIES

PREP: 50 MIN.
BAKE: 10 MIN./BATCH + COOLING
MAKES: 2½ DOZEN

These look so pretty at Christmas on a tea table with other decorated cookies. They taste as good as they look, and they are eaten quickly wherever and whenever I take them. They're also ideal for Valentine's Day, and every other day of the year!
—Stephanie Smith, Colorado Springs, CO

- ¾ cup butter, softened
- ½ cup sugar
- 1 large egg yolk
- 1 teaspoon vanilla extract
- 1½ cups all-purpose flour
- ¼ cup baking cocoa

FILLING
- 1 cup confectioners' sugar
- ¼ cup butter, softened
- 1 tablespoon maraschino cherry juice

TOPPING
- 30 maraschino cherries, patted dry
- ¼ cup semisweet chocolate chips
- 1½ teaspoons shortening

1. Preheat oven to 350°. In a large bowl, cream butter and sugar until light and fluffy. Beat in egg yolk and vanilla. In another bowl, whisk flour and cocoa; gradually beat into the creamed mixture.

2. Shape into 1-in. balls; place 2 in. apart on a greased baking sheets. Press a deep indentation in center of each ball with the end of a wooden spoon handle. Bake 7-9 minutes or until firm. Remove to wire racks to cool completely.

3. For filling, in a small bowl, beat confectioners' sugar, butter and cherry juice. Fill each cookie with ½ teaspoon of the filling. Top each cookie with a cherry. In a microwave, melt chocolate chips and shortening; stir until smooth. Drizzle over cookies. Let stand until set.

MINCEMEAT COOKIE BARS

PREP: 15 MIN.
BAKE: 30 MIN. + COOLING
MAKES: 3 DOZEN

My daughter won the grand champion title at the Alaska state fair with these bars when she was 10. The topping is delicious but crumbly—for neatly edged cookies, freeze before cutting.
—Mary Bohanan, Sparks, NV

- 1 teaspoon butter
- 2 cups all-purpose flour
- 1 cup sugar
- ½ teaspoon baking soda
- ½ teaspoon salt
- ½ cup canola oil
- ¼ cup 2% milk
- 1 jar (28 ounces) prepared mincemeat
- 1 cup chopped pecans

Preheat oven to 400°. Line an 8-in. square baking pan with foil; grease foil with butter. In a large bowl, whisk flour, sugar, baking soda and salt. Stir in oil and milk. Reserve 1 cup; press the remaining mixture onto bottom of the pan. Spread with mincemeat. Stir pecans into the reserved crumb mixture; sprinkle over top. Bake 30-35 minutes or until topping is golden brown. Cool completely in pan on a wire rack. Cut into bars.

HOLIDAY BUTTER MINT COOKIES

PREP: 15 MIN.
BAKE: 15 MIN./BATCH + COOLING
MAKES: 2½ DOZEN

My mom gave me this recipe in a special recipe collection when I got married. I make goodie boxes of them for holiday gifts for friends and neighbors—and everyone loves them!
—Sherry Flaquel, Cutler Bay, FL

- 1 **cup butter, softened**
- ¼ **cup confectioners' sugar**
- 1 **tablespoon water**
- 2 **teaspoons mint extract**
- 2 **cups all-purpose flour**
- ¾ **cup crushed butter mints, divided**

1. Preheat oven to 325°. In a large bowl, cream butter and confectioners' sugar until light and fluffy. Beat in water and extract. Gradually beat flour into creamed mixture. Stir in ¼ cup crushed mints.
2. Shape into 1-in. balls. Place 2 in. apart on ungreased baking sheets; flatten slightly. Bake 12-15 minutes or until bottoms are lightly browned.
3. Coat warm cookies with the remaining crushed mints. Cool on wire racks.

ORANGE & SPICE CUTOUT COOKIES

PREP: 45 MIN.
BAKE: 10 MIN./BATCH + COOLING
MAKES: 3 DOZEN

I've been making these cookies since I was a little girl. When my mother retired from baking the holiday cookies and passed the mantle on to me, she also passed along this recipe. In time, I will give it to my young niece. Just the aroma of them takes me back to when I was a little one, just as she is now.
—Lisa Rocco-Price, Bronx, NY

- 1 **cup butter, softened**
- 1½ **cups sugar**
- 1 **large egg**
- 2 **tablespoons dark corn syrup**
- 4 **teaspoons grated orange peel**
- 3 **cups all-purpose flour**
- 2 **teaspoons baking soda**
- 2 **teaspoons ground cinnamon**
- ½ **teaspoon salt**
- ½ **teaspoon ground cloves**
  ICING
- 4 **cups confectioners' sugar**
- 3 **tablespoons meringue powder**
- 5 **to 6 tablespoons warm water**
  Assorted decorations, as desired

1. Preheat oven to 350°. In a large bowl, cream butter and sugar until light and fluffy. Beat in egg, corn syrup and orange peel. In another bowl, whisk flour, baking soda, cinnamon, salt and cloves; gradually beat into the creamed mixture. Divide the dough in half.
2. On a lightly floured surface, roll each portion of dough into a 9-in. square. Cut into 18 rectangles, 3x1½-in. each. Place rectangles 2 in. apart on ungreased baking sheets. Bake for 10-12 minutes or until the edges are light golden. Remove from pans to wire racks to cool completely.
3. For icing, in a large bowl, combine confectioners' sugar, meringue powder and enough water to reach a piping consistency. Beat on high speed with a hand mixer for 10-12 minutes or on low with a stand mixer for 7-10 minutes or until peaks form. Frost the cookies. Using a #3 round tip, pipe designs on cookies; decorate as desired.

4. If desired, combine confectioners' sugar and milk until smooth. Drizzle over the cooled rugelach.

APRICOT VARIATION In a small bowl, combine ½ cup sugar and 1 tablespoon ground cinnamon. Spread ¼ cup of apricot jam over the dough; sprinkle with 2 tablespoons of the cinnamon sugar. Proceed as directed.

POTATO CHIP BANANA BREAD COOKIES

PREP: 25 MIN.
BAKE: 10 MIN./BATCH + COOLING
MAKES: 4 DOZEN

My 5-year-old wanted to bake a cake with potato chips and bananas. I couldn't quite manage that, but I did combine two cookie recipes to create these. They are stunningly delicious, and everyone tells me they are addictive!
—Rebecca Emmons, Tulsa, OK

- 1 **cup butter, softened**
- ¾ **cup sugar**
- ¾ **cup packed brown sugar**
- 1 **cup mashed ripe bananas (about 2 medium)**
- 2 **large eggs**
- 1 **teaspoon vanilla extract**
- 2½ **cups all-purpose flour**
- 1 **teaspoon baking soda**
- ½ **teaspoon salt**
- 2 **cups crushed baked potato chips**
- 1 **cup butterscotch chips**

1. Preheat oven to 350°. In a large bowl, cream butter and sugars until light and fluffy. Beat in bananas, eggs and vanilla. In another bowl, whisk flour, baking soda and salt; gradually beat into creamed mixture. Fold in potato chips and butterscotch chips.
2. Drop by heaping tablespoonfuls 2 in. apart onto greased baking sheets. Bake 10-12 minutes or until edges are golden brown. Cool on pans 5 minutes. Remove to wire racks to cool.
NOTE If you want more regular, round cookies, shape the dough into small balls and extend the baking time to about 15 minutes.

GRANDMA'S RASPBERRY RUGELACH

PREP: 45 MIN. + CHILLING
BAKE: 25 MIN./BATCH + COOLING
MAKES: ABOUT 5 DOZEN

I remember sitting down on the couch in my great-grandmother's house with a pad and pen as she told me each ingredient and measurement for her special rugelach. Some of its ingredients are different from the typical version.
—Dalya Rubin, Boca Raton, FL

- 1½ **cups margarine, softened**
- ⅓ **cup sugar**
- 3 **teaspoons vanilla extract**
  Pinch salt
- 1 **cup heavy whipping cream**
- 4 **to 4½ cups all-purpose flour**
- 1 **cup seedless raspberry jam**

OPTIONAL GLAZE
- 1 **cup confectioners' sugar**
- 4 **teaspoons 2% milk**

1. Beat margarine, sugar, vanilla and salt on medium-low until combined. Slowly beat in cream. Gradually beat in enough flour until the dough is no longer sticky. Divide dough into four portions; flatten each into a disk. Wrap each in plastic wrap; refrigerate at least 2 hours.
2. Preheat oven to 350°. On a lightly floured surface, roll each disk of dough into a 12-in. circle; spread each with ¼ cup raspberry jam. Cut each circle into 16 wedges.
3. Gently roll up wedges from the wide ends. Place 2 in. apart on parchment-lined baking sheets, point side down. Bake 25-30 minutes or until light golden. Remove to wire racks to cool.

PUMPKIN GINGERBREAD THUMBPRINT COOKIES

PREP: 20 MIN.
BAKE: 10 MIN./BATCH + COOLING
MAKES: ABOUT 4½ DOZEN

These cookies are the result of a recipe inspiration and an afternoon spent experimenting in the kitchen with my daughters. I took the cookies to a meeting and they were a hit. So yummy with a cup of coffee!
—Jennifer Needham, Woodstock, GA

  1 **package (14½ ounces) gingerbread cake/cookie mix**
 ¼ **cup hot water**
  2 **tablespoons unsalted butter, melted**
  1 **cup solid-pack pumpkin**
  1 **cup all-purpose flour**
  2 **to 3 teaspoons pumpkin pie spice**
58 **milk chocolate kisses**

1. Preheat oven to 375°. In a large bowl, combine cookie mix, hot water and butter. Stir in pumpkin. In a small bowl, whisk flour and pie spice; gradually stir into the mixture. Shape the dough into 1-in. balls.
2. Place balls 2 in. apart on ungreased baking sheets. Press a deep indentation in the center of each with your thumb. Bake 6-8 minutes or until set. Immediately press a chocolate kiss into center of each cookie. Remove to wire racks to cool.

ALMOND ROCA PINWHEELS

PREP: 20 MIN. + CHILLING
BAKE: 10 MIN./BATCH + COOLING
MAKES: ABOUT 2½ DOZEN

We all love Almond Roca! I use the candy crushed as ice cream topping, over pudding, and in cakes and cookies. My family expects these Almond Roca pinwheel cookies every Christmas. Use vanilla if you don't like rum extract.
—Nancy Heishman, Las Vegas, NV

 ½ **cup butter, softened**
 ¾ **cup sugar**
  1 **large egg**
  1 **teaspoon rum extract**
1½ **cups all-purpose flour**
 ¼ **teaspoon baking powder**
 ¼ **teaspoon salt**
  6 **Almond Roca candies, crushed or**
     ½ cup brickle toffee bits
 ¼ **cup miniature semisweet chocolate chips**

1. In a large bowl, cream butter and sugar until light and fluffy. Beat in egg and extract. In a second bowl, whisk flour, baking powder and salt; gradually beat into the creamed mixture. Shape dough into a disk; wrap in plastic wrap. Refrigerate 1 hour or until firm enough to roll.
2. On a sheet of waxed paper, roll disk into a 10-in. square. In a small bowl, combine crushed candies and chocolate chips; sprinkle over the dough to within 1 in. of edges. Using waxed paper, roll dough up tightly jelly-roll style, removing the paper as you roll. Wrap roll in plastic wrap; refrigerate 1 hour or until firm, or up to 24 hours.
3. Preheat oven to 375°. Unwrap roll and cut crosswise into ¼-in. slices. Place slices 2 in. apart on parchment paper-lined baking sheets. Bake 8-10 minutes or until edges are light brown. Cool on pans 2 minutes. Remove to wire racks to cool.

SOFT MOCHA DROPS

PREP: 30 MIN.
BAKE: 10 MIN./BATCH + COOLING
MAKES: ABOUT 6½ DOZEN

These delectable cakelike cookies are mild and not too sweet, with a smooth and flavorful frosting.
—Diane Wood, Kalispell, MT

- 1 cup shortening
- 2 cups packed brown sugar
- 2 large eggs
- 2 teaspoons vanilla extract
- 3½ cups all-purpose flour
- ½ cup baking cocoa
- 1 teaspoon baking soda
- 1 teaspoon salt
- 1 cup milk

FROSTING
- 3 cups confectioners' sugar
- ½ cup butter, softened
- ¼ cup baking cocoa
- ¼ cup strong brewed coffee
- 1 teaspoon vanilla extract

1. Preheat oven to 350°. In a large bowl, beat shortening and brown sugar until crumbly, about 5 minutes. Beat in eggs and vanilla. In a second bowl, whisk flour, cocoa, baking soda and salt; gradually add to creamed mixture alternately with milk.
2. Drop by tablespoonfuls 2 in. apart onto ungreased baking sheets. Bake for 9-11 minutes or until set. Remove to wire racks to cool completely.
3. In a small bowl, combine all frosting ingredients; beat until smooth. Spread over cool cookies.

APRICOT-HAZELNUT TRIANGLES

PREP: 25 MIN.
BAKE: 30 MIN. + COOLING
MAKES: ABOUT 2½ DOZEN

These crispy cookie treats can be changed up—try different nuts and jams, and dark or white chocolate depending on the holiday.
—Johnna Johnson, Scottsdale, AZ

- ⅓ cup butter, softened
- 1 cup sugar, divided
- 1 large egg
- 1 teaspoon vanilla extract
- 1¼ cups all-purpose flour
- ½ teaspoon baking powder
- 3 tablespoons apricot preserves (or flavor of your choice)
- ⅓ cup butter, melted
- 2 tablespoons water
- ¾ cup finely chopped hazelnuts (or nuts of your choice)
- 7 ounces dark chocolate candy coating, melted (or candy of your choice)

1. Preheat oven to 350°. In a small bowl, cream butter and ½ cup sugar until light and fluffy. Beat in egg and vanilla. In a second bowl, whisk together flour and baking powder; gradually beat into the creamed mixture.
2. Press the dough into a greased 8-in. square baking pan; spread with preserves. In a small bowl, mix melted butter, water and the remaining sugar; stir in hazelnuts. Spread over preserves.
3. Bake 30-35 minutes or until edges are golden brown and the center is set. Cool 15 minutes on a wire rack. Cut into sixteen 2-in. squares. Cut squares into triangles. Remove to wire racks to cool completely.
4. Dip one side of each triangle halfway into melted chocolate; allow excess to drip off. Place on waxed paper; let stand until set. Store in an airtight container.

CLASSIC CANDY CANE BUTTER COOKIES

PREP: 45 MIN. + CHILLING
BAKE: 10 MIN./BATCH + COOLING
MAKES: 3 DOZEN

To make cookies that look like candy canes, we color half the dough in classic red and twist away. They're fun to hang on the side of a coffee mug, or you can devour them all on their own.
—Shannon Roum, Milwaukee, WI

- 1 **cup butter, softened**
- ⅔ **cup sugar**
- ¼ **teaspoon salt**
- 1 **large egg yolk**
- 2 **teaspoons vanilla extract**
- 2¼ **cups all-purpose flour**
  Red paste food coloring

1. In a large bowl, cream butter, sugar and salt until light and fluffy. Beat in egg yolk and vanilla; gradually beat in flour. Divide dough in half; mix food coloring into one half. Roll each half into a 6-in. square. Wrap each square in plastic wrap; refrigerate at least 1 hour or overnight.

2. Preheat oven to 350°. Cut each square of dough into 36 squares. Work with a quarter of the dough at a time; keep the rest refrigerated. Roll a piece of plain dough into a 6-in. rope; roll a piece of red dough into a 6-in. rope. Place the ropes side by side. Lift left rope over the right; repeat to twist the entire length. Repeat with remaining dough. Curving the top of each into a hook, place 1 in. apart on parchment paper-lined baking sheets.

3. Bake 7-9 minutes or until set. Cool on pans 3 minutes. Remove to wire racks to cool completely.

GIVE IT A TWIRL

A roll here, a lift there, and a pretty little curve to finish it up—this simple method for making a twisted candy cane cookie is easy to master at home.

CHURCH WINDOW COOKIES

PREP: 20 MIN. + CHILLING
MAKES: 5 DOZEN

This is a hit with kids—the little ones just love the colored marshmallows!
—Emmilie Gaston, Wabash, IN

- 2 **cups semisweet chocolate chips**
- ½ **cup butter, cubed**
- 1 **package (10 ounces) pastel miniature marshmallows**
- ½ **cup chopped walnuts, toasted**
- 2 **cups flaked coconut**

1. In a large saucepan, melt chocolate chips and butter over low heat; stir until smooth. Cool slightly. Stir in marshmallows and walnuts.

2. Divide mixture into three portions; place each portion on a piece of waxed paper. Using waxed paper, shape each into a 10-in.-long roll; roll in coconut to coat. Wrap each roll tightly in waxed paper; refrigerate 2 hours or until firm. Cut crosswise into ½-in. slices.

NOTE To toast nuts, bake in a shallow pan in a 350° oven for 5-10 minutes or cook in a skillet over low heat until lightly browned, stirring occasionally.

2 cups all-purpose flour
½ teaspoon salt
FILLING/FROSTING
2 cups confectioners' sugar
4 to 5 tablespoons creme de menthe
1 cup semisweet chocolate chips

1. In a large bowl, cream margarine and sugar until light and fluffy. Beat in egg. In a second bowl, whisk flour and salt; gradually beat into the creamed mixture. Divide dough in half. Shape each into a disk; wrap each disk in plastic wrap. Refrigerate 1 hour or until firm enough to roll.
2. Preheat oven to 325°. Roll each disk of dough between two sheets of waxed paper to ¼-in. thickness (dough will be soft). Cut with a floured 2-in. round cookie cutter. Place 2 in. apart on ungreased baking sheets. Bake for 7-8 minutes or until set. Remove from pans to wire racks to cool completely.
3. In a small bowl, mix confectioners' sugar and enough creme de menthe to reach a spreading consistency. Spread evenly on bottoms of half of the cookies; cover with the remaining cookies. In a microwave, melt chocolate chips; stir until smooth. Frost cookies.

WHITE CHOCOLATE MAPLE PECAN MACAROONS

PREP: 30 MIN.
BAKE: 20 MIN./BATCH + COOLING
MAKES: 5 DOZEN

I love macaroons and wanted to add a different twist to them with white chocolate and pecans, some of my favorite ingredients.
—Patricia Harmon, Baden, PA

2 large egg whites
½ cup sugar
½ teaspoon maple flavoring
1⅓ cups flaked coconut
1 cup plus 1 package (10 to 12 ounces) white baking chips, divided
¾ cup chopped pecans
2 teaspoons shortening

1. Place egg whites in a large bowl; let stand at room temperature 30 minutes.
2. Preheat oven to 325°. In a large bowl, beat egg whites on medium speed until foamy. Gradually add sugar, 1 tablespoon at a time, beating on high after each addition until sugar is dissolved. Beat in

flavoring. Continue beating until stiff, glossy peaks form. Fold in coconut, 1 cup baking chips and pecans.
3. Drop by rounded teaspoonfuls 1 in. apart onto parchment paper-lined baking sheets. Bake for 18-20 minutes or until firm to the touch. Remove to wire racks to cool completely.
4. In a microwave, melt shortening and the remaining baking chips; stir until smooth. Dip bottoms of macaroons into melted baking chips; allow excess to drip off. Place on waxed paper; let stand until set. Store in an airtight container.

CREME DE MENTHE COOKIES

PREP: 15 MIN. + CHILLING
BAKE: 10 MIN. + COOLING
MAKES: ABOUT 2 DOZEN

This is my mother's recipe. She made these every Christmas, and whenever I smell them baking, I think of her.
—Beth Cates, Hampton, TN

¾ cup margarine, softened
½ cup sugar
1 large egg

CHOCOLATE CHIP & PECAN MERINGUE BARS

PREP: 30 MIN.
BAKE: 25 MIN. + COOLING
MAKES: 2 DOZEN

I've had recipes for chocolate chip cookies and pecan meringues in my personal collection for a number of years—and I combined them to make these bars! They're a lovely addition to any holiday cookie tray.
—Dawn Lowenstein,
Huntingdon Valley, PA

- 4 **large egg whites**
- ½ **cup butter, softened**
- 1½ **cups packed brown sugar, divided**
- ½ **cup sugar**
- 2 **large egg yolks**
- 3 **tablespoons 2% milk**
- 1 **teaspoon vanilla extract**
- 2 **cups all-purpose flour**
- 2 **teaspoons baking powder**
- 1 **teaspoon baking soda**
- ½ **teaspoon salt**
- 1 **cup semisweet chocolate chips**
- ¾ **cup chopped pecans or walnuts**

1. Place egg whites in a small bowl; let stand at room temperature for 30 minutes.

2. Preheat oven to 325°. In a large bowl, cream butter, ½ cup brown sugar and sugar until light and fluffy. Beat in egg yolks, milk and vanilla. In another bowl, whisk flour, baking powder, baking soda and salt; gradually beat into the creamed mixture. Press into a greased 15x10x1-in. baking pan.

3. With clean beaters, beat egg whites on medium speed until foamy. Gradually add remaining brown sugar, 1 tablespoon at a time, beating on high after each addition until the brown sugar is dissolved. Continue beating until thick and glossy. Stir in chocolate chips and pecans. Spread over the dough in the pan.

4. Bake on a lower oven rack for 25-30 minutes or until the meringue is lightly browned. Cool completely in pan on a wire rack. Using a serrated knife, cut into bars. Store in an airtight container.

"They're a true one-bite pleasure!"
—JOANIE FUSON

ORANGE-NUTELLA COOKIE CUPS

PREP: 30 MIN.
BAKE: 10 MIN./BATCH + COOLING
MAKES: 4 DOZEN

These cups are easy to put on a platter for impressive presentation—they're a true one-bite pleasure! Top them with the fresh fruit of your choice: Half a strawberry or a piece of mandarin orange complements the hazelnut chocolate flavor of the Nutella.
—Joanie Fuson, Indianapolis, IN

1 tube (16½ ounces) refrigerated sugar cookie dough
½ cup all-purpose flour
1 tablespoon grated orange peel
1 cup Nutella
48 fresh raspberries (about 2 cups)
   Toasted hazelnuts, optional

1. Preheat oven to 350°. In a small bowl, mix cookie dough, flour and orange peel. Shape the dough into 1-in. balls; press evenly onto the bottoms and up the sides of greased mini-muffin cups. Bake for 10-12 minutes or until light golden brown.

2. Cool cookies in pans 5 minutes; run a knife around the sides of the cups to loosen the cookies. Cool in pans completely before removing. Place 1 teaspoon Nutella in the center of each cookie; top with a raspberry. If desired, substitute toasted hazelnuts for the raspberries.

NOTE To toast nuts, bake in a shallow pan in a 350° oven for 5-10 minutes or cook in a skillet over low heat until lightly browned, stirring occasionally.

Holiday Helper
   I never throw away navel or thin-skinned orange peels; I freeze them in plastic bags to use in recipes that call for grated orange peel. The frozen peel grates beautifully and doesn't stick to the grater, making cleanup easier.
—F. Van Blarcom, Land O'Lakes, FL

SOFT PEPPERMINT SPRITZ COOKIES

PREP: 30 MIN.
BAKE: 10 MIN./BATCH + COOLING
MAKES: ABOUT 10 DOZEN

This quick recipe makes a lot of cookies, and the peppermint flavor is a change from traditional spritz cookies. I tint some of the dough green or red, and I leave the rest white. The decorating ideas are endless!
—Carole Resnick, Cleveland, OH

1 cup unsalted butter, softened
3 ounces cream cheese, softened
1 cup granulated sugar
1 large egg yolk
1 teaspoon vanilla extract
½ teaspoon peppermint extract
1½ cups all-purpose flour
1 cup cornstarch
½ teaspoon salt
   Paste food coloring of your choice
   Colored sugar, optional

1. Preheat oven to 350°. In a large bowl, beat butter, cream cheese and sugar until light and fluffy. Beat in egg yolk and extracts. In a second bowl, whisk flour, cornstarch and salt; gradually beat into the creamed mixture.

2. Divide the dough in half. Tint one portion with food coloring. Using a cookie press fitted with a disk of your choice, press dough 1 in. apart onto ungreased baking sheets. If desired, sprinkle with colored sugar.

3. Bake for 10-12 minutes or until the edges are light golden. Cool on pans for 5 minutes, then remove to wire racks to cool completely.

FREEZE OPTION Freeze cookies in freezer containers. Thaw before serving.

RED VELVET CRINKLE COOKIES

PREP: 30 MIN. + CHILLING
BAKE: 15 MIN./BATCH + COOLING
MAKES: 3½ DOZEN

This recipe is special to me because it is totally original, my very own! The cookies are firm but not crunchy on the outside, and they're tender inside. The powdered sugar makes them melt in your mouth.
—Jane Rundell, Alanson, MI

  1 **cup butter, softened**
2½ **cups sugar**
  4 **large eggs**
  2 **teaspoons white vinegar**
  2 **teaspoons red paste food coloring**
  1 **teaspoon vanilla extract**
  4 **cups all-purpose flour**
½ **cup baking cocoa**
  3 **teaspoons baking powder**
½ **teaspoon salt**
  1 **cup white baking chips**
     Confectioners' sugar

1. In a large bowl, cream butter and sugar until light and fluffy. Beat in eggs, one at a time. Beat in vinegar, food coloring and vanilla. In another bowl, whisk flour, cocoa, baking powder and salt; gradually beat into creamed mixture. Stir in chips. Refrigerate, covered, 1 hour or until firm.
2. Preheat oven to 350°. Shape dough into 1½-in. balls; roll in confectioners' sugar. Place 2 in. apart on parchment paper-lined baking sheets. Bake for 12-15 minutes or until tops are cracked and edges are set. Cool on pans for 5 minutes; remove to wire racks to cool.

PEANUT BUTTER PIE COOKIES

PREP: 45 MIN.
BAKE: 10 MIN. + COOLING
MAKES: ABOUT 2 DOZEN

I love the combination of chocolate and peanut butter, but my favorite—peanut butter pie—is tough to eat on the go. I dreamed up these cookies to get my favorite flavor combo in a bite-size package. They can be made ahead and taken to any holiday gathering.
—Ashley Moyna, Elkader, IA

  3 **ounces cream cheese, softened**
¼ **cup confectioners' sugar**
  2 **tablespoons creamy peanut butter**
  1 **large egg yolk**
½ **teaspoon vanilla extract**
COOKIES
½ **cup butter, softened**
½ **cup packed brown sugar**
  1 **large egg white**
15 **Oreo cookies, finely crushed (about 1½ cups)**
  1 **cup all-purpose flour**
1½ **teaspoons baking powder**

TOPPING
⅓ **cup semisweet chocolate chips, melted**
     Confectioners' sugar, optional

1. Preheat oven to 350°. For filling, in a small bowl, beat the first five ingredients until smooth; set aside.
2. For cookies, in a large bowl, cream butter and brown sugar until light and fluffy. Beat in egg white. In another bowl, mix crushed cookies, flour and baking powder; gradually beat into the creamed mixture.
3. Shape rounded tablespoons of dough into 1½-in. balls; place 2 in. apart on ungreased baking sheets. Flatten slightly to ½-in. thickness. Use your thumb to press a deep indentation in the center of each. Fill each indentation with 1 rounded teaspoon of the filling.
4. Bake 10-12 minutes or until the filling is almost set. Cool on pan for 5 minutes, then remove to wire racks to cool completely.
5. Drizzle generously with melted chocolate. If desired, sprinkle with confectioners' sugar. Refrigerate any leftovers.

HAWAIIAN DREAM COOKIES

PREP: 15 MIN. + CHILLING
BAKE: 15 MIN./BATCH + COOLING
MAKES: ABOUT 2 DOZEN

These cookies are lovely as they are, but I'll sometimes use a light-colored sanding sugar for the top: First, lightly brush the top cookie with cream, then sprinkle with sanding sugar. This can be done before or after placing the cookie on top of the filling.
—Lorraine Caland, Shuniah, ON

- ⅓ **cup shortening**
- ⅓ **cup butter, softened**
- ⅔ **cup sugar**
- 2 **large eggs**
- 1 **teaspoon vanilla extract**
- 1 **teaspoon grated lemon peel**
- 2 **cups all-purpose flour**
- 1½ **teaspoons baking powder**
- ¼ **teaspoon salt**

FILLING
- ¼ **cup sugar**
- 1 **tablespoon cornstarch**
- 1 **cup undrained crushed pineapple**
- ½ **teaspoon butter**
   Confectioners' sugar

1. In a large bowl, cream shortening, butter and sugar until light and fluffy. Beat in eggs, vanilla and lemon peel. In another bowl, whisk flour, baking powder and salt; gradually beat into the creamed mixture. Divide dough in half. Shape each half into a disk; wrap each disk in plastic wrap. Refrigerate for 1 hour.

2. Preheat oven to 350°. On a surface sprinkled with confectioners' sugar, roll out dough to ¼-in. thickness. Cut with a 2-in. round cookie cutter dusted with confectioners' sugar. Using a floured 1-in. star-shaped cookie cutter, cut out the centers of half of the cookies; re-roll scraps as needed. Place solid and window cookies 2 in. apart on greased baking sheets. Repeat with remaining dough.

3. Bake for 12-15 minutes or until edges are brown. Cool on pans 5 minutes; remove to wire racks to cool completely.

4. In a small saucepan, mix sugar and cornstarch. Stir in pineapple. Cook and stir over medium heat until thickened. Stir in butter. Cool completely. Spread filling on bottoms of the solid cookies; top with the window cookies. Dust with confectioners' sugar.

WHITE CHRISTMAS DESSERTS

Whether you're looking out at a snow-covered landscape or at palm trees on Christmas Eve, you can have the white Christmas of your dreams with these pristine desserts.

GINGER-CREAM BARS

PREP: 20 MIN.
BAKE: 20 MIN.
MAKES: 5-6 DOZEN

I rediscovered this nearly forgotten old-time recipe recently and found it's everyone's favorite. Even 4-year-olds have asked for these gingery frosted bars as nursery treats.
—Carol Nagelkirk, Holland, MI

> 1 **cup butter, softened**
> 1 **cup granulated sugar**
> 2 **cups all-purpose flour**
> 1 **teaspoon salt**
> 2 **teaspoons baking soda**
> 1 **tablespoon ground cinnamon**
> 1 **tablespoon ground cloves**
> 1 **tablespoon ground ginger**
> 2 **large eggs**
> ½ **cup molasses**
> 1 **cup hot brewed coffee**
> **FROSTING**
> ½ **cup butter, softened**
> 3 **ounces cream cheese, softened**
> 2 **cups confectioners' sugar**
> 2 **teaspoons vanilla extract**
> **Chopped nuts, optional**

1. Preheat oven to 350°. Cream butter and granulated sugar. Sift together flour, salt, baking soda and spices; add to the creamed mixture. Add eggs, one at a time, beating well after each addition, and molasses. Blend in coffee. Spread in a 15x10x1-in. baking pan.
2. Bake 20-25 minutes. Cool. For frosting, cream butter and cream cheese; add confectioners' sugar and vanilla. Spread over bars. If desired, top with nuts.

HOLIDAY EGGNOG PIE

PREP: 15 MIN. + FREEZING
MAKES: 8 SERVINGS

When I created this pie, I was just trying to use up a few things I had on hand—everyone loved it! With pumpkin pie spice and eggnog, this creamy, dreamy pie has fantastic holiday flavor.
—Shirley Darger, Colorado City, AZ

> 4 **ounces cream cheese, softened**
> 1 **tablespoon butter, softened**
> ½ **cup confectioners' sugar**
> ¼ **cup eggnog**
> 2 **tablespoons sour cream**
> 1 **teaspoon pumpkin pie spice**
> 1½ **cups whipped topping**
> 1 **graham cracker crust (9 inches)**
> ⅛ **teaspoon ground nutmeg**

1. In a small bowl, beat the cream cheese, butter and confectioners' sugar until smooth. Beat in eggnog, sour cream and pie spice. Fold in whipped topping; spread into crust. Sprinkle with nutmeg.
2. Cover and freeze for 4 hours or until firm. Remove from the freezer 15 minutes before slicing.
NOTE Commercially prepared eggnog was used in testing this recipe.

APRICOT-NUT WHITE FUDGE

PREP: 15 MIN. + CHILLING
MAKES: ABOUT 2½ POUNDS

My family looks forward to this luscious apricot-studded fudge every year. It's easy to make and it really does melt in your mouth. I like to wrap up small squares of the candy with ribbon and silk holly; it makes great gifts as well as a nice treat for the family!
—Betty Claycomb, Alverton, PA

- 1 **package (8 ounces) cream cheese, softened**
- 4 **cups confectioners' sugar**
- 12 **ounces white baking chocolate, melted and cooled**
- 1½ **teaspoons vanilla extract**
- ¾ **cup chopped walnuts or pecans**
- ¾ **cup chopped dried apricots**

1. Line a 9-in. square pan with aluminum foil. Coat the pan with cooking spray; set aside. In a large bowl, beat the cream cheese until fluffy. Gradually beat in the confectioners' sugar. Gradually add white chocolate. Beat in the vanilla. Fold in nuts and apricots.

2. Spread mixture into the prepared pan. Cover and refrigerate for 8 hours or overnight. Using foil, lift fudge from pan; cut into squares.

Holiday Helper
Cutting fudge outside of the pan prevents the knife from scratching the pan and also allows for more evenly cut pieces. Lift the fudge from the pan, place it on a cutting board, remove the foil and cut—a pizza cutter makes quick work of it!

COCONUT CREAM CAKE

PREP: 20 MIN. + CHILLING
BAKE: 20 MIN. + COOLING
MAKES: 15 SERVINGS

Have the urge to splurge? Try this moist and mouthwatering cake. No one who's ever eaten a piece can believe it's from a lower-fat recipe.
—Deborah Protzman, Bloomington, IL

- 1 **package white cake mix (regular size)**
- 3 **large egg whites**
- 1¼ **cups water**
- ⅔ **cup flaked coconut, divided**
- 1 **can (14 ounces) fat-free sweetened condensed milk**
- 1 **teaspoon coconut extract**
- 1½ **cups reduced-fat whipped topping**

1. Preheat oven to 350°. Beat cake mix, egg whites, water and ⅓ cup coconut on low speed for 30 seconds. Beat on medium for 2 minutes.

2. Transfer to a 13x9-in. baking pan coated with cooking spray. Bake until a toothpick inserted in the center comes out clean, 20-25 minutes. Cool on a wire rack for 10 minutes.

3. Meanwhile, combine milk and coconut extract. Using a large meat fork, punch holes in cake. Gently spread half of the milk mixture over cake; let stand for 3 minutes. Spread the remaining milk mixture over cake; cool for 30 minutes.

4. Toast the remaining coconut. Spread whipped topping over cake; sprinkle with toasted coconut. Refrigerate, covered, at least 4 hours.

NOTE To toast coconut, bake in a shallow pan in a 350° oven for 5-10 minutes or cook in a skillet over low heat until golden brown, stirring occasionally.

I'M DREAMING OF A...

To make your dreams of a white Christmas come true, set out a gorgeous (and tasty!) display of white desserts framed by white linens, white lights, and clear crystal. Stunning!

EGGNOG MARSHMALLOWS

PREP: 1 HOUR + STANDING
MAKES: 8 DOZEN

These easy-to-make marshmallows are a lovely holiday treat with the flavor of eggnog. When my children were young, we always set aside one day each holiday season to bake treats for their schoolmates; for a kid-friendly version, we used vanilla in place of the rum extract.
—Kelly Ciepluch, Kenosha, WI

- 2 **teaspoons butter, softened**
- 1 **cup confectioners' sugar**
- 1 **teaspoon ground nutmeg, divided**
- 3 **envelopes unflavored gelatin**
- ½ **cup cold water**
- 2 **cups granulated sugar**
- 2 **cups light corn syrup**
- ½ **cup water**
- ¼ **teaspoon salt**
- 1 **teaspoon rum extract**

1. Line a 13x9-in. pan with foil; grease foil with butter. Combine confectioners' sugar and ½ teaspoon nutmeg; sprinkle 2 tablespoons of the mixture over the prepared pan.

2. In a heatproof bowl of a stand mixer, sprinkle gelatin over cold water; set aside. Meanwhile, in a large heavy saucepan over medium heat, combine granulated sugar, corn syrup, remaining water and salt. Bring to a boil, stirring occasionally. Cook, without stirring, over medium heat until a candy thermometer reads 240° (soft-ball stage).

3. Remove from heat; slowly drizzle into gelatin, beating on high. Continue beating until very stiff and doubled in volume, 10-15 minutes. Immediately beat in the extract and the remaining nutmeg. With greased hands, spread the marshmallow mixture into the prepared pan. Sprinkle with 2 more tablespoons confectioners' sugar mixture. Cool, covered, at room temperature 6 hours or overnight.

4. Using foil, lift the marshmallows out of the pan. Cut into 1-in. pieces with a lightly buttered knife; toss in remaining confectioners' sugar mixture. Store in an airtight container in a cool dry place.

EASY PUMPKIN SPICE PUDDING PIE

PREP: 20 MIN. + CHILLING
MAKES: 8 SERVINGS

Caramel, pumpkin, nuts and cream cheese—classic winter flavors combine in a no-bake pie that couldn't be easier or more delicious.
—Cynthia Brabon, Mattawan, MI

- ⅓ **cup hot caramel ice cream topping, warmed**
- 1 **9-inch graham cracker crust (about 6 ounces)**
- ⅓ **cup chopped walnuts**
- 3 **tablespoons chopped pecans**

FILLING

- 1 **cup cold whole milk**
- ¼ **cup refrigerated Italian sweet cream nondairy creamer**
- 1 **package (3.4 ounces) instant pumpkin spice pudding mix**
- ½ **cup Philadelphia ready-to-serve cheesecake filling**
- ½ **teaspoon pumpkin pie spice**
- ¼ **teaspoon ground ginger**

TOPPINGS

- 1 **carton (8 ounces) frozen whipped topping, thawed**
- 1 **tablespoon hot caramel ice cream topping**
- 1 **tablespoon coarsely chopped walnuts**
- 1 **tablespoon coarsely chopped pecans**

1. Spread caramel topping over the bottom of crust. Sprinkle with nuts.

2. For the filling, whisk milk, creamer and pudding mix for 2 minutes. Stir in cheesecake filling and spices until blended. Pour over the nut mixture. Let stand for 10 minutes.

3. Spread whipped topping over filling. Refrigerate until set, at least 4 hours or overnight. Before serving, drizzle the pie with 1 tablespoon of caramel topping; sprinkle with chopped walnuts and pecans.

1/3 cup water
1½ teaspoons almond
    extract, divided
1½ teaspoons vanilla extract,
    divided
¾ cup cake flour
1 teaspoon baking powder
¼ teaspoon salt
2 cups heavy whipping cream
¾ cup confectioners' sugar
1¼ cups slivered almonds,
    toasted and divided
2/3 cup seedless raspberry jam
    Fresh raspberries and mint
    leaves, optional

1. Preheat oven to 375°. Line a greased 15x10x1-in. baking pan with waxed paper. Grease paper; set aside.
2. Beat eggs 3 minutes. Gradually add granulated sugar; beat until the mixture becomes thick and lemon-colored, about 2 minutes. Stir in water, 1 teaspoon of the almond extract and ½ teaspoon of the vanilla. In another bowl, combine the dry ingredients; fold into egg mixture. Spread batter evenly in prepared pan.
3. Bake until the cake springs back when lightly touched, 12-15 minutes. Cool in the pan for 5 minutes, then invert onto a kitchen towel dusted with confectioners' sugar. Gently peel off the waxed paper. Roll up the cake in the towel jelly-roll style, starting with a short side. Cool completely on a wire rack.
4. Beat cream, confectioners' sugar and the remaining extracts until soft peaks form. Refrigerate half of the whipped cream. Chop 1 cup almonds; fold into the remaining cream. Unroll the cake; spread with jam to within ½ in. of edges. Top with the almond mixture.
5. Roll up cake again. Place seam side down on a serving platter. Frost the top, sides and ends with the remaining whipped cream. Refrigerate, covered, for about 1 hour. Top with remaining almonds. Serve with raspberries and mint, if desired.
NOTE To toast nuts, bake in a shallow pan in a 350° oven for 5-10 minutes or cook in a skillet over low heat until lightly browned, stirring occasionally.

PEAR CAKE WITH SOUR CREAM TOPPING

PREP: 20 MIN.
BAKE: 30 MIN.
MAKES: 16 SERVINGS

This is a great way to combine bread and fruit for an all-in-one breakfast cake that does double duty as an elegant and simple dessert. The cake is very tasty and the topping is simply delicious.
—*Norma Bluma, Emporia, KS*

½ cup butter, softened
½ cup granulated sugar
3 large eggs, lightly beaten
1 teaspoon grated lemon peel
1¾ cups all-purpose flour
2 teaspoons baking powder
1 teaspoon salt
½ cup milk
1 can (29 ounces) pear
    halves, drained
TOPPING
1 cup sour cream
2 tablespoons brown sugar
1 tablespoon grated lemon peel

1. Preheat oven to 350°. Cream butter and sugar until fluffy. Add eggs and lemon peel; mix well. In another bowl, combine flour, baking powder and salt; add to creamed mixture alternately with milk, beating well after each addition.
2. Spread batter into a greased 13x9-in. pan or 3-qt. baking dish. Slice pear halves; arrange slices in rows on top of batter. Mix topping ingredients until smooth; spread over pears. Bake until a toothpick inserted in center comes out clean, 30-35 minutes.

RASPBERRY-ALMOND JELLY ROLL

PREP: 20 MIN. + COOLING
BAKE: 15 MIN.
MAKES: 10 SERVINGS

With a whipped cream, almond and raspberry filling, the lovely swirled slices taste as good as they look.
—*Gloria Warczak, Cedarburg, WI*

3 large eggs
1 cup granulated sugar

*"The lovely swirled slices
taste as good as they look."*
—GLORIA WARCZAK

"A melt-in-your-mouth delight."
—CHRISTINE VENZON

MERINGUE TORTE WITH PEPPERMINT CREAM

PREP: 30 MIN.
BAKE: 20 MIN. + COOLING
MAKES: 8 SERVINGS

I made this torte to surprise my brother-in-law one Christmas after his mother passed away—a melt-in-your-mouth delight, this was a specialty of hers. He was so touched.
—Christine Venzon, Peoria, IL

- 3 **large egg whites**
- 1 **teaspoon water**
- 1 **teaspoon white vinegar**
- 1 **teaspoon vanilla extract**
  Dash salt
- 2 **drops red food coloring, optional**
- 1 **cup sugar**
- ½ **cup semisweet chocolate chips**
- 1 **teaspoon shortening**
- 1 **cup heavy whipping cream**
- ⅔ **cup crushed soft peppermint candies**
  Chocolate curls
  Additional crushed soft peppermint candies

1. Let the egg whites stand at room temperature 30 minutes. Add water, vinegar, extract, salt and, if desired, food coloring; beat on medium speed until soft peaks form. Gradually beat in sugar, 1 tablespoon at a time, on high speed until stiff glossy peaks form and sugar is dissolved.
2. Preheat oven to 300°. With a pencil, draw three 8x5-in. rectangles—with space between them—on parchment paper. Place paper, pencil marks down, on baking sheets. Spread meringue over each rectangle. Bake 20 minutes. Turn oven off; leave meringues in oven for 1½ hours. Remove from oven; let cool on baking sheets. When completely cool, remove from paper.
3. In a microwave, melt chocolate and shortening; stir until smooth. Spread a third of the chocolate mixture over each meringue. In a large bowl, beat cream until stiff peaks form; fold in candies.
4. Place a chocolate-covered meringue on a serving plate; top with a third of the peppermint cream. Repeat layers twice. Top with chocolate curls and additional crushed candies.

MINT BROWNIE PIE

PREP: 20 MIN. + CHILLING
BAKE: 20 MIN. + COOLING
MAKES: 8 SERVINGS

I first served this treat to my family on St. Patrick's Day, and it was an instant success. Now I serve it year-round; in the winter, I leave out the green coloring to make a cool white mint pie.
—Karen Hayes, Conneaut Lake, PA

- 6 **tablespoons butter**
- 2 **ounces unsweetened chocolate**
- 1 **cup sugar**
- 2 **large eggs, lightly beaten**
- ½ **teaspoon vanilla extract**
- ½ **cup all-purpose flour**
  FILLING
- 1 **package (8 ounces) cream cheese, softened**
- ¾ **cup sugar**
- ½ **teaspoon peppermint extract**
  Green food coloring, optional
- 1 **carton (8 ounces) frozen whipped topping, thawed**
- ¼ **cup semisweet chocolate chips, melted**
  Additional whipped topping and chocolate chips, optional

1. Preheat oven to 350°. In a large saucepan over low heat, melt butter and chocolate. Stir in the sugar until smooth. Add eggs and vanilla. Stir in flour until well blended.
2. Pour chocolate mixture into a greased 9-in. springform pan. Bake until a toothpick inserted in center comes out clean, 18-20 minutes. Cool on a wire rack.
3. Meanwhile, for filling, beat cream cheese and sugar until smooth. Beat in extract and, if desired, food coloring. Fold in the whipped topping. Spread the filling evenly over the brownie layer. Refrigerate, covered, for at least 1 hour.
4. Remove the sides of the springform pan just before serving. Melt chocolate chips; drizzle over top of the pie. Serve with additional whipped topping and chocolate chips if desired.

MARSHMALLOW CREAM WITH CUSTARD SAUCE

PREP: 25 MIN. + CHILLING
COOK: 20 MIN.
MAKES: 6 SERVINGS

The original recipe for this dessert came from my great-grandmother and has been passed down through the generations. It has always been a favorite of my husband and children.
—Penny Klusman, Richmond, IN

- 2 **large egg whites**
- ¼ **cup sugar**
  Dash salt
- ¼ **teaspoon vanilla extract**

CUSTARD SAUCE

- 1½ **cups whole milk**
- 2 **large egg yolks**
- 1 **large egg**
- ¼ **cup sugar**
- 2 **teaspoons vanilla extract**
  Fresh raspberries

1. In a small heavy saucepan over medium-low heat, combine the egg whites, sugar, salt and vanilla. Beat with a hand mixer on high until the mixture reaches 160°. Continue beating until stiff peaks form, about 1 minute. Spoon into dessert glasses; refrigerate until chilled.
2. For the custard sauce, heat milk in a small saucepan over medium heat until small bubbles form around the sides of the pan. Remove from heat. In a small bowl, combine egg yolks, egg and sugar. Whisk a small amount of hot milk into the egg mixture; return all to pan, whisking constantly. Cook and stir on low until mixture reaches 160° and coats a spoon, about 20 minutes. Remove from heat; stir in vanilla. Refrigerate at least 1 hour.
3. Serve custard sauce over marshmallow cream; top with raspberries.

CHERRIES IN THE SNOW

PREP: 10 MIN.
COOK: 40 MIN. + CHILLING
MAKES: 6 SERVINGS

Dried local Oregon cherries dot this light, creamy rice pudding. We created this for guests with dietary concerns who still want a treat. Sugar-free and fat-free—what's not to love?
—Barbara Sidway, Baker City, OR

- 6 **cups fat-free milk**
- ¾ **cup uncooked arborio rice**
  Sugar substitute equivalent to
  ¾ **cup sugar**
- ½ **vanilla bean**
- ½ **cup dried cherries**
- 2 **tablespoons dark rum**
- ¼ **teaspoon salt**
- 1 **cup fat-free whipped topping**

1. In a large saucepan, combine milk, rice and sugar substitute. Scrape seeds from vanilla bean; add the bean and the seeds to the milk mixture. Bring to a boil. Reduce heat; simmer, uncovered, for 40-45 minutes or until the rice is tender and the pudding is thickened, stirring occasionally.
2. Transfer to a small bowl; discard the vanilla bean. Stir in cherries, rum and salt. Cover and refrigerate until chilled. Fold in whipped topping before serving.
NOTE This recipe was tested with Splenda no-calorie sweetener.

ungreased 10-in. tube pan. Cut through the batter with a knife to remove any air pockets. Bake on lowest oven rack until lightly browned and entire top appears dry, 40-50 minutes. Immediately invert pan, but do not remove the cake from the pan. Cool completely, about 1 hour.

4. In a small saucepan, combine ¼ cup crushed candies and water. Cook and stir over medium heat until the candies are melted and syrupy. In a large bowl, beat cream until stiff peaks form.

5. Run a knife around the side and center tube of the pan. Remove the cake to a platter; cut horizontally into three layers. Place the bottom layer on a serving plate; drizzle with 2 tablespoons mint syrup. Spread with ½ cup whipped cream; sprinkle with 1 tablespoon crushed candies. Repeat layers.

6. Top with the third cake layer. Frost the top and sides of cake with the remaining whipped cream. Top with mint leaves and remaining candies. Store in refrigerator.

CHRISTMAS FRUITCAKE BARS

PREP: 10 MIN.
BAKE: 25 MIN.
MAKES: 2 DOZEN

I have baked this cookie every Christmas for at least 25 years. I've had the recipe for so long, I don't even remember where it came from!
—Jeaune Hadl, Lexington, KY

 ¼ cup butter, softened
 1 cup sugar
 2 large eggs
 1¼ cups biscuit/baking mix
 1¼ cups chopped mixed candied fruit
 1 cup chopped pecans
 ½ cup flaked coconut
  Confectioners' sugar

1. Preheat oven to 350°. Beat butter, sugar and eggs until fluffy. Add biscuit mix. Stir in candied fruit, pecans and coconut.

2. Spoon batter into a greased 13x9-in. baking pan. Bake until a toothpick inserted in center comes out clean, 25-30 minutes. Remove to a wire rack to cool. Dust with confectioners' sugar and cut into bars.

MINT ANGEL CAKE

PREP: 20 MIN.
BAKE: 40 MIN. + COOLING
MAKES: 16 SERVINGS

One look at this lovely cake will have guests saving room for dessert! For an easy garnish, sprinkle the bright white frosting with crushed mint candies.
—Agnes Ward, Stratford, ON

 12 large egg whites
 1 cup cake flour
 1 teaspoon cream of tartar
 1 teaspoon almond extract
 ¼ teaspoon salt
 1¼ cups sugar
 ¼ cup plus 3 tablespoons crushed peppermint candies, divided
 ¼ cup water
 1¾ cups heavy whipping cream
  Fresh mint leaves

1. Let the egg whites stand at room temperature 30 minutes. Sift flour twice; set aside.

2. Preheat oven to 350°. Add cream of tartar, almond extract and salt to the egg whites; beat on medium speed until soft peaks form. Gradually add sugar, about 2 tablespoons at a time, beating on high until stiff peaks form. Gradually fold in flour, about ½ cup at a time.

3. Gently spoon the batter into an

CHOCOLATE HAZELNUT PUDDING TORTE

PREP: 15 MIN. + CHILLING
MAKES: 8 SERVINGS

This recipe is a busy mom's twist on one of my favorite desserts—tiramisu. The dish is simple to assemble and great to make the day before you want to serve it. The hardest thing about this recipe is waiting for it to chill so you can eat it!
—Cheryl Snavely, Hagerstown, MD

24 soft ladyfingers
½ cup Nutella
1½ cups half-and-half cream
1 package (3.4 ounces) instant French vanilla pudding mix
1 carton (12 ounces) frozen whipped topping, thawed Grated or shaved chocolate

1. Arrange 12 ladyfingers in an 11x7-in. dish. Spread with half of the Nutella.
2. In a large bowl, whisk cream and pudding mix 2 minutes. Stir in whipped topping. Spread half the mixture over the Nutella. Top with the remaining ladyfingers, then the remaining Nutella, and then the remaining pudding mixture. Sprinkle with grated or shaved chocolate. Refrigerate, covered, for 8 hours or overnight. Refrigerate any leftovers.

LEMON NOODLE KUGEL

PREP: 25 MIN.
BAKE: 55 MIN. + STANDING
MAKES: 12 SERVINGS

Comforting kugel is a traditional dessert at our family's Polish Christmas Eve supper. Rich with butter, sugar, sour cream and cinnamon, it suits any special-occasion meal.
—Romaine Smith, Garden Grove, IA

5 cups uncooked egg noodles
2 tablespoons butter
4 large eggs
2 cups sour cream
2 cups 4% cottage cheese
1 cup milk
¾ cup plus 1½ teaspoons sugar, divided
1½ teaspoons lemon extract
1 teaspoon vanilla extract
½ teaspoon ground cinnamon

1. Preheat oven to 350°. Cook noodles according to the package directions; drain and return to pan. Toss with butter; set aside.
2. Beat eggs, sour cream, cottage cheese, milk, ¾ cup sugar and the extracts until well blended. Stir in the noodles. Transfer to a 13x9-in. baking dish coated with cooking spray. Combine cinnamon and the remaining sugar; sprinkle over the noodles.
3. Bake, uncovered, until a thermometer reads 160°, 55-60 minutes. Let stand 10 minutes before cutting. Serve warm or cold. Refrigerate leftovers.

ALMOND CUSTARD FONDUE

START TO FINISH: 25 MIN.
MAKES: 2 CUPS

I've served this smooth, rich fondue for nearly 40 years. It's a wonderful way to bring people together at the end of a meal. Grapes, pineapple and pound cake cubes make delightful dippers.
—Patricia Swart, Galloway, NJ

- ½ cup sugar
- 2 tablespoons cornstarch
- ¼ teaspoon salt
- 2 cups half-and-half cream
- 2 large egg yolks
- 1 tablespoon butter
- 1¼ teaspoons almond extract
  Prepared brownie and angel food cake cubes, thawed mini waffles, pretzel rods and mini Oreo cookies

1. In a heavy saucepan over medium-high heat, combine sugar, cornstarch and salt. Stir in cream until smooth. Cook and stir until thickened and bubbly. Reduce heat; cook and stir 2 minutes longer.

2. Remove from heat. Stir a small amount of the hot mixture into egg yolks; return all to the pan, stirring constantly. Bring to a gentle boil; cook and stir 2 minutes longer. Remove from heat; stir in butter and extract. Keep warm. Serve with brownie and cake cubes, mini waffles, pretzel rods and cookies for dipping.

PINEAPPLE & MACADAMIA NUT CAKE

PREP: 20 MIN.
BAKE: 25 MIN. + COOLING
MAKES: 16 SERVINGS

This delicious cake is one of my own invention. It's been a huge hit among family and friends and it even inspired fierce bidding at a local charity auction!
—Greta Kirby, Carthage, TN

- 1 package white or yellow cake mix, regular size
- 1¼ cups unsweetened pineapple juice
- ½ cup canola oil
- 3 large eggs

FILLING
- ¾ cup granulated sugar
- 4 teaspoons all-purpose flour
- 2 large egg yolks
- ¼ cup butter, melted
- 1 can (8 ounces) unsweetened crushed pineapple, undrained
- ¼ cup chopped macadamia nuts, toasted

FROSTING
- ½ cup butter, softened
- 4 cups confectioners' sugar
- 2 to 4 tablespoons 2% milk
  Additional chopped macadamia nuts, optional

1. Preheat oven to 350°. Combine cake mix, pineapple juice, oil and eggs; beat on low for 30 seconds. Beat on medium for 2 minutes. Pour into three greased and floured 8-in. round baking pans.

2. Bake until a toothpick inserted in the center comes out clean, 25-30 minutes. Let cool for 10 minutes in the pans before removing to wire racks to cool completely.

3. For filling, combine sugar and flour in a large saucepan. Whisk in egg yolks, butter and pineapple until blended. Bring to a boil over medium heat; cook and stir until thickened and bubbly, about 2 minutes. Remove from heat; cool to room temperature. Reserve ⅓ cup of the pineapple mixture for frosting; gently stir nuts into the remaining pineapple mixture.

4. Place one cake layer on a serving plate; spread with half of the filling. Top with the second cake layer, then the remaining filling; finish with the third cake layer.

5. For the frosting, cream the butter, confectioners' sugar, reserved pineapple mixture and enough milk to reach a good spreading consistency. Spread over the top and sides of the cake. If desired, chop and toast additional nuts; sprinkle on the top and around the bottom of the cake.

NOTE To toast nuts, bake in a shallow pan in a 350° oven for 5-10 minutes or cook in a skillet over low heat until lightly browned, stirring occasionally.

OLD-WORLD RICOTTA CHEESECAKE

PREP: 20 MIN.
BAKE: 1 HOUR + CHILLING
MAKES: 12 SERVINGS

I reconstructed this dessert based on an old recipe that had been in the family for years but was never written down. The subtle cinnamon flavor of the zwieback crust and the dense texture of the ricotta cheese are reminiscent of the cheesecake I enjoyed as a child.
—Mary Beth Jung, Hendersonville, NC

1⅔ cups zwieback crumbs
 3 tablespoons sugar
 ½ teaspoon ground cinnamon
 ⅓ cup butter, softened
FILLING
 2 cartons (15 ounces each)
   ricotta cheese
 ½ cup sugar
 ½ cup half-and-half cream
 2 tablespoons all-purpose flour
 1 tablespoon lemon juice
 1 teaspoon finely grated lemon peel
 ¼ teaspoon salt
 2 large eggs, lightly beaten
TOPPING
 1 cup sour cream
 2 tablespoons sugar
 1 teaspoon vanilla extract

1. Combine zwieback crumbs, sugar and cinnamon; mix in butter until the mixture is crumbled. Press onto bottom and 1½ in. up sides of a greased 9-in. springform pan. Refrigerate until chilled.
2. Preheat oven to 350°. Beat all filling ingredients except eggs until smooth. Add eggs; beat on low until combined. Pour into the crust. Place the pan on a baking sheet.
3. Bake until the center is set, about 50 minutes. Remove from oven; let stand 15 minutes, leaving oven on. Combine the topping ingredients; spoon around edge of cheesecake. Carefully spread over filling. Bake 10 minutes longer. Loosen sides from pan with a knife; cool for 1 hour. Refrigerate 3 hours or overnight, covering when completely cool. Remove rim from pan. Refrigerate any leftovers.

CREAMY COCONUT SNOWBALLS

PREP: 40 MIN. + CHILLING
MAKES: 1½ POUNDS

My grandmother made these little cheesecake-like bites for years. They keep nicely in the refrigerator so you can have them on hand for drop-in guests.
—Yvonne Schaney, Alliance, OH

 ½ teaspoon plus ½ cup butter,
   softened and divided
1¾ cups flaked coconut, divided
 4 ounces cream cheese, softened
3¾ cups confectioners' sugar
 8 ounces white candy
   coating, chopped
 2 tablespoons shortening

1. Line a 9x5-in. loaf pan with foil. Grease foil with ½ teaspoon butter; set aside. Pulse ¾ cup coconut in a food processor until coarsely chopped. Add the cream cheese and remaining butter; pulse until blended. Gradually add confectioners' sugar; pulse until blended. Press into prepared pan. Refrigerate, covered, at least 3 hours.
2. Microwave the candy coating and shortening until melted; stir until smooth. Cool slightly. Use foil to lift coconut mixture out of pan. Gently peel off foil; cut into 36 pieces. Taking a few pieces at a time, roll each into a ball; keep remaining pieces refrigerated.
3. Using a toothpick, dip each ball in the melted coating mixture, allowing excess to drip off. Roll each ball in the remaining coconut and place on waxed paper-lined baking sheet. Refrigerate until set. Store in an airtight container in refrigerator.

> *"So quick, so easy and so very, very good!"*
> —MARCIA SNYDER

HOLIDAY KIPFERL COOKIE

PREP: 30 MIN. + CHILLING
BAKE: 15 MIN. + COOLING
MAKES: 4 DOZEN

My family has been making the classic Kipferl cookie on December 1 every year since I can remember. During the last two weeks of December, we make them with the addition of dried cranberries and toasted pecans for Christmastime.
—Brooke Maynard, Poughkeepsie, NY

- ⅔ cup blanched almonds
- 2 cups all-purpose flour
- ½ cup granulated sugar
- ½ teaspoon salt
- ¾ cup plus 2 tablespoons cold butter, cubed
- 3 large egg yolks
- 2 tablespoons cold water
- ½ cup chopped pecans, toasted
- ½ cup dried cranberries, chopped
  Confectioners' sugar

1. Pulse almonds in a food processor until finely ground. Add flour, granulated sugar and salt; pulse until combined. Add butter; pulse until mixture resembles coarse crumbs. In a small bowl, whisk egg yolks and water. Add to the almond butter mixture, and pulse until dough forms. Shape the dough into a disk and wrap in plastic. Refrigerate until easy to handle, about 1 hour.

2. Preheat oven to 325°. Divide dough into fourths. On a lightly floured surface, roll each portion of dough into an 8-in. circle. Sprinkle each circle with pecans and cranberries; lightly press into dough. Cut each circle into 12 wedges. Roll up wedges, starting from the wide end. Place rolls point-side down 1 in. apart on greased baking sheets. Curve the ends to form crescents.

3. Bake crescents until lightly browned, 12-15 minutes. Carefully roll the warm cookies in confectioners' sugar; set on wire racks to cool completely. Sprinkle with additional confectioners' sugar. Store in an airtight container.
NOTE To toast nuts, bake in a shallow pan in a 350° oven for 5-10 minutes or cook in a skillet over low heat until lightly browned, stirring occasionally.

WHITE CANDY BARK

PREP: 20 MIN. + CHILLING
MAKES: 2 POUNDS

You can change up this speedy candy recipe depending on what fruits or nuts you have on hand. We have a walnut tree, so I use walnuts, but pecans could also be substituted, and dried cherries are an easy swap for the cranberries. So quick, so easy and so very, very good!
—Marcia Snyder, Grand Junction, CO

- 1 tablespoon butter, melted
- 2 packages (10 to 12 ounces each) white baking chips
- 1½ cups walnut halves
- 1 cup dried cranberries
- ¼ teaspoon ground nutmeg

Line a 15x10x1-in. baking pan with foil. Brush with butter. Microwave white chips on high until melted; stir until smooth. Stir in walnuts, cranberries and nutmeg. Spread into prepared pan. Chill until firm. Break into pieces.
NOTE This recipe was tested in a 1,100-watt microwave.

Holiday Helper

To melt semisweet chocolate, set the microwave to high (100%) for 1 minute; stir. Microwave at additional 10- to 20-second intervals, stirring until smooth. For milk chocolate and vanilla or white chocolate, use 70% power. Stir frequently until the chocolate is melted; do not overheat.

HOLIDAY GIFT MIXES

Just right for teachers, co-workers and friends,
these mixes for soups, spice rubs, cakes, cookies and
muffins are truly gifts from the heart.

SALT-FREE HERB BLEND

START TO FINISH: 5 MIN.
MAKES: ⅓ CUP

A handful of seasonings, from paprika to poppy seed, make up this salt-free mix that will perk up poultry, meat and vegetables, too!
—Eva Bailey, Olive Hill, KY

- 4 teaspoons sesame seeds
- 2 teaspoons celery seed
- 2 teaspoons dried marjoram
- 2 teaspoons poppy seeds
- 2 teaspoons coarsely ground pepper
- 1½ teaspoons dried parsley flakes
- 1 teaspoon onion powder
- 1 teaspoon dried thyme
- ½ teaspoon garlic powder
- ½ teaspoon paprika

Combine all ingredients. Store in an airtight container up to 6 months.

LEMON-GINGER SALT

PREP: 10 MIN.
BAKE: 20 MIN. + COOLING
MAKES: 1 CUP

Sprinkle a bit of this zingy lemon-ginger combo on hot buttered corn on the cob for a salty twist.
—Taste of Home *Test Kitchen*

- ¾ cup kosher salt
- ½ cup grated lemon peel (from about 5 large lemons)
- 1 teaspoon ground ginger
- 2 tablespoons lemon juice

Preheat oven to 200°. Pulse salt, lemon peel and ginger in a food processor until blended. Transfer to an 8-in. square baking dish. Stir in lemon juice. Bake, stirring occasionally, until dry, 20-25 minutes. Cool completely. Stir with a fork to break up. Store in an airtight container in a cool, dry place for up to 3 months.

HOMEMADE CAJUN SEASONING

START TO FINISH: 5 MIN.
MAKES: ABOUT 3½ CUPS

We in Louisiana love seasoned foods. I use this in gravy, over meats and with salads. It makes an excellent gift for teachers.
—Onietta Loewer, Branch, LA

- 1 carton (26 ounces) salt
- 2 containers (1 ounce each) cayenne pepper
- ⅓ cup pepper
- ⅓ cup chili powder
- 3 tablespoons garlic powder

Combine all ingredients; store in an airtight container. Use to season pork, chicken, seafood, steaks or vegetables.

ZIPPY DRY RUB

START TO FINISH: 5 MIN.
MAKES: ABOUT ¾ CUP

This spicy blend has broad appeal—it can be used as a rub on all meats or added to rice while it's cooking for a boost of flavor.
—Gaynelle Fritsch, Welches, OR

- ¼ **cup salt**
- 4 **teaspoons mustard seed**
- 4 **teaspoons pepper**
- 4 **teaspoons chili powder**
- 4 **teaspoons paprika**
- 2 **teaspoons ground cumin**
- 2 **teaspoons dried coriander**
- 1 **teaspoon garlic powder**

Combine all ingredients; store in an airtight container. Rub the desired amount onto surface of uncooked meat. Cover meat and refrigerate at least 4 hours before grilling.

CHILI-SCENTED SEASONING

START TO FINISH: 5 MIN.
MAKES: 1 CUP

This pleasantly mild blend, with its mix of chili, mustard and smoky paprika, is a versatile complement to fish, poultry and different kinds of meat. Use it at the table, just as you would salt.
—Millie Osburn, Winona, MO

- 6 **tablespoons onion powder**
- 3 **tablespoons poultry seasoning**
- 3 **tablespoons paprika**
- 2 **tablespoons ground mustard**
- 1 **tablespoon garlic powder**
- 2 **teaspoons dried oregano, crushed**
- 1 **teaspoon chili powder**

- 1 **teaspoon black pepper**
- ¼ **teaspoon cayenne pepper**

Combine all ingredients. Store in an airtight container.

SAVORY STEAK RUB

START TO FINISH: 5 MIN.
MAKES: ¼ CUP

Marjoram stars in this rub. I use it on different beef cuts; it locks in natural juices for mouthwatering results.
—Donna Brockett, Kingfisher, OK

- 1 **tablespoon dried majoram**
- 1 **tablespoon dried basil**
- 2 **teaspoons garlic powder**
- 2 **teaspoons dried thyme**
- 1 **teaspoon dried rosemary, crushed**
- ¾ **teaspoon dried oregano**

Combine all ingredients; store in a covered container. Rub over steaks before grilling or broiling.

SPLIT PEA SOUP MIX

PREP: 10 MIN.
COOK: 1¼ HOURS
MAKES: 13 BATCHES (13 CUPS MIX);
4 SERVINGS PER BATCH

This hearty soup is thick with lentils, barley and peas, and chicken is a nice change from the usual ham.
—Susan Ruckert, Tangent, OR

- 1 package (16 ounces) dried green split peas
- 1 package (16 ounces) dried yellow split peas
- 1 package (16 ounces) dried lentils, rinsed and dried
- 1 package (16 ounces) medium pearl barley
- 1 package (12 ounces) alphabet pasta
- 1 jar (½ ounce) dried celery flakes
- ½ cup dried parsley flakes

ADDITIONAL INGREDIENTS (FOR EACH BATCH)
- 4 cups chicken broth
- ¼ teaspoon pepper
- 1 cup cubed cooked chicken, optional

Combine the first seven ingredients. Transfer to airtight containers, or divide them equally among 13 plastic bags. Store in a cool, dry place for up to 1 year.

TO PREPARE SOUP In a large saucepan, combine 1 cup of the soup mix with broth, pepper and, if desired, cubed chicken. Bring to a boil. Reduce heat; simmer, covered, until peas and lentils are tender, 1-1¼ hours.

Holiday Helper
Split peas and lentils don't have to be soaked, like many legumes, but should be rinsed to remove dust. Rinse the peas in cold running water, then spread them out on a clean kitchen towel and pick out any shriveled peas or debris. Let them dry before bagging them.

SAND ART BROWNIES

PREP: 15 MIN.
BAKE: 30 MIN. + COOLING
MAKES: 1 BATCH (4 CUPS MIX);
16 SERVINGS

A jar of this layered mix produces a yummy batch of fudgy brownies dressed up with chocolate chips and M&M's. If you need a sweet gift for a neighbor or teacher, this is a delicious solution!
—Joan Hohwald, Lodi, NY

- 1 cup plus 2 tablespoons all-purpose flour
- ½ teaspoon salt
- ½ teaspoon baking powder
- ⅓ cup baking cocoa
- ⅔ cup sugar
- ⅔ cup packed brown sugar
- ½ cup semisweet chocolate chips
- ½ cup holiday milk chocolate M&M's

ADDITIONAL INGREDIENTS
- 3 large eggs
- ⅔ cup vegetable oil
- 1 teaspoon vanilla extract

Combine flour, salt and baking powder. In a 1-qt. glass container, layer the flour mixture, cocoa, sugar, brown sugar, chocolate chips and M&M's, packing down well between each layer. Cover and store in a cool dry place for up to 6 months.

TO PREPARE BROWNIES Preheat oven to 350°. Beat eggs, oil and vanilla. Stir in brownie mix. Pour into a greased 8-in. square baking dish. Bake until center is set, 26-28 minutes (do not overbake). Cool on a wire rack.

a boil. Reduce heat; cover and simmer until rice is tender, 18-20 minutes. In another saucepan, heat tomato sauce and sausage. Cook shrimp in boiling water until pink; drain. Stir into sausage mixture. Serve with rice mixture.

DOUBLE CHOCOLATE HOT COCOA MIX

START TO FINISH: 10 MIN.
MAKES: 6⅔ CUPS MIX; 20 SERVINGS

I gave this away at our neighborhood Christmas party in cute gift bags and was thrilled that I was able to give something to everyone. The next week I started getting calls from the neighbors who'd made it; I was blown away at the response. Everyone loved it! The white chocolate makes it extra creamy.
—Mandy Rivers, Lexington, SC

> 4 **cups nonfat dry milk powder**
> 2 **cups white baking chips**
> 2 **cups baking cocoa**
> 1½ **cups confectioners' sugar**
> ½ **teaspoon salt**
> **ADDITIONAL INGREDIENT (FOR EACH SERVING)**
> 1 **cup hot 2% milk**

Pulse the first five ingredients in a food processor until the baking chips are finely ground. Transfer to a large airtight container. Store in a cool, dry place up to 6 months.
TO PREPARE HOT COCOA Place ⅓ cup hot cocoa mix in a mug. Stir in hot milk until blended.

JAMBALAYA MIX

START TO FINISH: 25 MIN.
MAKES: ABOUT 3 BATCHES (3⅓ CUPS MIX);
4-6 SERVINGS PER BATCH

This zippy mix is the starting point for a full-flavored meal. Add shrimp, smoked sausage and a few other easy ingredients to the rice mix to create a skillet sensation. A jar of the mix along with a copy of the recipe makes a great gift!
—Sybil Brown, Highland, CA

> 3 **cups uncooked long grain rice**
> 3 **tablespoons dried minced onion**
> 3 **tablespoons dried parsley flakes**
> 4 **teaspoons beef bouillon granules**
> 1 **tablespoon dried minced chives**
> 1 **tablespoon dried celery flakes**
> 1½ **teaspoons pepper**
> ¾ **teaspoon cayenne pepper**
> ¾ **teaspoon garlic powder**
> ¾ **teaspoon dried thyme**
> **ADDITIONAL INGREDIENTS (FOR EACH BATCH)**
> 2 **cups water**
> ½ **cup chopped green pepper**
> 1 **can (8 ounces) tomato sauce**
> 1 **pound smoked sausage, cut into ¼-inch slices**
> 1 **pound uncooked shrimp (31-40 per pound), peeled and deveined**

Combine the first 10 ingredients. Divide into three equal batches; store in airtight containers in a cool, dry place for up to 6 months.
TO PREPARE JAMBALAYA In a small saucepan, bring water and green pepper to a boil. Stir in 1 cup jambalaya mix; return to

PANCAKE MIX IN A JAR

START TO FINISH: 30 MIN.

MAKES: 2 BATCHES (3 CUPS MIX);
8 PANCAKES PER BATCH

*At Christmas, I like to present friends
and family with this special mix and
a bottle of pure maple syrup. The
pancakes that it makes are fluffy
and fruity.*
—Diane Musil, Lyons, IL

3 **cups all-purpose flour**
3 **tablespoons sugar**
2 **tablespoons baking powder**
4½ **teaspoons ground cinnamon**
1 **teaspoon salt**

**ADDITIONAL INGREDIENTS
(FOR EACH BATCH)**

1 **large egg**
¾ **cup milk**
3 **tablespoons canola oil**
¼ **cup chopped dried apples or
cranberries, optional**

Combine the first five ingredients.
Transfer to a 1-qt. jar with a tight-fitting
lid. Cover and store in a cool, dry place
for up to 6 months.

TO PREPARE PANCAKES Place 1½ cups
mix in a large bowl. In another bowl, whisk
the egg, milk and oil. Stir in dried fruit, if
desired. Stir egg mixture into pancake
mix just until moistened. Pour the batter
by ¼ cupfuls onto a greased hot griddle.
Turn when bubbles on top begin to pop;
cook until second side is golden brown.

GINGERBREAD CAKE MIX

PREP: 15 MIN.
BAKE: 35 MIN.
MAKES: 5 BATCHES (10 CUPS MIX);
9 SERVINGS PER BATCH

This mix makes moist, nicely spiced gingerbread in no time. I use it myself during the hectic holiday season, and love giving it in pretty jars as a gift.
—Ruth Seitz, Columbus Junction, IA

- 6⅔ cups all-purpose flour
- 1½ cups sugar
- ¾ cup plus 1 tablespoon nonfat dry milk powder
- ¼ cup baking powder
- 1 tablespoon salt
- 2½ teaspoons ground cinnamon
- 2 teaspoons cream of tartar
- 1¼ teaspoons ground cloves
- 1¼ teaspoons ground ginger
- 1½ cups shortening
  ADDITIONAL INGREDIENTS
  (FOR EACH BATCH)
- 1 large egg
- ½ cup water
- ½ cup molasses

Combine the first nine ingredients. Cut in shortening until mixture resembles coarse crumbs. Store in an airtight container in a cool, dry place for up to 6 months.
TO PREPARE CAKE Preheat oven to 350°. Lightly beat egg, water and molasses. Add 2 cups cake mix; beat until well blended. Spread batter into a greased 8-in. square baking pan. Bake until a toothpick inserted in the center comes out clean, 35-40 minutes. Cool on a wire rack.
NOTE Contents of mix may settle during storage. When preparing recipe, spoon mix into measuring cup.

Holiday Helper
When cutting in shortening, start by chilling the shortening and cutting it into smaller pieces. Add the pieces to the flour mixture and toss to coat. Then use a pastry blender, two knives, or your fingers to work the shortening into the flour mixture until it has a coarse, crumblike texture.

CHIPPY CHOCOLATE COOKIE MIX

PREP: 10 MIN.
BAKE: 15 MIN./BATCH
MAKES: 1 BATCH (4 CUPS MIX);
2 DOZEN COOKIES

I've had this recipe for a long time; I have yet to meet the person who doesn't rave over the cookies! I sometimes use M&M's instead of the peanut butter chips.
—Francine Wingate,
New Smyrna Beach, FL

- 1 package chocolate cake mix (regular size)
- 1 cup peanut butter chips

ADDITIONAL INGREDIENTS
- ½ cup canola oil
- 2 large eggs

In a 1-qt. glass container, layer half of the cake mix, the peanut butter chips and the remaining cake mix. Cover and store in a cool, dry place up to 6 months.
TO PREPARE COOKIES Preheat oven to 350°. Combine cookie mix, oil and eggs. Drop by rounded tablespoonfuls 2 in. apart onto ungreased baking sheets. Bake until the tops are cracked, 14-16 minutes. Remove to wire racks to cool.

"...moist, nicely spiced gingerbread in no time."
—RUTH SEITZ

HEARTY PASTA SOUP MIX

PREP: 15 MIN.
COOK: 1¼ HOURS
MAKES: 1 BATCH (4 CUPS MIX);
14 SERVINGS (3½ QUARTS)

Warm up loved ones on frosty winter nights with a gift of this hearty, stick-to-the-ribs soup mix from our Test Kitchen. Pack it into pretty glass jars, and include preparation instructions and a list of additional ingredients needed with your gift card.
—Taste of Home *Test Kitchen*

- ½ cup dried split peas
- 2 tablespoons chicken bouillon granules
- ½ cup dried lentils
- 2 tablespoons dried minced onion
- 1 teaspoon dried basil
- 1 teaspoon dried parsley flakes
- 1 envelope savory herb with garlic soup mix or vegetable soup mix
- 2 cups uncooked tricolor spiral pasta

ADDITIONAL INGREDIENTS
- 10 cups water
- 3 cups cubed cooked chicken
- 1 can (28 ounces) diced tomatoes, undrained

In a half-pint glass container, layer the first seven ingredients in the order listed; seal tightly. Place the pasta in a 1-pint resealable jar; seal.

TO PREPARE SOUP Place water in a Dutch oven; stir in soup mix. Bring to a boil. Reduce heat; cover and simmer for 45 minutes. Add chicken, tomatoes and pasta. Cover and simmer until pasta, peas and lentils are tender, 15-20 minutes longer.

MAKE A GIFT MIX COMBO

Looking for a new way to package gift mixes? Check out transparent ornaments at your local craft store. Load up one or more with a selection of mixes and present them as a set!

APPLESAUCE MUFFIN MIX

START TO FINISH: 30 MIN.
MAKES: 1 BATCH (2 CUPS MIX); 9 MUFFINS

I adapted one of my favorite muffin recipes to create a homemade mix I can give to my family for holiday gifts. Now they can make my muffins any time of year!
—*Barbara Opperwall, Wyoming, MI*

　½ cup sugar
　1¼ teaspoons baking powder
　1 teaspoon ground cinnamon
　½ teaspoon ground nutmeg
　¼ teaspoon salt
　1½ cups all-purpose flour, divided
　2 tablespoons quick-cooking oats
ADDITIONAL INGREDIENTS
　1 large egg, lightly beaten
　1 cup unsweetened applesauce
　½ cup butter, melted
　1 teaspoon vanilla extract
　1 tablespoon sugar

Combine the first five ingredients. In a 1-pint glass jar, layer ¾ cup flour, oats, sugar mixture and the remaining flour. Cover and store in a cool dry place for up to 6 months.
TO PREPARE MUFFINS Preheat oven to 375°. Combine egg, applesauce, butter and vanilla. Stir in muffin mix just until moistened. Fill greased muffin cups three-fourths full. Sprinkle with sugar. Bake until a toothpick comes out clean, 15-20 minutes. Cool 5 minutes before removing from pan to a wire rack.

APPLE-CINNAMON OATMEAL MIX

START TO FINISH: 5 MIN.
MAKES: 8 CUPS MIX; 16 SERVINGS

Oatmeal is a breakfast staple at our house. It's a warm, nutritious start that keeps us going all morning. We used to buy oatmeal mixes, but we think our homemade version is better! Feel free to substitute raisins or other dried fruit for the apples.
—*Lynne Van Wagenen, Salt Lake City, UT*

　6 cups quick-cooking oats
　1⅓ cups nonfat dry milk powder
　1 cup dried apples, diced
　¼ cup sugar
　¼ cup packed brown sugar
　1 tablespoon ground cinnamon
　1 teaspoon salt
　¼ teaspoon ground cloves
ADDITIONAL INGREDIENT (FOR EACH SERVING)
　½ cup water

In a large bowl, combine the first eight ingredients. Store in an airtight container in a cool, dry place for up to 6 months.
TO PREPARE OATMEAL Shake mix well. In a small saucepan, bring water to a boil; slowly stir in ½ cup mix. Cook and stir over medium heat for 1 minute. Remove from the heat. Cover and let stand for 1 minute or until oatmeal reaches desired consistency.

CONFETTI BEAN SOUP MIX

PREP: 20 MIN. + STANDING
COOK: 1 HOUR 25 MIN.
MAKES: 4 BATCHES; 9 SERVINGS
(2¼ QUARTS) PER BATCH

With its colorful variety of beans, this mix looks great in the jar and tastes great in the bowl! I give it to friends each Christmas.
—Rebecca Lambert, Staunton, VA

- 1 **pound each dried navy beans, great northern beans, red kidney beans, pinto beans and green split peas**
- 12 **beef bouillon cubes**
- ¾ **cup dried minced chives**
- 4 **teaspoons dried savory**
- 2 **teaspoons ground cumin**
- 2 **teaspoons coarsely ground pepper**
- 4 **bay leaves**

ADDITIONAL INGREDIENTS
(FOR EACH BATCH)
- 12 **cups water, divided**
- 1 **can (14½ ounces) stewed tomatoes, undrained**
- 1½ **teaspoons salt**
- ¼ **teaspoon hot pepper sauce, optional**

1. Combine beans and peas; place 3 cups of the mixed beans in each of four large resealable plastic bags. Set aside.

2. In each of four snack-size resealable plastic bags, place 3 bouillon cubes, 3 tablespoons chives, 1 teaspoon savory, ½ teaspoon cumin, ½ teaspoon pepper and 1 bay leaf. Seal the bags.

TO PREPARE SOUP Place the contents of one bag of beans in a Dutch oven; add 7 cups of water. Bring to a boil; boil for 2 minutes. Remove from the heat; cover and let stand for 1 hour. Drain the beans and discard the liquid. Add the remaining water and the contents of one seasoning bag. Bring to a boil. Reduce heat; cover and simmer, stirring occasionally, until the beans are tender, about 1 hour. Add tomatoes, salt and, if desired, pepper sauce. Simmer, uncovered, for 20 minutes. Discard the bay leaf.

OATMEAL CHIP COOKIE MIX

START TO FINISH: 30 MIN.
MAKES: 1 BATCH (4 CUPS MIX);
2½ DOZEN COOKIES

I like to give a jar of this oatmeal cookie mix, along with a cookie sheet, for a bridal shower or housewarming gift.
—Joan Airey, Rivers, MB

- 1¼ **cups quick-cooking oats**
- 1 **cup all-purpose flour**
- ½ **teaspoon baking powder**
- ½ **teaspoon baking soda**
- ¼ **teaspoon salt**
- ¾ **cup milk chocolate chips**
- ⅓ **cup white baking chips**
- ½ **cup slivered almonds**
- ¼ **cup flaked coconut**
- ½ **cup packed brown sugar**
- ½ **cup granulated sugar**

ADDITIONAL INGREDIENTS
- ½ **cup butter, softened**
- 1 **large egg**
- ½ **teaspoon vanilla extract**

1. Pulse oats in a food processor until finely ground; set aside. Combine flour, baking powder, baking soda and salt.

2. In a 1-qt. glass jar, layer the oats, flour mixture, chips, almonds, coconut, brown sugar and granulated sugar, packing well between each layer. Cover and store in a cool, dry place for up to 6 months.

TO PREPARE COOKIES Preheat oven to 375°. Cream butter until light and fluffy. Beat in egg and vanilla. Add the cookie mixture; blend well (mixture will be dry). Drop by rounded tablespoonfuls 2 in. apart onto ungreased baking sheets. Bake until lightly browned, 10-15 minutes. Cool for 2 minutes before removing to wire racks.

HOMEMADE GIFTS & DECOR

*Add a personal touch to holiday gifts
and entertaining with these
fun and easy homemade crafts.*

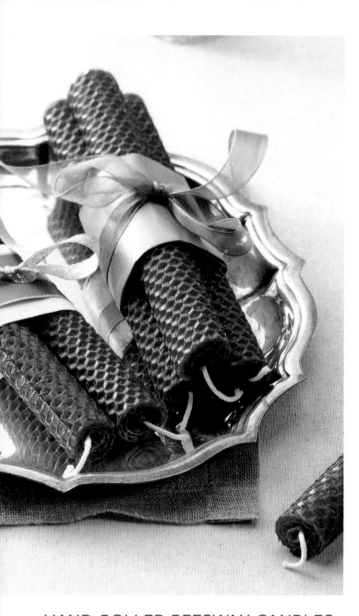

FLOWERS & FRILLS VASES

Dress up old jars with hand-me-down doilies for a lacy new look. To make your vase pop with color, perk up the doily using bright and cheerful fabric dye.

MATERIALS
Mason jars or vases
Doilies or lace
Decorative ribbon, raffia or twine
Spray adhesive

DIRECTIONS (FOR EACH)
1. Thoroughly clean the jar or vase inside and out. Let it dry completely.
2. Measure the doily or lace to cover the exterior of the jar. Trim if needed.
3. Place doily right-side down on a work surface. Spray the back side with adhesive. Apply the doily to the jar, smoothing out wrinkles as much as possible.
4. Decorate as desired with ribbon, raffia or twine.

HAND-ROLLED BEESWAX CANDLES

These beautiful, long-burning candles make a thoughtful holiday or hostess gift. Easy to make, they're calming to burn, so keep a few for your own table, too!

MATERIALS
16x8-in. beeswax craft sheets*
2/0 wick (18 in. per pair of candles)

*Available online. Ours are from *brushymountainbeefarm.com.*

DIRECTIONS
1. Set wax sheets out at room temperature for several hours.
2. Cut desired number of wicks to 9 in. each.
3. Cut wax sheets in half crosswise.
4. For each candle, lay wick along one edge of the wax square, leaving roughly 1 in. extending beyond top edge of the wax. Roll the wax tightly and evenly around the wick, keeping the top and bottom edges of the candle even. Roll completely; press gently along the seam with fingertips to secure.

CHRISTMAS JOURNAL

Keep track of all the many things on your to-do list in the run-up to the holidays with this homemade journal. Afterward, add mementos to the book and preserve memories of a beautiful season.

MATERIALS
Scrapbook
Printed copies of digital downloads
Choice of holiday papers and stickers
Choice of recipes and recipe cards

NOTE Different holiday checklists can be found online and are available for free download; search for "Christmas planner free" and you'll have lots of choices that will let you customize the journal.

DIRECTIONS
1. Use holiday papers and stickers to decorate the scrapbook as desired.
2. Fill each page with lists to keep your family and yourself organized throughout the holiday season.
3. Some examples of things to include are a Christmas card checklist, favorite family recipes, holiday meal plans, a gift list and a budget plan.

BUTTON-TRIMMED CHRISTMAS CARDS

Use ready-to-embellish cards and buttons to create one-of-a-kind Christmas cards.

MATERIALS

Ready-to-embellish 5x7-in. blank cards
Assorted colored card stock
Paper doily
Green felt

Vintage Christmas-themed printouts (sheet music, Santa, etc.)
Various Christmas-themed scrapbook stickers
Scrapbook letter stickers
Assorted buttons
Washi tape
Baker's twine
Glue tape roller
Hot glue gun

DIRECTIONS (FOR EACH)
SANTA BUTTON WREATH CARD

1. Find royalty-free Christmas carol sheet music online to use as background and a royalty-free Santa image online to use in the wreath center. Print the music and trim it to fit within the front of the ready-to-embellish card. Print and cut out the Santa image.

2. Use the glue tape roller to attach the sheet music to the card, the paper doily to the sheet music, and the Santa image to the center of the doily.

3. Hot-glue large green buttons in a circle around the Santa image, as a wreath. Add small red buttons, as holly berries.

4. Trim a piece of washi tape and place it across the bottom of the sheet music.

5. Adhere a holiday scrapbook sticker on top of the washi tape, centered below the wreath.

WASHI TAPE CHRISTMAS TREE CARD

1. Trim colored card stock to fit within the front of a ready-to-embellish 5x7-in. card. Roll glue tape on the back of the card stock and attach it to the card.

2. Cut 4-in. to 1-in. pieces from a variety of washi tapes. Tape the pieces onto a piece of card stock, layering the tape pieces on top of each other with the longest at the bottom and working upward in a rough triangle. Trim to a triangular tree shape. Use the glue tape roller to adhere tree to the card stock.

3. Hot-glue buttons to the tree, as ornaments. Layer 2 buttons on the top of the tree as the tree topper.

4. Add scrapbook elements as desired to finish the card.

HANGING ORNAMENT CARD

1. Trim colored card stock to fit within the front of a ready-to-embellish 5x7-in. card. Roll glue tape on the back (bottom only) of the card stock; adhere the card stock to the card.

2. Select a variety of 6 buttons.

3. Cut 6 pieces of various colors of baker's twine. Gently pull the top of the card stock forward and apply roll tape to the back. Adhere the ends of the twine, spaced out across the top of the back side of the card stock. Press to adhere the top of the card stock to the card, hiding the ends of the twine.

4. Trim the hanging twine to desired lengths, varying the lengths.

5. Hot-glue a button to the end of each piece of hanging twine.

6. Add a scrapbook holiday message.

UPCYCLED DOILY RUNNER

Stitched together, doilies from thrift or dollar stores—or your old linen drawer!—make an elegant and eye-catching runner. Keep it pristine white, or throw in dashes of color in holiday-appropriate shades. Substitute lace doilies for even more variation.

MATERIALS

Several crocheted or knit cotton doilies
Sewing pins
Needle and thread
Household iron

DIRECTIONS

1. Iron all the doilies flat and arrange them in a long, roughly rectangular runner shape.

2. Use sewing pins to secure the doilies.

3. Use a needle and a coordinating colored thread to stitch the doilies together one at a time where their edges meet.

4. Remove the sewing pins; if needed, iron the runner flat.

SANTA & MRS. CLAUS PAINTED SPINDLES

Create a front porch holiday display by painting stairway spindles as Santa and Mrs. Claus. Add a North Pole sign to let everyone know your house is Holiday Central!

MATERIALS

2 unfinished wood spindles (stairway or porch spindles)
Railing spindle (for North Pole sign)
Gothic post top finial (for Santa hat)
Wood rectangle and decorative trim (for North Pole sign)
Wooden letters (for "North Pole")
Various wooden notions (carved appliqués, heart shapes, round shapes, knobs, beads, spools, popsicle sticks and clothespins)
Wooden planter or pot
Rock salt or sand
Acrylic craft paint, various colors
Various paintbrushes
Painter's tape
Hot glue gun (or wood glue)
Screw gun
Fine-tooth hand saw

NOTE Stairway and porch spindles come in various designs. A Gothic post top is the perfect shape for Santa's hat. If you can't find a spindle with a Gothic top, replace the finial as instructed below. A rounded post top is the perfect shape for Mrs. Claus' hair bun. Be creative to make a whimsical Santa and Mrs. Claus with a variety of wood shapes and appliqués.

DIRECTIONS

SANTA CLAUS HAT ASSEMBLY

To set a Gothic finial on one spindle, first use a fine-tooth handsaw to remove the existing finial. Then use a screw gun to screw a hole in the top center of the post, and attach the Gothic finial.

PAINTING (ALL SPINDLES)

1. Apply a base coat of acrylic paint to all unfinished wood. Then apply as many coats as needed in the desired colors to paint the spindles; allow the paint to dry between coats.
2. Use the photo as a guide for color placement. For the Santa and Mrs. Claus spindles, use white paint for hair and fur trim, red paint for Santa's suit and black paint for his boots, and green and red paint for Mrs. Claus' dress. Be sure to paint Santa's suit before painting his boots. When the red paint is dry, use painter's tape to tape off straight lines around the bottom of the spindle, and then paint the black boots.
3. For the North Pole sign, use the photo as a guide for color placement. Paint the spindle base, letters, wooden sign piece and trim.
4. Paint the planter box in red and white candy-cane stripes; use green for the trim.
5. Paint any wooden appliqués, notions and other embellishments. Let all dry completely.

FINAL ASSEMBLY (ALL SPINDLES)

1. While the paint dries, lay out wooden notions on a flat surface to be sure you have all the face elements and costume embellishments you desire.
2. Once the paint is completely dry, use hot glue (or wood glue) to fasten wooden embellishment pieces on the Santa and Mrs. Claus spindles as desired.
3. Use hot glue to attach the decorative trim and letters to the rectangular wood piece to make the North Pole sign. Then glue the sign to the spindle post.
4. Partially fill the planter box with rock salt or sand. Create mounds to resemble snow. Insert the spindle ends deep in the base for stability. Display on a covered front porch or somewhere protected from the weather.

CLEARLY CHRISTMAS CENTERPIECE

Bowl over your party guests with these last-minute table trims! The starting point is a fishbowl or a bowl-shaped vase—if you don't have one, you can find one at a craft store. For a dramatic effect, use bowls or vases of different heights and sizes, or place one or two on cake stands or platters.

MATERIALS

Glass bowl-shaped vase or fishbowl
Greens
Cranberries
Spider mum (or other flower)

DIRECTIONS

Fill a clear bowl-shaped glass vase nearly full with cold water. Submerge arborvitae leaves (or local greenery like pine or holly boughs); float cranberries on top. Snip the stem from a spider mum or other flower and place the flower in the middle of the cranberries.

Roasted Acorn Squash & Brussels
Sprouts, 60
Slow Cooker Butternut Squash
Soup, 134

STUFFING
Corn & Onion Stuffing, 28
Slow Cooker Mushroom Stuffing, 33

SWEET POTATOES
(*also see Potatoes*)
Brown Sugar Sweet Potatoes with
Apples, 30
Grilled Sweet Potato
Casserole, 140
Roasted Sweet Potatoes with
Balsamic Vinegar and Rosemary, 63

TURKEY & TURKEY SAUSAGE
Holiday Turkey Gravy, 24
Roasted Sage Turkey with Vegetable
Gravy, 59
Slow-Cooked Turkey Breasts with
Cranberry Sauce, 72
Spiced & Grilled Turkey, 144
Turkey-Cranberry Monte Cristo, 73

VEGETABLES (*also see specific
kinds*)
Antipasto Marinated Vegetables, 55
Truly Tasty Turnip Greens, 26
Sweet and Tangy Beets, 34

WHITE CHOCOLATE
Creamy Coconut Snowballs, 183
White Candy Bark, 184
White Chocolate Cranberry Orange
Bars, 136
White Chocolate Maple Pecan
Macaroons, 162

p. 162

Alphabetical Recipe Index
This index lists every recipe in the book in
alphabetical order. Just search for the titles
when you want to find your favorites.

A
Almond Custard Fondue, 181
Almond Roca Pinwheels, 158
Antipasto Marinated Vegetables, 55
Apple & Brown Sugar Glazed
Carrots, 36
Apple Cinnamon Cake, 114
Apple-Cinnamon Oatmeal Mix, 197
Apple-Cranberry Breakfast Risotto, 81
Applesauce Muffin Mix, 197
Apricot Ham Balls, 118
Apricot-Hazelnut Triangles, 159
Apricot-Nut White Fudge, 171
Aunt Nancy's Cream of Crab Soup, 93
Aunt Rose's Fantastic Butter
Toffee, 100

B
Bacon Lima Beans, 33
Bacon-Wrapped Blue Cheese
Shrimp, 11
Baked Brie with Mushrooms, 15
Blackberry Brandy Slush, 50
Bourbon-Infused Fingerling
Potatoes, 43
Broiled German Chocolate Cake, 141
Brown Sugar Sweet Potatoes with
Apples, 30
Butter Pecan Ice Cream Torte, 135

C
Calabrian Holiday Soup, 54
Camembert & Cranberry Pizzas, 14
Canadian Bacon with Apples, 106
Cappuccino Party Punch, 132
Caramel Apple Pie with Streusel
Topping, 44
Caramel Creme Brulee, 148
Cheese-Stuffed Sweet Onions, 24
Cheesy Scalloped Potatoes &
Ham, 87
Cherries in the Snow, 178
Chewy Caramel-Coated Popcorn, 114
Chicken & Bacon Roll-Ups, 113
Chicken & Blue Cheese Pizza, 131
Chicken-Cranberry Hot Dish, 82
Chicken Marsala Bake, 60
Chicken Marsala Lasagna, 132

Chili-Scented Seasoning, 189
Chippy Chocolate Cookie Mix, 194
Chocolate Cherry Candies, 128
Chocolate-Cherry Thumbprint
Cookies, 154
Chocolate Chip & Pecan Meringue
Bars, 163
Chocolate Hazelnut Pudding
Torte, 180
Christmas Fruitcake Bars, 179
Church Window Cookies, 161
Cinnamon-Apple Cider Monkey
Bread, 107
Cinnamon Roll Cream Cheese Coffee
Cake, 90
Citrus-Herb Roast Chicken, 88
Classic Candy Cane Butter
Cookies, 161
Coconut Cream Cake, 172
Company Mashed Carrots, 44
Confetti Bean Soup Mix, 199
Coriander-Crusted Beef with Spicy
Cranberry Relish, 82
Corn & Onion Stuffing, 28
Cran-Almond Loaf, 71
Cran-Marnier Truffles, 78
Cranberry Amaretto Bread
Pudding, 71
Cranberry Apple-Nut Pie, 74
Cranberry-Apple Red Cabbage, 31
Cranberry Beef Brisket, 80
Cranberry-Berry Sauce, 72
Cranberry Bourbon, 68
Cranberry Cake with Caramel Sauce, 77
Cranberry Caramels, 79
Cranberry Cocktail, 13
Cranberry Eggnog Salad, 59
Cranberry Green Beans, 77
Cranberry-Orange Cake with Lemon
Glaze, 79
Cranberry-Orange Rice Pudding, 99
Cranberry-Orange Roast Ducklings, 68
Cranberry-Pecan Holiday Cheese
Ball, 11
Cranberry Pesto, 48
Cranberry Short Ribs, 78
Creamy Chocolate Fudge, 129
Creamy Coconut Snowballs, 183

Creamy Orange Gelatin, 91
Creamy Ranchified Potatoes, 27
Creme de Menthe Cookies, 162
Creme de Menthe Squares, 64
Crispy Sriracha Spring Rolls, 127
Crunchy Spinach Casserole, 41
Curried Mushroom Empanadas, 16

D
Double Chocolate Hot Cocoa Mix, 192
Dove Dinner Rolls, 49

E
Easy Parmesan Biscuits, 111
Easy Pumpkin Spice Pudding Pie, 173
Eggnog Marshmallows, 173
Eggnog Pancakes, 106
Eggnog Pound Cake, 96

F
Favorite Marinated Brisket, 127
Fluffed Fruit Salad, 100
Four-Cheese Baked Eggs, 108
Four-Cheese Sausage Rigatoni, 94
Frozen Pineapple-Cranberry Salad, 77

G
Garlic-Herb Smashed Spuds, 61
Ginger Applesauce, 34
Ginger-Apricot Tossed Salad, 117
Ginger-Cream Bars, 170
Gingerbread Cake Mix, 194
Gingerbread Men Cookies, 95
Goat Cheese & Onion Pastries, 21
Gooey Old-Fashioned Steamed
    Molasses Bread, 33
Grandma's Molasses Fruitcake, 86
Grandma's Raspberry Rugelach, 156
Grapefruit & Fennel Salad with Mint
    Vinaigrette, 63
Grilled Bananas Foster, 140
Grilled Brussels Sprouts, 142

p. 156

Grilled Cauliflower Wedges, 147
Grilled Gorgonzola Pear Salad, 149
Grilled Sweet Potato
    Casserole, 140

H
Ham and Cheese Puffs, 16
Hash Brown Broccoli Bake, 119
Hawaiian Dream Cookies, 167
Hearty Pasta Soup Mix, 196
Hoisin Meatballs, 124
Holiday Beef Bourguignon, 61
Holiday Butter Mint Cookies, 155
Holiday Eggnog Pie, 170
Holiday Hot Buttered Rum Mix, 15
Holiday Kipferl Cookie, 184
Holiday Stuffed Baby Portobellos, 8
Holiday Turkey Gravy, 24
Homemade Cajun Seasoning, 188
Homemade Peanut Butter Cups, 101
Homemade Spicy Hot Sauce, 142
Honey-Glazed Carrots with
    Cranberries, 74
Honey-Mint Lamb Skewers, 18
Hot Fruit Salad, 36
Hubbard Squash Pie, 98

I
Insalata Caprese, 53
Italian Herb-Crusted Pork Loin, 47

J
Jambalaya Mix, 192

L
Lemon-Ginger Salt, 188
Lemon Herb Game Hens, 41
Lemon Noodle Kugel, 180
Lemon Snowball, 136
Louisiana Jambalaya, 125

M
Make-Ahead Marinated Shrimp, 118
Maple-Pecan Pork Chops, 124
Marshmallow Cream with Custard
    Sauce, 178
Meatball Submarine Casserole, 112
Mediterranean Pastry Pinwheels, 128
Meringue Torte with Peppermint
    Cream, 177
Mincemeat Cookie Bars, 154
Mini Crab Cakes, 21
Mint Angel Cake, 179
Mint Brownie Pie, 177
Mixed Nut Clusters, 99
Mocha Mint Coffee, 108

p. 108

Mocha Punch, 98
Mulled Wine, 134

N
Napoleon Cremes, 120
Never Fail Cutout Cookies, 111
New England Lamb Bake, 129
Nicole's Slow Cooker Broccoli, 27
Nutty Pumpkin Bisque, 42

O
Oatmeal Chip Cookie Mix, 199
Old-Fashioned Scalloped Pineapple, 88
Old-World Ricotta Cheesecake, 183
One-Bite Tamales, 10
Orange & Spice Cutout Cookies, 155
Orange-Chili Chocolate Cookies, 145
Orange-Nutella Cookie Cups, 165

P
Pancake Mix in a Jar, 193
Peanut Butter Pie Cookies, 166
Pear & Pecan Salad with Cranberry
    Vinaigrette, 74
Pear Cake with Sour Cream
    Topping, 174
Pear Chutney Chicken, 133
Pear-Stuffed French Toast with Brie,
    Cranberries & Pecans, 105
Pepper-Crusted Beef Tenderloin with
    Mushrooms, 147
Pepper Parmesan Beans, 56
Pepper-Stuffed Pork Tenderloin, 117
Peppermint Lava Cakes, 150
Pimiento Cheese Deviled Eggs, 14
Pina Colada Bundt Cake, 50
Pineapple & Macadamia Nut Cake, 181
Pork Tenderloin with Cranberry Apple
    Chutney, 81
Portobello Wellingtons with Spinach
    Pistachio Pesto, 62

Potato Chip Banana Bread Cookies, 156
Potluck Macaroni and Cheese, 36
Pretzel Bread Bowl with Cheese Dip, 13
Pumpkin Gingerbread Thumbprint
    Cookies, 158
Pumpkin Spice Loaves, 91

Q
Quick & Easy au Gratin Potatoes, 48

R
Ramen Noodle Salad, 113
Raspberry-Almond Jelly Roll, 174
Red Velvet Crinkle Cookies, 166
Rich Rum Cake, 64
Ricotta Puffs, 10
Roasted Acorn Squash & Brussels
    Sprouts, 60
Roasted Sage Turkey with Vegetable
    Gravy, 59
Roasted Sweet Potatoes with
    Balsamic Vinegar and Rosemary, 63
Rustic Tuscan Pepper Bruschetta, 54

S
Salt-Free Herb Blend, 188
Sand Art Brownies, 191
Savory Steak Rub, 189
Shrimp in Phyllo Cups, 19
Slow-Cooked Big Breakfast, 96
Slow-Cooked Cheesy Cauliflower, 28
Slow-Cooked Green Beans, 35
Slow-Cooked Turkey Breasts with
    Cranberry Sauce, 72
Slow-Cooked Wild Rice, 31
Slow Cooker Butternut Squash
    Soup, 134
Slow Cooker Chipotle Beef
    Carnitas, 150
Slow Cooker Corn Pudding, 30
Slow Cooker Italian Mushrooms, 28
Slow Cooker Mushroom Beef
    Stroganoff, 93
Slow Cooker Mushroom Stuffing, 33
Smoky Braised Chuck Roast, 131
Smoky Hash Brown Casserole, 34
Smoky Pineapple Cheese Ball, 94
Soft Mocha Drops, 159
Soft Peppermint Spritz Cookies, 165
Sparkling Oranges, 105
Spice Up My Life Chili, 148
Spiced & Grilled Turkey, 144
Spiced Cranberry Crisp Cake, 80
Spiced Orange-Cranberry Chutney, 43
Spicy Sausage & Apple Overnight
    Casserole, 145

Spinach Salad with Raspberries &
    Candied Walnuts, 47
Spinach Souffle Dip, 8
Split Pea Soup Mix, 191
Spumoni Torte, 56
Steaks with Cherry-Chipotle
    Glaze, 149
Strawberry-Champagne Punch, 8
Sugar Cookies, 87
Sweet and Tangy Beets, 34

T
Tangy Cranberry Beans, 26
Texas Garlic Mashed Potatoes, 133
Tropical Candy Cane Freeze, 19
Truly Tasty Turnip Greens, 26
Turkey-Cranberry Monte Cristo, 73

U
Ultimate Chocolate Bread
    Pudding, 120

W
Wasabi Crab Cakes, 141
Wassail Bowl, 99
White Candy Bark, 184
White Chocolate Cranberry
    Orange Bars, 136
White Chocolate Maple Pecan
    Macaroons, 162
White Seafood Lasagna, 53
Winter Fruit Compote, 35

Z
Zippy Dry Rub, 189

Craft Index

This index lists every craft project in the book by
craft category, technique and/or main materials,
so you can easily find the project you're looking for.

BEADING
Winter Rose Mixed-Media Choker, 227

CANDLES
Hand-Rolled Beeswax Candles, 202

CARDS & BOOKS
Button-Trimmed Christmas Cards, 204
Christmas Journal, 203

**CENTERPIECES &
TABLE ACCENTS**
Bling Rings, 222
Clearly Christmas Centerpiece, 207
Felt Candy Favors, 210
Flowers & Frills Vases, 202
Place of Grace Utensil Holders, 209
A Touch of Glitter Vase, 213
Upcycled Doily Runner, 205
Wonderful Winter Coasters, 218

FABRIC & FIBER
Bobble Knit Infinity Scarf, 217
Felt Candy Favors, 210
Felt-Wrapped Christmas Wreath, 216
Flowers & Frills Vases, 202

Holiday Hoop Wall Hangings, 224
Knit Mitten Garland, 211
Upcycled Doily Runner, 205
Whimsical Woolen Elf, 220
Wonderful Winter Coasters, 218

FASHION & ACCESSORIES
Bobble Knit Infinity Scarf, 217
Winter Rose Mixed-Media
    Choker, 227

FLORAL/NATURAL CRAFTS
Clearly Christmas Centerpiece, 207
Green Stamps, 223
Snowman's Best Friend Holiday
    Wreaths, 221

GARLANDS
Deck the Halls Garlands, 226
Knit Mitten Garland, 211

GENERAL CRAFTS
Button-Trimmed Christmas
    Cards, 204
Christmas Journal, 203
Cute-as-a-Button Ornaments, 208

Deck the Halls Garlands, 226
Felt Candy Favors, 210
Felt-Wrapped Christmas Wreath, 216
Hand-Rolled Beeswax Candles, 202
Holiday Wine Bottle Labels, 229
Knit Mitten Garland, 211
Muffin Tin Advent Calendar, 212
Seasonal Magnet Set, 228
Sentimental Bookmarks, 222
Snowman Jar, 213
A Touch of Glitter Vase, 213
Whimsical Woolen Elf, 220
Wonderful Winter Coasters, 218
Wrapped Cookie Cutter
   Ornaments, 225

GIFT PACKAGING
Folded Paper Candy Boxes, 215
Holiday Wine Bottle Labels, 229
Painted Treat Tins, 219
Snowman Jar, 213

GIFTS (*also see Gift Packaging*)
Bobble Knit Infinity Scarf, 217
Christmas Journal, 203
Flowers & Frills Vases, 202
Hand-Rolled Beeswax Candles, 202
Holiday Hoop Wall Hangings, 224
Seasonal Magnet Set, 228
Sentimental Bookmarks, 222
Winter Rose Mixed-Media Choker, 227
Wonderful Winter Coasters, 218

HOME DECOR
Clearly Christmas Centerpiece, 207
Deck the Halls Garlands, 226
Felt-Wrapped Christmas
   Wreath, 216
Flowers & Frills Vases, 202
Holiday Hoop Wall Hangings, 224
Holiday Wine Bottle Labels, 229
Knit Mitten Garland, 211
Muffin Tin Advent Calendar, 212
Santa & Mrs. Claus Painted
   Spindles, 207
Seasonal Magnet Set, 228
Snowman Jar, 213
Snowman's Best Friend Holiday
   Wreaths, 221
A Touch of Glitter Vase, 213
Upcycled Doily Runner, 205
Whimsical Woolen Elf, 220
Wonderful Winter Coasters, 218

KNITTING
Bobble Knit Infinity Scarf, 217

PAINTING
Painted Treat Tins, 219
Santa & Mrs. Claus Painted
   Spindles, 207

PAPER
Button-Trimmed Christmas
   Cards, 204
Christmas Journal, 203
Folded Paper Candy Boxes, 215
Green Stamps, 223
Holiday Wine Bottle Labels, 229
Muffin Tin Advent Calendar, 212
Place of Grace Utensil Holders, 209
Seasonal Magnet Set, 228
Sentimental Bookmarks, 222

SEWING
Bling Rings, 222
Holiday Hoop Wall Hangings, 224
Wonderful Winter Coasters, 218

STAMPING
Green Stamps, 223
Holiday Hoop Wall Hangings, 224
Place of Grace Utensil Holders, 209
Upcycled Doily Runner, 205

TREE ORNAMENTS
Cute-as-a-Button Ornaments, 208
Wrapped Cookie Cutter
   Ornaments, 225

UPCYCLED PROJECTS
Bling Rings, 222
Deck the Halls Garlands, 226
Flowers & Frills Vases, 202
Knit Mitten Garland, 211
Muffin Tin Advent Calendar, 212
Painted Treat Tins, 219
Seasonal Magnet Set, 228
Snowman Jar, 213
A Touch of Glitter Vase, 213
Upcycled Doily Runner, 205
Wrapped Cookie Cutter
   Ornaments, 225

WOOD
Santa & Mrs. Claus Painted
   Spindles, 207

WREATHS
Felt-Wrapped Christmas
   Wreath, 216
Snowman's Best Friend Holiday
   Wreaths, 221

p. 207